ŚIKṢĀ SAMUCCAYA

ŚIKṢĀ SAMUCCAYA

A Compendium of Buddhist Doctrine

Compiled by

ŚĀNTIDEVA

Chiefly from Earlier Mahāyāna Sūtras

Translated from the Sanskrit by

CECIL BENDALL

W. H. D. ROUSE

MOTILAL BANARSIDASS PUBLISHERS
PRIVATE LIMITED • DELHI

Reprint : Delhi, 1981, 1990, 1999, 2006
Second Edition: Delhi, 1971
First Edition: London, 1922

ISBN: 81-208-0732-4 (Cloth)
ISBN: 81-208-1633-1 (Paper)

MOTILAL BANARSIDASS
41 U.A. Bungalow Road, Jawahar Nagar, Delhi 110 007
8 Mahalaxmi Chamber, 22 Bhulabhai Desai Road, Mumbai 400 026
236, 9th Main III Block, Jayanagar, Bangalore 560 011
203 Royapettah High Road, Mylapore, Chennai 600 004
Sanas Plaza, 1302 Baji Rao Road, Pune 411 002
8 Camac Street, Kolkata 700 017
Ashok Rajpath, Patna 800 004
Chowk, Varanasi 221 001

Printed in India
BY JAINENDRA PRAKASH JAIN AT SHRI JAINENDRA PRESS,
A-45 NARAINA, PHASE-I, NEW DELHI 110 028
AND PUBLISHED BY NARENDRA PRAKASH JAIN FOR
MOTILAL BANARSIDASS PUBLISHERS PRIVATE LIMITED,
BUNGALOW ROAD, DELHI 110 007

PREFACE

THE manuscript of this book was brought from Nepal by Mr. Cecil Bendall, and edited by him for the Russian Bibliotheca Buddhica (St. Petersburg, 1897). When Mr. Bendall returned to Cambridge as Teacher of Sanskrit, he began a translation of it, in which Mr. E. B. Cowell, then Professor of Sanskrit, seems to have helped, since a part of the MS. was in his handwriting. This portion, which was delivered to me as complete, proved to be in need of revision; indeed, a good deal of it has been re-written. On the death of Mr. Cowell, when Mr. Bendall succeeded him as Professor, I began to work with him upon the translation, and continued the work until his death. The part we did together was chapters III, IV, V, and part of VI, pp. 44–125 of the Sanskrit text.

On his deathbed, Mr. Bendall asked me to finish the work, and I undertook the task as a sacred duty, although I was well aware of my own insufficiency for the task unaided. Indeed, for me unaided it would have been impossible; but I have had the most generous and ungrudging aid of the chief living authority on Buddhism, Buddhist Sanskrit, and Tibetan—Mr. L. de la Vallée Poussin, Professor of Sanskrit at Brussels. During his residence in Cambridge, from 1914 to 1918, M. de la Vallée has revised every passage in which I felt a difficulty. The acknowledgment which I make here to him is quite inadequate to express my gratitude for his kindness. If the work meet with the approval of scholars, the credit is his: any errors that remain will be mine. We have to thank Mr. F. W. Thomas, Librarian of the India Office, for the loan of the Tibetan translation of this work.

W. H. D. ROUSE.

CONTENTS

ŚIKSHĀ-SAMUCCAYA

CHAPTER I

SALUTATION TO ALL BUDDHAS AND BODHISATVAS !

[1] To hear that jewel of the Good Law through not hearing which you, mine honoured readers, have suffered the pain of consuming-fire in the terrible flames [1] of hell, agony awful, renewed, unending, this I say to hear bestow your most respectful care. When that one has given ear to it with mind not puffed up, one puts away all one's offence [2] for the future and completely destroys the sin formerly accumulated, yea all, great though it be. Such men as hear gain delight that they never had before, and never come to lack true joy ; they gain the highest deathless sweets of the Sambodhisatvas and the stage of Buddha, incomparable combination of blessings : this jewel of the Law, hard though it be to get, to-day [3] gotten, yet now to this give respectful ear, now ye have gotten acceptable time and it is told to you.

And let there approach for to hear the word of him who alone is the Saviour of the Three Worlds, the beings of the Suras and Nāgas all full of faith, the lords of the Gandharvas, Yakshas, Garudas and Suras and Kinnaras, yea, let the Manes come with joy when once the thirst for hearing is aroused. After humble reverences to the blessed Buddhas with their sons [4] and the Law, [5] and all the Worshipful ones, I will now set

[1] Read °महाप्रताप°.

[2] Word lost in MS. Perhaps श्रुत्वापि यत्त्यजति°.

[3] Read °द्य° for °प्य° with Tib.

[4] After the spirit, cf. *Jinasūnu* in Pali.

[5] The Buddha, the Order, and the Law (dharmakāya).

forth the entrance into the discipline of the Bodhisatvas, in collected sayings of deep purport. And in this book I have naught that is new to tell; nor have I skill in composing; for this very cause I am not making an effort for the welfare of others; this book of mine is intended to cultivate my own mind, yet through this my work the impulse of faith to cultivate the good gains increase; and if but one fellow-creature fashioned of like elements to myself may behold that truth, and another should see him, then this book will have been not in vain.

[2] The happy conjuncture [1] is exceedingly hard to win; once gotten it can achieve all the aims of a man. If one use it not for thinking of salvation, how can it be found again? [2]

For so we hear in the holy *Gandavyuha Sutra*, in the passage called *Holy Jayoshmāyātanavimoksha*: "Hard to attain is the prevention of the eight untoward moments; [3] hard is the attainment of birth as a man; hard to get is the perfection of the favourable conjuncture; hard is the production of a Buddha; hard to secure is full perfection in one's bodily senses; [4] hard to gain is the hearing of the Buddha's Law; hard to gain is the society of good men; hard to gain is the true Good Friend; hard to attract to oneself the means of instruction in the true rule of life; hard to attain is the true [5] life; hard to attain is the good law, yea, and the effort that leads to it in this world of men."

Accordingly when a man has attained this assemblage of favourable conjunctures, knowing well both practically and metaphysically [6] the suffering of transmigration, desiring the

[1] This and the whole passage following should be compared with the passage from the Pali *Jinālankāra* cited by Burnouf, *Lotus*, p. 305.

[2] See Bodhicaryāvatāra, 1–4, and Barnett, *The Path of Light*.

[3] These are detailed in the *Mahāvyutpatti*, f. 120 (ed. Minaev, p. 36), and Dh.-s. § 134, and really give the states of existence unfavourable for living the ideal life. The Pali has nine (C. s.v. *akkhaṇa*).

[4] *Avikalendriyatā*. This amounts to a repetition, as the contrary is one of the eight *akshaṇaṣ* above which have to be prevented (indriyavaikalya, *Mahāvy.*; indriyavikalatā, *Dh.-s.*).

[5] *Bhūta* and *samyak* are not widely different in meaning. The same Tibetan phrase (yaṅ-dag-pa) represents both.

[6] On *Saṃvriti* and *paramārtha* as used by Buddhist schools, see Taran. ap. Wassiljew, "Buddhism," p. 321 *sqq*.

happiness of extinction, inasmuch as such a mighty being has his lot in the spiritual family of the Buddha, so thus he communes with himself: "Since I and my fellow-men abhor pain and fear alike, what distinction can I rightly make for self, that I should preserve it and not another?"[1] Hence both for oneself and the world of the living it is true that "when one desires to make an end of pain and to go to the end of joy, one must make firm the root of faith, and fix the spirit firmly on enlightenment."[2]

For it is said in the *Ratnolka-dhāraṇi:*

"Believing in the Buddhas and their qualities, he believes in the practice of the sons of the Buddhas. Believing in the supreme Bodhi the thought of the Great Beings is born in him. Faith is the guide, the mother, the producer, the protector and increaser of all virtues.

[3] "Desire-expelling, bringing across the stream, faith shews the city of bliss. Faith is the calm of the undefiled thought—firmly rooted in honour, void of pride. Faith is the best foot to go and find the wealth of the treasury, it is a hand to grasp happiness. Faith gives joy even in renunciation, faith gives delight in the law of the Jina. Faith causes preeminence in knowing virtues, guides and brings to attainment the destiny of the Buddha; for the keenness and clearness of the five moral qualities it is a force, also that they be not extinguished; not to be vanquished by the passions, faith seeks the qualities of the Buddhas. Faith is not attached to the joys that attach, delivered from all unfavourable states, it is the best and unique happy state. Faith goes beyond the path of Māra, reveals the path of supreme deliverance. As a cause, faith has the undecaying seed of virtues, faith causes the tree of wisdom to grow, increases the felicities of perfect knowledge; Faith shews all the Jinas. They who have always faith and respect for the Buddha never abandon moral conduct or discipline. And they who abandon not moral conduct and discipline give themselves without jealousy to praise of those

[1] Kārikā 1. [2] Kārikā 2.

who possess the virtues. They who have always faith and respect for the Law are unsatiated in hearing [1] of the qualities of the Jinas. They who are unsatiated aspire to their qualities inconceivable. They who have always faith and respect to the Sangha are resolutely devoted to the Sangha. They who are resolutely devoted to the Sangha will never fall from the strength of the faith.

[4] "Whoso lose not the strength of the faith, their senses are keen and clear. They who have senses keen and clear shun sinful friends. Whoso shun sinful friends theirs is it to hold fast righteous friends. They who hold fast righteous friends amass great merit. They who amass great merit are possessed of the knowledge of causes mighty of soul. In them are the sublime aspirations. They in whom are sublime aspirations are ever guarded by the Jinas all. They who are ever guarded by all the Jinas, the thought of enlightenment is produced in them. They in whom the thought of enlightenment is produced are devoted to the virtues of the great Rishis. They who are devoted to the virtues of the great rishis for a birth are subsequently born in the Buddha's family.[2] They who are born subsequently in the family of Buddha are released from wrong thoughts and filled with right ones. They who are released from wrong thoughts and filled with right ones, in them there is a calm and pure will. In whom there is a calm and pure will, in them there is the very best desire. They in whom there is the very best desire always walk in the perfections. They who ever walk in the perfections embrace here the Great Vehicle. They who embrace here the Great Vehicle worship the Buddhas by a holy life. They who worship the Buddhas by a holy life, their memory of the Buddha can never be destroyed. They whose memory of the Buddhas cannot be destroyed ever behold the incomprehensible Buddhas. They who ever behold the incomprehensible Buddhas, the Buddha never ceases to abide in them. They in whom the Buddha never ceases to abide, from them the Law is never

[1] Read शृणोन्ति.

[2] Page 4^{10} read जात ते, 4^{11} जात ये.

absent They from whom the Law is never absent are ever guarded by all the Jinas."

[5] Thus the development of the guṇas is based on Faith. He again sums this up: "It is difficult to find worldly men who believe such doctrines. But they who have done good deeds and gained merit, they believe in the Buddhas by the force of merit. He who ministers with all kinds of pleasure for an æon to beings as numerous as the dust of ten fields, there is still not for him such a pre-eminent merit as there is in him who believes these dharmas."

Thus, too, we are taught in the holy *Daśadharma Sūtra:* "For faith is the sublimest vehicle, whereby the leaders escape from the world. For this cause the prudent man should embrace the following of the Buddha. In a faithless man no pure conduct thrives, even as there is no green shoot from seeds that have been scorched."

Hence, too, we are taught in the *Lalita-vistara:* "Ānanda, one must apply oneself to faith, this the Tathagata enjoins." So, too, in the *Siṃha-paripṛcchā:* "By faith one immediately avoids the unfavourable condition."

Thus having made firm the root of faith one must make firm the thought of enlightenment, for it comprehends all merit. So, too, in the *Siṃha-paripṛcchā:* "The Blessed One was asked by Prince Simha,[1] 'By what act does a man take upon himself all that is good and becomes endeared to one's fellow-creatures wheresoever he is born?' The Blessed One replied: 'One should incline one's mind to enlightenment for the emancipation of all creatures. That is to take upon oneself all good and to become endeared to all.'"

Likewise we find it set forth in the *Gaṇḍa-vyūha Sūtra:* "The thought of enlightenment, fair youth, is the seed of all qualities of a Buddha; [6] it is the soil for growing all the white qualities of all the world; it is the earth, in that it is the refuge of all the world; . . . it is a father, in that it protects all bodhisatvas," . . . and so forth. "It is the Wealth-god, in that it dissipates all poverty; it is the philosopher's stone, in

[1] Son of Ajātaśatru.

that it accomplishes all purposes; it is the miraculous pot, in that it fulfils all aims; it is a force for the vanquishing of our foes the passions; it is a chariot of righteousness, in that it dissipates incorrect judgments; it is a sword, in that it cuts off the heads of the passions; it is an axe, in that it hews the tree of pain; it is a weapon in preserving from all mischances; it is a hook, for that it catches and destroys transmigration like a fish; it is a whirlwind, in that it scatters all lets and hindrances [1] like grass; it is a catalogue as summing up all longings after the godliness of the saints; it is the shrine of the world of gods, men and asuras. Thus, fair youth, is the thought of enlightenment attended with these and other unmeasured excellencies."

Now how is it known that the thought of enlightenment arises for the worldling? It is no mere phrase, as we see from several scriptures. As, for instance, is shown in the *Vimalakīrti-nirdesa*. "When one has caused the heresy of individuality to arise as high as Sumeru, even then the thought of enlightenment can arise; thus can the qualities of a Buddha grow." And from the *Ratnakaraṇḍa Sūtra* we know that even a worldling may be a Bodhisatva.

Even as it has been said: "Truly, O Mañjuśrī, a tiny sparrow cast forth from the egg-membrane, without the shell fully broken and without as yet having stepped forth from the egg, utters just a sparrow's cry; even so. Mañjuśrī, a Bodhisatva wrapt in the membrane of ignorance, without breaking the heresy of a self, or stepping forth from the triple world, utters the cry of a Buddha, the cry of void, unconditional and untrammelled."

In the *Sarvadharmapravṛttinirdeśa*, too, it is narrated how the earth opened her jaws for the Bodisatva Jayamati, and that he being dead fell into a great Hell: for that he had not set his faith on the doctrine of the Void, and showed hatred against him whosoever confessed it.

[7] Likewise we are told in the *Niyatāniyatāvatāra-mudrā Sūtra*: "'Who is the Bodhisatva that rides on the cattle-

[1] Rh. Davids (*Tevijjo-sutta*, p. 182 (*q.v.*)) translates āvaraṇa "veils."

cart? Just as a certain man might be desirous to approach the world spheres in number like to the dust of the ultimate atoms of the five Buddha-fields. He mounts his cattle-cart and gains the road. By a long tedious way he may go for a hundred leagues. There and then he may be torn away and turned back again for a space of eighty thousand leagues by a whirlwind.[1] At that rate how could this man be able to traverse the spheres with his car, yea, even[2] with countless, countless myriads of cars to traverse one?'

"The disciple said: 'He could not, Master.'

"The Master replied: 'Even so, Mañjuśrī, whosoever after producing the thought of enlightenment holdeth not fast, neither studieth the Great Vehicle, but hath intercourse with such as follow the Disciples' Vehicle,[3] and is intimate with them; and readeth their doctrine, and maketh his study therein, and proveth it, and informeth him thereof, and reciteth its topics . . .' and so forth down to '. . . teacheth them, he thereby becometh dull of wit, and is torn away and cast back from the Road of the Highest Wisdom. And whatsoever organ of wisdom, eye of wisdom this Bodhisatva may have gained through meditating upon enlightenment, this eye becomes dull and obstructed. Such is the Bodhisatva in the parable of the cattle-cart.'"

Thus the absence of conviction that the world is but void and of acquiescence in the Great Vehicle is generally not observable even in a Bodhisatva who has not completed the stage of aspiration,[4] much less in a Bodhisatva of intense aspiration. For in the *Ratnamegha* he [the imperfect Bodhisatva] is described as "having passed by all the errors of folly and making child's-play of infinite mystical exercises,[5]

[1] For the image compare the Jain work *Somadeva's Yaśastilaka*, ap. Peterson, Rep. II. (1884) p. 43, note ‡.

[2] For yāvad-api with a number, cf. Mhv. I. 317, and Senart's note.

[3] Dhamasangr, t. II.; cf. Saddh. xviii. 25 (p. 269, Kern).

[4] On the *Adhirmukticarya* see Article *Bodhisatva* in Hastings' *Encyclopædia*, and Mahāyānasūtrālaṃkāra, Bibl: de l'école des hautes études, preface). It is *adhimātra*, "intense;" *madhya*, "middle;" or *mṛdu*, "weak."

[5] The five categories named are: samādhi, dhāraṇī, vimoksha, abhijñā, vidyā.

having received the perception of the impulse of affection, feeling love and delight in the everlasting law, without doubt and without special effort for infinite ages free from sensual taint, having in the infinite years of olden time accomplished the various kinds of meditation in the system of supreme Mahāyāna by dying for others' good."

But that needs explanation; why not admit at this stage others who produce the thought of enlightenment? You have no right to consider as explicit according to your wish a text of eulogy. The mention of intense aspiration implies also the categories middle and weak. But what of the passage in the *Tathāgataguhya Sūtra*,[1] [8] where we read: "'In whom is there the thought of enlightenment, Master?' 'In him, O King, who has the intact resolve to gain it.' 'And who has such a resolve?' 'He in whom is the spring of great mercy.' 'In whom is this?' 'He who never neglects all sentient beings.' 'And how are they kept safe from neglect?' Quoth he: 'When one's own comfort is renounced.'" The preceding is said in order to produce the desire for compassion in such as are content with mere thought of enlightenment:[2] as it is said, "None are truly devoted to the religion of Buddha who have not self-renunciation." So in all this a depreciation of the thought of enlightenment is observable, but it does not amount to saying that the thought of enlightenment is produced in no other way. As is shown in the *Daśadharmaka Sūtra*: "In this world, my son, one who is destined to become[3] a Bodhisatva, without having gotten spiritual enlightenment, being by some Tathāgata or a pupil of such an one aroused, instructed, encouraged, produces thought towards the highest illumination, this is the first cause of producing that thought; or he has heard recounted the glory of full illumination or enlightenment, this is the second cause; again, he had beheld living beings without

[1] This is explained by Yoga Sūtra I. 22, मृदुमध्याधिमात्रत्वात्ततो ऽपि विशेषः speaking of devotion in Yogis. The glossator less aptly seems to refer to a twelve-fold division.

[2] *i.e.* non-merciful, gloss

[3] Read बोधिसत्वगो°.

protection,[1] without refuge, without haven. and has called up feelings of compassion till that he produces thought of perfect enlightenment, this a third cause; or when he has beheld how complete in every form is the state of a Tathāgata this is a fourth cause." Moreover, the thought of enlightenment has two stages: (1) the resolution thereunto; and (2) the advancement toward the same. As the holy *Gaṇḍavyūha* says: "Rare, my son, in all the world are such beings as make resolution toward the highest illumination, yet rarer than these and rarest are they that have started toward the same."

The first of these, the thought of the resolution towards enlightenment, is produced by the decision of the mind: "I must become a Buddha," for the *Śūraṅgama Sūtra* says that the thought of enlightenment produced by actual deception is a cause of Buddhahood, how much more shall we say this if one has done ever so little good?" So says the *Bhadrakalpika Sūtra*:[2] [9] "There was the Bodhisatva called Ghoshadatta, in whose case the thought of enlightenment was kindled by the Tathāgata Nakshatrarāja under the guise of a herdsman by giving him a betel leaf; so, too, Yaśas in the case of Vidyutpadīpa, by giving him a hem-fringe under guise of a weaver; and Anantaprabha, to whom Arcishmant gave a rush-light under guise of an inhabitant of the outskirts of the town; and Dṛdhavikrama, to whom Duspradarśa as a wood-carrier gave a piece of tooth-wood.[4] Furthermore, even when the thought of enlightenment is deficient in corresponding conduct, we need think no scorn of it; for [though it cannot then emancipate] it may yet engender happiness through an endless chain of births. To this effect is the description in the holy *Maitreyavimoksha*: "Verily, my son, even when broken[5] the diamond-gem is distinguished above all others and outweigheth a golden ornament, and does not lose the name of

[1] Read सत्त्वानत्राणानाश्र°.

[2] Examples of such causation by means of (small) acts of kindness.

[3] Read सम्यक्संबोधै चित्तं.

[4] Read दन्त°.

[5] Read भिन्नं for चित्तं, text quoted in Bodhicaryâvatārapañjika, i. 17.

diamond-gem; it turneth back all poverty. So also the diamond of the production of the thought of perfect enlightenment, even though divorced from good intention and conduct, outweigheth the gold ornament of the virtues of mere Śrāvakas and Pratyekabuddhas, and does not lose the name of thought of enlightenment,[1] but turneth the affliction of all re-births." From what follows we see that even without practice the thought of enlightenment is to be recognized as a helpful thing, since we are told in the second [2] *Rājāvavādaka Sūtra:* "Forasmuch also as thou, O King, hast much to do, many duties to perform, thou art not capable of being instructed in every time, manner and place in the perfection of liberality . . ." (and so on down to) "in the perfection of wisdom; therefore, O King, for ever and aye mark, learn and practise desire for full enlightenment, cultivate faith [striving for thine object] and earnest aspiration; when thou walkest, standest, sittest, sleepest, wakest, eatest, or drinkest, for ever and aye mark, learn and inwardly digest. Add, weigh and count up thine own merits past, future and present, and those of all Buddhas, Bodhisatvas, Pratyekabuddhas, disciples and laics, rejoice in them with exceeding great joy, yea, as if they were equal to pure ether or nirvāna itself rejoice therein, and when thou hast rejoiced devote those merits to doing worship to Buddhas, Bodhisatvas, and disciples, [10] and this done, make them common to all creatures; then apply them day by day, morning, noon and night, to perfect enlightenment, for the sake of all creatures fulfilling all the qualities of the Buddha and acquiring omniscience. Thus, O King, so equipped thou shalt truly rule, and shalt never be lacking in all the duties of royalty and shalt fully attain the requisites of Buddhahood." In the same passage, the fruit of all this is described: "Moreover thou, O King, by the fruit of the meritorious action, consisting in the thought of enlightenment, wast re-born many an hundred times amongst the devas; and as oft among men; and in all thy re-births thou barest

[1] Read बोधिचित्तनाम°, Bodhic. i. 17.

[2] This probably refers to the book forming No. 988 in Namjio's Cat., apparently distinct from the work of the same name described at 248–50.

sovereignty. And for thee, O King, no failing or incompleteness of this merit is foreknown. Yea, even a single thought of enlightenment, in that it forms the basis of the deliverance, loosening, consolation and final salvation of all creatures, bears in itself the accumulation of boundless, countless good; how much more shall we say this of producing such thought in many cases?"

And this thought of enlightenment is produced by the sight of the Visible Body of Buddha, as we read in the *Pūrvāvadāna*: "So much concerning the thought of resolution towards enlightenment. But the following is to be said: 'For a man who has not entered on the "stages" is there any qualification for taking the Bodhisatva's vow of restraint or not?' 'Yes, there is,' it must be known, because we hear in the *Ākāśagarbha Sūtra* of 'a radical sin' [which consists in hurting one's neighbour for one's personal gratification] for the sake of honour and gain."

Now, in the *Daśabhūmika Sūtra* at the first stage the matter is set forth thus: "And he doth not at all long for honour from any one, thinking to himself, 'It is I who must minister unto all creatures yonder a plenitude of succour.'" So too the author says: "The same *bodhisatva* in the stage named *Pramuditā* becometh fully stablished in unswerving devotion. . . ." And again: [11] "Fixed in the family of the Tathāgata he becomes predestined to full enlightenment." In the *Ākāśagarbha Sūtra* he says: "He has now no 'Disciples' vehicle, much less the Great Vehicle," [1] So too in the holy *Ugraparipṛcchā*. The duties are enjoined even on one "tied and bound" [2] by uncharitableness. But in the *Pramuditā* we read: "And after losing the notion of a self, he has no self-love, how much less love for any service;" and it is said

[1] Taken in connexion with the gloss (partly lost), I understand this to mean that when he has reached the first (*muditā*) stage any real Buddhist is void of all spiritual pride so as to desire homage as a saint; and if this be true of the inferior sect, much more must it apply to the follower of the true Mahāyāna.

[2] Or "overgrown with"; of. Divyāv. 125, where it is used of spiritual blindness: but cf. the Anglican Lenten Collect.

here that he gives his head for a fellow-man. In these and other sūtras we find the rules of conduct declared for the Bodhisatva who has entered the Stages. Then where [1] the teaching concerns the Bodhisatvas in general, the beginner should not have to observe the rules (1) when he is unfit to observe them, (2) when he is prohibited. When, however, neither of these two obstacles are present, he should in all cases observe the rule. But when one is observing one rule there is no fault in not observing another, in case one is not able.[2]

In the holy *Akshayamati Sūtra*, too, the Master speaks thus: "At the time for giving one can overlook the practice of morality and so forth.[3] But for all that he must not be lax, and he does not practise other rules 'according to his strength, as he is fit,' as says the *Daśabhūmaka*. And this discipline is attained even in the case of women, when their sinful inclinations are not violent, and their minds have a longing for enlightenment. For it is said in the *Bodhisattva-prātimoksha*: "When attended by four qualities of righteousness, O Sāriputra, the Bodhisatvas become truthful," so he says at first, and continues: "In this world, Sāriputra, either noble youth or maid, when either has applied his thoughts to the highest full enlightenment, lives strenuous in the pursuit of good." With this exordium all the due instruction follows.

And the taking of a vow of discipline should be made in the presence of one who is himself under this discipline, who is intent on the practice of the precepts of the Bodhisatva. [12] For by this means, in case of his contravening a precept keen shame and fear of breaking faith with his guru arise in his mind. And as to this, it may be noted that the general principle of a vow of restraint is that without special effort, there comes the attainment of reverence and love. Hence it is that Bodhisatvas take the vow upon themselves in presence of Tathāgatas, out

[1] Read यत्र तु न्य°.

[2] See *Bodhic. ad* v. 42. On p. 11[9] read *opekshā*:

[3] "Here is enforced a contempt for mere meditation when a person in need has come from afar and one has to make him a pious gift"—gloss. Read न त्यागः as in *Bodhic.*

of desire for the completion of one or other of the precepts. Otherwise in the absence of a spiritual guide he should take the vow of restraint before the Bodhisatvas and Buddhas of the ten regions, imagining their presence, well weighing the vow and his own strength; otherwise he might break faith with the Buddhas and Bodhisatvas and the world and the devas.

For in the *Saddharma-smṛtyupasthāna Sūtra* we hear of banishment to the Preta-world as the punishment for refusing to give some trifle spontaneously, and to hell for refusing what one has promised. How much more, then, when one has promised the highest weal of all the world and then does not carry it out ? [1]

Hence, too, the *Dharmasaṅgīti Sūtra* says : " A Bodhisatva, fair sir, must reverence truth. To be in concert with truth is to be in concert with the Law. In this expression, what is meant by 'truth'? When a Bodhisatva, after applying his thought to supreme enlightenment, will not give up that thought even to save his life nor deceive the world, that is the Bodhisatva's truth : but when after such application he does give up or waver, it is his vile falsehood."

In the holy *Sāgaramati Sūtra*, too, it is shown : " It may be that a king or titular king,[2] after having summoned all the townsfolk with an invitation for a feast on the morrow, may then become negligent and not produce the food and drink, and break faith with the whole body of the people. Therefrom they would depart, sneering at not receiving the nourishment of food and drink. In like manner, O Sāgaramati, acts the Bodhisatva, who, after giving confidence to all men for helping those to cross who have not crossed, for liberating the unliberated, for giving confidence to those that lack confidence . . . does not devote himself to religious erudition, nor yet to the other duties besides this that form sources of merit connected with enlightenment ; such a Bodhisatva breaks faith with the world of men and devas. [13] Accordingly, the deities, who have witnessed all the former Buddhas,

[1] See *Bodhic.* iv. 6.

[2] Rājamātra, v. index to Divyāv.

sneer at him and abjure him. Hard to find are the patrons of the sacrifice, who, when they have promised a mighty sacrifice, fully carry it out. Hence, I say, Sāgaramati, that the Bodhisatva should not speak any such word as may make him deceive the world of gods, men and asuras. Moreover, Sāgaramati, a Bodhisatva is often asked to render services. Then the Bodhisatva so speaks to such an effect that the Bodhisatva sacrifice his own life: but then no being is to be deceived." Hence, we learn that man must have due regard to his own powers in undertaking even one meritorious act and then keep to it. As the holy *Kshitigarbha Sūtra* says: "Buddhaship is to be got by those ten salutary courses of conduct; but not by such an one as does not even keep during his life to even one good path of action, and then, on the other hand, makes such speeches as: 'I am one of the Great Vehicle,' or 'I am pursuing the Highest enlightenment.' That man is a thorough impostor, an utter liar and deceiver of the world before all the venerable Buddhas, in asserting that death ends all, that fool dies with the doom of suffering before him." Accordingly, as long a time as one can, one should undertake good and hold unto it.

That also one may observe in the *Bhaishajyaguru-Vaidūryaprabha Sūtra:* "But the great man who has not only heard of but fathomed for himself by wisdom the difficulty of the walk of the Bodhisatva, and yet dares to bear the yoke of the salvation of afflicted mankind, such an one, when he has achieved homage, worship, confession of crime, delight in virtue, solicitation and entreaty of Buddhas, application of the merit to the attainment of enlightenment, should then say, either after asking[1] his teacher and repeating his word or else of himself: 'Consider well, O Teacher, I am named so and so. . . .'[2] Beginning with these words he must produce the thought of spiritual enlightenment; just as in the *Mañjuśrī-Buddhakshetraguṇavyūhālaṃkāra Sūtra*, in the chapter dealing with his

[1] Read *mitram adhyeshya tad. . . .* in 13^{16}.

[2] Here apparently a lacuna, or else to be supplied from next extract though none is marked. The actual vow is not stated.

previous birth, the venerable Mañjuśrī has produced the thought of enlightenment. For thus spoke he: "As the chain of births is endless from beginning to end,[1] so long shall I live that holy life for the well-being of all creatures. [14] Let us produce the thought of enlightenment in the presence of our Leader. I invite all the world; for I shall deliver it from poverty. No mind of malice and stubbornness, neither envy and grudging, will I cherish from this day as long as I have enlightenment. I will practise continence and avoid criminal lusts and imitate the self-restraint and morality of the Buddhas. Not as one that is hurried do I undertake to gain enlightenment. I will remain until the end of the chain of being for one living being's sake. I will purify[2] a measureless, an unimaginable Buddha's field. I will gain me a name renowned in the ten quarters. I will alway make pure the works of both act and word. I will purify my mind and work; yea, I will not work a work that shall be bad."

And in this connection we must not raise a doubt that, after taking a vow relating to all time, there may be a violation of it in some future birth, from the fact that in this sūtra Akshobhya's vow is allowed. For it is said as follows: Akshobhya the Tathāgata, when he was a Bodhisatva, spoke this word: "May all the venerable Buddhas be forsworn by me, if I do not in every single birth renounce the world." As it is said, "One birth must be diligently made pure by the enlightened sage; the other births that same birth will purify down to the time of enlightenment." "Thus, O Śāriputra, a Bodhisatva must imitate the Tathāgata Akshobhya; thus living the Bodhisatva in each successive birth renounces the world; yea, whether there uprise Tathāgatas or not, he must needs sally forth from the householder's state in all his existences. What causes this? For this is the highest gain, I mean the abandonment of householding," and so forth down to "he has no yearning for wife, sons and daughters." And as

[1] The meaning is "infinite as Samsāra," but the exact meaning of the line is uncertain.

[2] See Pali, visodheti="convert," Ch. s.v.

we shall be further told in the same passage that this fault is not to occur in another birth, we may now dismiss the topic.

[15] Accordingly, a universal characteristic [1] of sin is declared for the man who has taken the vow, so that when he has seen any object possessing that mark he may shun it, and he is not to bewilder himself in matters which may resemble sin or sinlessness.

[2] The Bodhisatva makes an effort guilelessly with all the forces of body, word and mind for assuaging all bodily and mental pain, both present and future, for all beings, and for producing bodily and mental happiness present and to come. But if he does not search for the complicated causes leading to all this, nor strive for the remedy of obstacles in its way; if he does not engender a little pain and grief in himself which becomes the remedy of much grief in others; nor relinquishes a little wealth for the sake of great prosperity, yea, if he overlook these duties for even a moment, then is he guilty of sin.

To state it briefly: There is no sin as concerns matters that are beyond one's power, because there the effort would be fruitless, and because there is no injunction of rule But owing to the faultiness of human nature one might take a wrong path. Thus, in a case where there would be sin, because, although the matter is beyond one's power, nevertheless there is efficacity of effort, one must not pay attention to his sin; one is made free from it, because it is included in the general confession of sin.[3]

The above is the body [4] of the rules for the Bodhisatva put concisely. But should one desire it at full length, the exposition of it would not end in a thousand ages. Putting the matter otherwise, in brief, there are two cases of sin on the part of

[1] Viz. the appearance of it is to be avoided.

[2] In *Bodhicaryāvatāra*, iv. 48 (Bibl. Ind. p. 93) with better readings; in line 8 of the present text read वान्यद् for त्वसद्, and यत्र तु स्व° . . योगसा° . . . °देशनान्तर्भावात्तो . . .

[3] This means that one need not waste one's energies on a thing quite fruitless and beyond our powers, *e.g.* draining the sea; but in cases where, though the main object cannot be fully realized, good may result from self-sacrifice, we must not excuse ourself on the score of inability. This may be illustrated by the Spartan army at Thermopylæ.

[4] I have found no authority for this use (like Lat. corpus) of *śarīra*.

the Bodhisatva: first, where he commences his action without having first considered its adaptability or the reverse to his powers, does not come back, or takes no account of it;[1] the second is where he has fully weighed the act on its merits, yet transgresses and incurs the reproach of even the pariah slave. How can this be? This point may be cleared up from the pronouncement in the *Adhyāśayasamcodana Sūtra*:[2] "Moreover, O Maitreya, by four causes the word of the Buddhas may be recognised. What four? (1) O Maitreya, it refers to truth, not to untruth; (2) to the Law, not the not-Law; (3) it lessens sin, not increases it; (4) it shows the advantages of nirvāna, not indicates those of continued re-birth; by these four," and so forth down to "When some one, O Maitreya, utters or shall utter a word endowed with these four qualities, the believing young men and women will produce the idea of Buddha, of Master; they will hear this Law as he preaches. Why? Anything, Maitreya, that is well said, is a word of Buddha. And any one who shall reject such utterances, and say, 'They are not spoken by Buddha,' and produce disrespect towards them; such a hateful person does really reject all the utterances pronounced by all Buddhas; and having rejected the Law, he will go to hell, on account of a deed which is by nature an injury to the Law."

[16] Should, however, any student desire proficiency in order to train himself, he must just give attention to the present work, the *Sikshāsamuccaya*, in order to get training in the preliminary practice, because there is so much profit if we only begin to be trained. As the *Praśāntaviniścayaprātihārya Sūtra* says: "There is one Bodhisatva, O Mañjuśrī, who might give to Buddhas innumerable as the sands of the Ganges Buddha-worlds[3] likewise numberless to each and all of them, worlds filled full of mighty jewels and gems of magic potency, and will give in this way for ages likewise numberless; and another

[1] Read चारभते । न निवर्तते । उपेक्षते वा.

[2] Extant in Tib.; v. Feer, Analyse du K. p. 216. Quoted *ad Bodhicar.* IV. 48 (p. 94) where we read ०भाषितं वेदितव्यं । कतमैश्चतुर्भिः ।.

[3] See Childers, s.v. *Khetta*.

Bodhisatva who hears such doctrine, and goes aside, and ponders thereon in mind, saying, 'I will train myself in those doctrines.' The latter, although untrained, engenders in the process of training a far larger [1] merit than is the merit that consists in mere giving of gifts." Hence, a Bodhisatva seeing the advantages must not go back. As the scripture says in the same passage: "O Manjuśrī, there are beings like in number to the dust of the least atoms of thousands of worlds. Suppose each of them became a king and ruler in Jambudvīpa, and all them proclaimed thus: 'Whosoever shall take knowledge [2] of the Great Vehicle, shall bear in mind, recite, study or sound it abroad, him we will torture by the quick [3] of his nails for a month, and the torture of five *palas* by day,[4] and by this manner of departure will we banish him from life."

If the Bodhisatva, O Mañjuśrī, at such a proclamation feels no fear or alarm, yea, by so much as a single thought within him is not afraid nor dejected nor wavering, and, furthermore, is devoted to the mastering of the True Law and lives in devotion to reading and study, such a Bodhisatva, O Mañjucrī, is worthy to be called a hero in mind, in liberality, in conduct, forbearance, prowess, meditation, wisdom, and contemplation.

"If, O Mañjuśrī, when yonder men are murderously inclined toward him, he is not angry nor wroth, nor cherisheth an heart to harm them, such an one is like Brahma or Indra, inflexible."

So at this day devotion to the true teaching ripens unto mighty fruit. For so we hear in the *Candrapradīpa Sūtra:* [17] "I will minister unto myriads of Buddhas, proffering water with mind serene, sunshades, flags, and festoons of lamps, yea, for myriads of ages as many as the Ganges sand, and whoso, when the good Law is abused and precepts of the Buddha let and hindered by night and day, even though alone

[1] Read बहुतरं.

[2] *Divy.* index.

[3] Cf. the various *chedanas* in the list of tortures in Milinda-pañha.

[4] *Divasena* is perhaps corrupt. I have not found out the torture implied in the adj. *pañcapalika.*

practiseth the teaching, becometh everywhere [1] renowned for holiness."

For this cause we must give all devotion. Moreover, the rules for the Bodhisatva's instructions are given in the scriptures. Thus the *Ratnamegha* teaches: "And how, fair sir, do Bodhisatvas become restrained with the restraints of the true Bodhisatva? In this case the Bodhisatva reflects thus: 'It is not by the restraint of the monk's code alone that I can gain the highest enlightenment. How then? I must learn in all the Sūtrāntas the various rules and precepts of conduct enjoined in each by the Tathāgata for the Bodhisatva.' This point is further enlarged on, and he adds: 'We must conclude that the precise system of discipline of the Bodhisatva is hard to grasp, for limited intelligence like ours, owing to the detailed manner of its injunctions." What, then, is right? One should know their vital points; and thus become free from guilt.[2]

"And what are those 'vital points' that are laid down in the scriptures for the good of such as take pleasure in the Great Vehicle? This stanza tells us:

> "Give freely for all creature's sake
> Thy person, thy enjoyments too,
> Thy merit's store throughout all time
> Guard each and grow in holiness." [3]

There we find the summary of the vows of restraint for the Bodhisatva, and in it is laid down sin in case of slackness of conduct on the part of Bodhisatvas.

As it is said in the *Bodhisatva-Prātimokṣa*: "Whatsoever road is taken by the Bodhisatva for the sake of all beings, a road destroying pain, if after the Bodhisatva has taken that road and has stood firmly upon it for a myriad ages, one thought of happiness and one thought of despondency should arise, then the Bodhisatva must thus think within himself, 'Having taken upon myself the troubles of all beings, putting away this thought from myself, I am despondent.' And comprehending this, Mañjuśrī said: These are the five 'continuities' in

[1] Cf. Ved. idam . . . idam. [2] Kārikā 3*b*. [3] Kārikā 4.

virtue of which Bodhisatvas quickly gain perfect enlightenment. What five do I mean?

(1) When a Bodhisatva devotes himself to the highest enlightenment and has given his mind to it, [18] and does not intermediately give his mind to the spiritual stage of the mere Disciple or Pratyeka-buddha.

(2) When he has made up his mind to the sacrifice of all he has, and does not meantime put it down with a grudging heart; this, my son, is the second 'continuity.'

(3) When he has made up his mind that he will be the protector of beings, and does not meanwhile become slack.

(4) When he has made up his mind that he will gain full knowledge of all the laws not [suddenly] evolved and unhindered [in their development], and does not meanwhile follow in the ways of false doctrines.

(5) When he has resolved that he will gain knowledge of these laws with wisdom well equipped for each single moment, and does not stay nor take rest till all knowledge is attained."

Therefore the growth of purity should be fostered in due manner by constantly preserving thus the renunciation of self, goods, and merit. In this connection surely to promote renunciation of goods one should produce a passionless state by means of meditating on the sin of grasping greed, and should meditate on the praises of self-sacrifice. On this point we are told in the *Candrapradīpa Sūtra*: " The fools that cling to this foul body, to life that must needs be unsteady and like to illusions, dreams and phantasm, these pass into the power of delusion and commit hideous crime, and thus go to fearsome hells. Fools are they and in the way of death."

So too it is said in the *Anantamukha-nirhāradhāraṇī*: " Wherever conflicts arise amongst living creatures, the sense of possession is the cause. For this cause let a man leave any place where desire may arise. For the world is at the feet of him who is rid of desire."

In the *Bodhisattva-prātimoksha* we are told: "Again, Śāriputra, in all business of life the Bodhisatva has the thought, This belongs to others, without attaching any personal feeling. How so? Because attachment is a danger." [1]

In the holy *Ugradatta-paripṛcchā*, too, we hear: [19] "The thing that is given one has not to guard any longer, whereas what is in one's house has to be guarded. What is given is for the destroying of desire, what is at home increases desire. The one never excites greed nor fear, not so the other. The one helps the path of enlightenment, the other the path of the Evil One. The one is lasting, the other is impermanent. The one is a source of happiness, the other of pain. The one makes for deliverance from sin, the other increases sin. What we give, not what we keep by us, tends to our true enjoyment. The giver is the true hero, the miser the coward; thus to give makes us gain a hero's heart, to keep, a coward's. By giving we gain the praise of all the Buddhas, by keeping that of foolish folk. . . .

"Again, if he comes to feel an excessive affection for his son and not for others, he must admonish his mind with three admonitions. What are these? Wisdom belongs to the Bodhisatva who is properly employed and even-minded, not to him who is disturbed and improperly employed; wisdom belongs to him who is consistent, not to the inconsistent. Admonishing his mind with these three admonitions, he must attach to his son the notion of no-friend, 'for that is no friend to me, not friendly, when I for its sake shake off the yoke of the doctrine instituted by Buddha, and feel excessive affection for this my son and not for others.'

"Thus he must educate his mind that he may feel in each case the same affection for all creatures that naturally centres in his son, or in himself. He must thoroughly consider the matter in this way: 'He comes from one place and I from another. All creatures are also my sons, and I their child. In this life no one is really a son or a stranger to any one. . . .' Thus, O goodman of the house, the Bodhisatva when a householder

[1] *Upādāna* comes between *trishṇā* and *bhava* in the *pratityasamutpāda*.

must not feel for any given object that it is his and he means to keep it, neither attachment to it; nor feel that it is fated to be his or that his lust inclines to it. Again, O goodman of the house, suppose that a beggar come up to the householding Bodhisatva and beg for any object whatsoever, and that object be not already given up to another, in this case he must not allow himself to reason in such wise as this: 'Whether I give this thing up or no, I shall come to be without substance; whether I will or no I must some day submit to death, [20] and then that object will leave me, and I shall leave it.' 'If I give up that object I shall have to end my days poverty-stricken'; 'Well, if I once do give it up it will not haunt [1] my mind when I come to die; on the contrary, it will give rise to satisfaction, joy without a tinge of grudging.' If it be only such considerations as these that enable him to give up the object, he must make to the suitor the fourfold frank avowal that here follows, saying: 'I am but a weak vessel, and goodness is but stunted in me. I am but a beginner [2] in the Great Vehicle. I have no command over my heart to make it give up. I am full of the heresy of attachment to this world; for I am sunk in pride and selfishness. Be patient with me, good sir, and be not wroth. I will act, perform, and exert all vigour to fulfil thy desire and that of all mankind.' So must he avow to the suitor. And over and above he may say to himself thus, so as to remove all sin: 'Let not the Bodhisatva feel displeasure in this act, nor let the suitor feel it towards the Bodhisatva.'" But at that rate we must not suppose that a niggard spirit is free from blame; and, in fact, our Master does reprehend it in Bodhisatvas, as, for example, in this passage of the *Bodhisattva-prātimoksha*: "In the true Bodhisatva four qualities are never found. What are they? Guile, niggardliness, envious slander,[3]

[1] Exact counterpart of a Pali phrase; see Ch. s.v. pariyādāti.

[2] For the phr. cf. Divy.-index where however the connotation of meaning is somewhat different.

[3] Cf. Dharm.-s. § 69, where *īrshyā*, *mātsarya* and *śāṭhya* are successively mentioned as vices.

and the heart that cleaveth to earth and says, 'I cannot gain the highest illumination.' In whomsoever, Śāriputra, these four *are* found, of him the wise must take knowledge, saying: 'Yonder man, my son, is a deceitful babbler, his good qualities are ruined, yea, they are but sin, his belly is heavy with the 'fleshpots of Egypt,' his mind is all for food and raiment.'

"Thus, Śāriputra, Bodhisatvas become spiritual heroes (and so on . . .), thus such an one sacrifices his own hand, his foot, nose, head, limbs greater and lesser, son, daughter, wife, love, servant, mind, ease, house, wealth, country, treasure and all that is his."

[21] And in the *Nārāyaṇa-paripṛcchā* likewise it is said: "One must not take to oneself anything of which one will have no thought of sacrifice, no understanding of sacrifice; no such acquisition is to be acquired as to which he would have not the heart to let go. He must not take articles of which there arises in him, when asked by beggars, the thought of possession. Nor must he grasp kingdom, enjoyments, treasure . . . or anything whatever which would make the Bodhisatva unready to give it up. Moreover, noble sir, the Bodhisatva must think thus: 'I have devoted and abandoned my frame to all creatures. Much more my outward possessions: any being who shall require it for any purpose, it being recognised for a good, I will give hand, foot, eye, flesh, blood, marrow, limbs great and small—my head itself to such as ask for them; not to mention outward things. wealth, corn, gold, silver, gems, ornaments, horses, elephants, chariots, cars, villages, towns, markets, peoples, kingdoms, capital cities, menservants, maidservants, messengers, sons, daughters and retinue. Whoever shall want it to him I will give so it be for his good. Without regret, and without grudging, without waiting for merit to mature, I will abandon them, without respect of persons, to show them kindness, out of compassion and pity, to be theirs to possess, so that these beings, well entreated by me as by one who has attained wisdom, may learn to know the law. . . . Even so, my son, when the tree of healing is cut

by root, trunk, branch, bark, or leaf, flower, fruit or pith, it never flinches nor complains that aught from root to pith is cut away; but rather unflinchingly devotes them to taking away the diseases of beings of every degree. Even so the Bodhisatva must regard as medicine this his frame composed of the four great elements, and say, 'Let all creatures take it of me as they require it, a hand, for such as need it, or a foot, for such as need it.'"

And so, too, it is shown in the *Akshayamati Sūtra*: "I must wear out even this my body for the behests of all creatures. And as these Four Outward Elements, *i.e.* earth, air, fire and water, [22] go to the varied enjoyment of creatures through many directions and turnings, supports, appliances and uses: so I purpose to make this my body, itself an aggregation of the four great elements, fit for the enjoyment of all creatures through the many directions and other means. He, seeing that it is to be used for a purpose, looks fixedly at the misfortunes of the body and is not distressed thereby through care for all creatures."

And in the holy *Vajradhvaja Sūtra* he says:

"So indeed the Bodhisatva, giving himself amongst all creatures, by aiding all roots of good, regarding all creatures in their roots of good, offering himself as a lamp amongst all creatures, establishing himself amongst all creatures as their happiness, keeping himself in all the world like the womb of the Law, behaving himself amongst all creatures like a light, looking upon himself as the asylum of the world, behaving himself in the world as a cause of the root of good, appointing himself as a friend amongst all beings, showing himself amongst all creatures as the road to supreme happiness, purifying himself amongst all creatures as a communication of supreme happiness, making himself like unto the sun in all the world—offering himself amongst all creatures in those capacities, regarding himself in all the world as ready for service as they wish, regarding himself as the abode of the world,[1] producing equanimity for all beings in all the world, regarding himself as a means for all

[1] Text uncertain.

service, looking on himself as the giver of happiness to the whole world, resolving to be the generous benefactor of all the world, making himself as wisdom for the whole world, showing himself to be devoted to the practices of the Bodhisatva, showing himself as one whose deeds are as his words, regarding himself as girt about with the armour of omniscience, keeping the thought which he entertained, and establishing himself in his duties, [23] keeping in mind the Bodhisatva's thought of renunciation, regarding himself as being a pleasure-garden for all creatures, showing himself amongst all creatures as delighting in the Law, establishing himself as the giver of contentment to all creatures, yielding himself to all the world as producing supreme delight, keeping himself as the storehouse for all pure righteousness in the whole world, placing himself as the giver of Buddha's wisdom to all creatures, giving himself as a father to all creation, establishing himself in all the region of creatures as a store of all help and sufficiency.

"Thus, indeed, is the Bodhisatva, giving himself for service, having a mind humble and attentive for those who ask, having a mind to rest on as upon a carpet, with attention fixed on supporting all unhappiness like the earth, with mind devoted to unwearied service for all creatures, firm amidst the evil acts of the foolish, of firmly abiding nature, not resting, endowed with the root of good, unattached, the support of all the worlds, sacrificing ears and nose to suitors who ask it, having a mind because of his attaining the Bodhisatva's discipline, noble as the Tathāgata's race, intent upon the exercise of remembering all the Bodhisatvas, considering what is essential [1] apart from the three unessential worlds, his chain of thought not being fixed upon his own body, homeless,[2] spending his time in remembering all the attributes of the Buddha, with the intention of taking what is essential from this unessential body.

"Thus, indeed, if the Bodhisatva is asked for his tongue,

[1] Tib. implies °सारंप्रत्य°.

[2] But the Tib. gives this as an epithet of "qualities."

[he sits down, and speaks [1]] with lovable and friendly voice, prompted by friendly thoughts,[2] and seating him in a goodly couch fit for a king, he addresses that suitor with pleasure. He becomes unangered in mind, unoffended, not vexed, with mind absorbed in magnanimity, with mind partaking of the Buddha's race, with the chain of his thought unwavering in nature, full of strength and power, with mind not fixed upon his body, not devoted to talking, his body resting on the knees; putting all his body at the service of the suitor he speaks from his own mouth, uttering words that are affectionate, gentle, and lovely, a friendly service. 'Take thou my tongue, do with it as seemeth thee good. Do so as pleaseth thee, [24] that thou be pleased at heart and satisfied with thyself, contented and delighted with pleasure:' with these words, he sacrifices his head, bringing about the highest knowledge which is the topmost head of all things, attaining the wisdom which is the head of the salvation of all creatures, craving incomparable knowledge which is the chiefest head of all the world, resolved to obtaining the king of knowledge, the head of all regions, desirous of accomplishing the culmination of lordship over transcendent things, with a mind bursting with affection for an endless number of applicants.

"Thus, indeed, the Bodhisatva, sacrificing hands and feet to those that ask, by doing kindness with the hand of faith, with the outstretched hand of sacrifice, the heroism of a noble Bodhisatva, finding pleasure in renunciation, by sacrificing hand and foot, placing his foot on the great basis [3] by the resolution of following the practice of a Bodhisatva, by the fact of not being troubled by suffering, by ability to take pleasure in the giving, with the restraint that consists in pure thought; he cherishes the idea of a body uncut, unbroken, undiminished, which consists in the body of the Law formed of knowledge without obstacle [4]; he has a mind not low, preserved from all the

[1] From Tib.

[2] So Tib. for °चित्ततया.

[3] Tib. rten chen.po.la rkaṅ.par hdor.ba.

[4] Tib. ye.ses yons.su dkrigspa med.pa daṅ chos.kyi.lus rgyad. mi. hchad. pa mi.sigs.pa mi.chad.paḥi lus daṅ ldan.pa—as obscure as the Sanskrit.

machinations of Māra, cherished and saved by the good friend, delivered by the whole-hearted renunciation which is praised by all Bodhisatvas.

"Thus, indeed, the Bodhisatva, sacrificing his own body, offering his blood to those that ask, has a mind delighting in wisdom, desiring to behave as a Bodhisatva, not casting away a thought that was made clear to him, ready and eager for all that ask, not hated by any one who receives, walking in the path of the renunciation of all the Bodhisatvas, not regarding his own body because of unconquerable joy and contentment, offering the blood from his own body, devoted to the Great Vehicle as the abode of knowledge, with mind unspoilt in the Great Vehicle, agreeable, pleased, delighted, joyful, friendly, happy, contented, and becoming joyful, pleased, and content, sacrificing the very marrow from his body for those who ask, with good renunciation, addressing those suitors with welcome voice: 'Let your honours take the marrow and the flesh, to use as you will,' with equal increase of pleasure and sacrifice, with a great root of merit practised by a company that has the knowledge of a Bodhisatva, [25] with excellent resolve that removes the filth of the world; with efforts towards great generosity undertaken in the spirit of equanimity of all the Bodhisatvas, with suitors longed for, gifts given without repentance, without expecting the reward of merit, with worship of the mass of gloriously adorned Buddha-fields, not disregarding any of the worlds, with mercy and salvation directed towards all the world, towards the enlightenment of all the Buddhas; with the [strength] of the Daśabala, with attention only to the root of merit, directed towards all the Bodhisatvas past, present and future, with the sound of a bull's or lion's roar directed towards all skill, in the three times,[1] with equanimity and knowledge in all ways, with determination through infinite number of ages directed towards the world, with the Bodhisatva's resolve, by producing a mind free from distress directed towards fearlessness, the Bodhisatva sacrificing his own heart to those that ask, his mind

[1] Past, present, future.

instructed as to the kinds of gifts, developing the Perfections, his mind humble and well established in the gifts of all Bodhisatvas, resolved to be attentive to all that ask, purifying his resolve, undertaking the great resolve which is the cause of the ripening of all the world, abiding in the conduct of the Bodhisatva, gathering the elements of omniscience, not relaxing his resolve, he then sacrifices to those that ask liver, heart, and lungs, with intelligence pleased with those that ask, with eyes looking happy and glad, with affection sent forth to the Bodhisatva, with unflagging attention, renunciation, with a well-thought-of idea of taking the essence from the non-essential body, attentively remembering that the body has its end in the cemetery, regarding his body as food for wolves, jackals and dogs, remembering that it is the share of others; because of the body's impermanency, with the thought that the body is the share of others when it is cast forth, even so, applying his reflection to the Law, the Bodhisatva steadily observing those suitors, thus begins to think: 'If I should give to the suitor from the body intestines, liver, heart, or lungs, or if I should not give them, at the end of my life this body is not eternal, it is owed to the cemetery.' [26] Thus he with nature content and satisfied, with knowledge of the law, with resolve, established in the idea of the good friend, at the instance of a suitor desirous of extracting the essence from this non-essential body, through love of the law, even when he sacrifices only a nail from his own flesh with the thought, 'This is applied to the root of good,' thus renounces his own body."

And the renouncing of one's enjoyments and merits is described in the same place, thus: "So, indeed, the Bodhisatva amongst various recipients worthy of gifts, who come from all sorts of places, amongst the innumerable poor beggars, who have heard of the renown of the Bodhisatva, who have come after hearing the rumour of the Bodhisatva, who have an opportunity of confidence in a Bodhisatva, who have heard the resolve of the Bodhisatva after giving, who have been invited by the resolve of the Bodhisatva's mind, men desired by him with his mind set upon renunciation, with the thought welcomed by doing honour to the delighted suitors, with the thought of propitiating the suitors who come. 'It is I who should have shown respect to you, now that I have come into this region, to save you the trouble of coming:' thus he propitiates all the suitors by doing a complete prostration, and after propitiating them invites them to bathe and gives repose to their bodies and offers them any service they wish: namely, jewel-waggons full of choice and beautiful girls of Jambudvīpa, namely, gold-waggons full of choice and virtuous girls of the country, namely, jewel-waggons full of a quantity of singing and music all sounding together: so he gives crystal waggons full of choice maidens of charming and agreeable looks, all adorned with fair faces and fair dress." Then in the same place it is explained: "giving jewel-waggons provided with noble elephants covered with jewelled nets, and carriages; giving sandal-wood waggons with jewelled wheels and trappings, provided with jewelled seats" . . . as far as "quantities of all sorts of jewelled sunshades with coloured canopies outspread, adorned with banners and flags in all four directions, [27] scented with all sorts of perfumes, anointed with precious fragrant ointments, bespread with multitudes of all manner of flowers, prolonged with hundreds of thousands of maidens like strings of jewels, steady in movement, provided with steady animals all alike, . . ." and so on to "agreeable charming scents in the air, with pleasant civilities and greetings by daughters and sons, with civilities and gifts of quantities of perfumed powders of all sorts."

Again, in the same place he says: "And presenting himself to all creatures, or giving service to all Buddhas, or relinquishing a kingdom, or citadel,[1] or the habitation of the king of a city all gloriously adorned, or performing all service properly for those that ask, or giving sons, daughters and wife to thos that ask, or leaving his house utterly" . . . and so on to "giving all indulgence and enjoyments: so the Bodhisatva gives his drink or his dainty dishes of all sorts, fine, noble, pure, perfect, pungent,

[1] Tib. *mk'ar*. See B.R. *puṭabhedana*.

tasty, bitter,[1] astringent, full of all sorts of excellent savours, soft, full of the various kinds of flavours, establishing the equilibrium of the troubled humours,[2] supporting the strength of body and mind, causing ability to please, gratify, and delight" . . . and so on to "preventing all the attacks of others, causing health and the appeasing of all diseases.[3] So with gifts of clothing, flowers, scents, ointments, garlands; gifts of beds, dwellings, pillows, and lights; the Bodhisatva offering requisites for the sick, medicines and utensils," . . . and so on to "vessels of all sorts, various necessaries, copper vessels filled up with infinite provisions, filled with powdered silver and gold, —giving these things to the Blessed Buddhas, his heart confident in those worthy of infinite offerings; or giving to the precious Bodhisatvas, by cherishing the mind of the good friend so hard to attain; or giving to the noble Order; or giving to a man who is the support of the Buddha's teaching; or giving to disciples and Pratyekabuddhas with heart pleased with their noble virtues, or to mother and father; or with the idea of obeying or waiting upon a teacher, giving to teachers and preceptors worthy of gifts, devoted to the practice of the admonitions and instructions which are the preceptor's task, or giving food and clothing to poor mendicants and beggars, not turning his eyes from any creature, cherishing friendship in his heart. . . ."

"And so the Bodhisatva giving thorobred elephants strongly grown in their seven parts, of sixty years, [28] provided with six carts [4] of lotus colour, with clean faces, adorned with gold, their bodies covered with golden nets, multitudes of nets of all sorts of jewels thrown over the trunks, various ornaments and filagree work, glorious with gold, beautiful and lovely to behold, doing their duty unwearied for a thousand leagues, or giving thorobred horses, provided with goodly vehicles and goodly bodies, gifted with speed, with speed to go and fetch from the four quarters of the earth, with riders on their backs, covered with all adornments like those of beautiful, lovely,

[1] Read *kaṭuka*.
[2] Read *śamana*.
[3] Restoring health.
[4] The Tib. has *mče*, tusk, *shaḍḍantopetān*.

divine beings. As he gives these, offering them with respect to teachers, good friends, father and mother, poor mendicants and beggars, to recipients from all the world, giving with heart emancipated, relinquishing them with no niggardly mind, with a nature that manifests great mercy, walking in the Bodhisatva's virtues which extend even unto the great renunciation, purifying the resolves of a wise Bodhisatva," . . . and so on to "And so the Bodhisatva, giving a seat, renouncing it, gives auspicious royal seats with feet of beryl, thrones with canopies of golden chains and jewelled nets, supplied with plenty of robes soft to the touch, with provision of all good food and perfume, with banners all over diamonds, and heaps of jewels by the million, bespread with golden nets, utensils scented with sandalwood, circlets of golden bells in masses giving forth a lovely sound of music, mighty seats, a sight for the eye uplifted and wide-ranging, consecrated as thrones of commandment for the whole earth united under one dominion; and he flourishes in universal sovereignty for the rule and admonition of his empire, having taken his seat with all dominion and power:" . . . and so on to "so indeed the Bodhisatva giving sunshades and renouncing them, gives sunshades adorned with heaps of grand jewels, jewelled stems, covered with festoons of bells hung with strings of jewels and beryl drooping over ear and neck, [29] providing a merry noise of cries of joy, clean coverings within the golden nets, spread over hundreds of thousands of ribs jewelled and ornamented, fitted in jewelled sockets, of fragrant aloes and sandalwood, provided with millions and millions of choice perfumes all of the same fine quality scattered abroad, of clear bright gold: of such glorious sunshades in millions and millions giving those that are left over in countless millions on millions with indifference and renouncing them, relinquishing them, offering them, to great personages who are present or to adorn the shrines of the Tathāgatas who come no more to earth, or to the Bodhisatvas, good friends, for searching after righteousness, or to the noble Bodhisatvas who preach the Law, or to mother and father, or to the precious Order, or to the gospel of all

Buddhas . . . or to all recipients: thus he applies the merit of these acts."

Just as in the first application of merit it was explained whenever we dealt with the root of good, so he makes his resolution. "How could these roots of good provide life and help for the whole world, ending in the pure Law, in such a way that through those roots of good there might be for all beings removal of hell and unhappy states; so that by these they could keep away from them the mass of pain which consists in birth as an animal or Yama's world? He applying these roots of good thus applies the root of good in this case, 'By this root of good may I become a rest of all beings to keep them away from all the mass of pain: may I become the protector of all beings by setting them free from all sin: may I become a shelter for all beings to save them from all fear: may I become a path for all beings that they may go in every place: may I become a refuge for all beings that they may attain peace in the infinite meditation: may I become a light to all beings by showing knowledge without darkness: may I become a fire for all beings by driving away the darkness and gloom of ignorance: may I become a radiance for all beings by establishing infinite purity: may I become a guide for all beings by bringing them into the interpretation of the Law surpassing thought: may I be a leader for all beings by bringing them to the elements of knowledge revealed;'" . . . and this he applies with intention not in word only, this he applies with uplifted heart, with heart delighted, with heart pleased, [30] with heart rejoicing and glad, with mercy and love in his heart, with favour and kindness at heart, with happy heart. And this he applies as follows: "May this very root of good turn out for purifying the ways of all beings, for purifying their achievements, for purifying their merit and magnanimity; may it so turn out that they be unconquered, that they be never grasping, that their thoughts be unapproachable, that their memory be not distracted, for decision of conduct and thought, for unlimited wisdom, for perfecting all the ornaments of good qualities in deeds of body and of mind: By this my root of good may all beings please all the Buddhas, and having pleased may they not displease; and in those blessed Buddhas may they acquire unbreakable satisfaction; and in the presence of those holy Tathāgatas the supreme Buddhas may they hear the preaching of the Law, and hearing may they put away all errors, and may they observe it as heard; and observing it may they accomplish their undertakings, and find favour with the Tathāgatas; may they obtain activity of thought, and accomplish blameless deeds; may they establish themselves in the great roots of good, and keep away endless poverty, and may they accomplish the seven receivings of wealth; may they be taught by all the Buddhas, and may they attain the good moral qualities, and develop lofty equanimity of resolution, and receive opportunity in omniscient knowledge; may they develop unhindered vision in all the world, and receive the endowment of all the distinguishing marks, which is the perfection of body; may they lay hold of purified speech adorned with all virtues, may they receive self-restraint and the soundness of thought coupled with the ten powers; [1] [31] may they carry out an independent mode of life; and may all beings receive that supply of happiness which all Buddhas are endowed with."

As the sixth application, he applies in the way described. "May all beings by the food of knowledge be endowed with detachment of mind, diligent in making proper distinction in food, not clinging to food, feeding on affection, living without meat . . . extinguishing desire and thirst. May all beings be sprinkled as from a cloud with the essence of righteousness, their natures delighted with love for the supreme Law. May all beings have all choice flavours on their tongues, enamoured [2] of its flavour, their thoughts dwelling on all the attributes of the Buddhas, going not astray, being in the chief path, the supreme path, the quick path, the Great Path. May all beings be never satisfied with looking, possessing the love of the Buddha. May all beings be unhindered in seeing the good friend. May all beings be like sovereign medicines and drugs. May all beings

[1] See Pali Dict., s.v. Balam. [1] See Pali Dict., *nimittaṃ gaṇhāti.*

keep far away the poison of sin. May all beings be like the sun's orb arising, by scattering the veil of darkness and gloom for all beings."

Thus having offered himself he must recite in conformity with his meditation. "I make the application that all beings may see most clearly, that they may see cheerfulness and good, that they may see what is desired and agreeable, and not see what is disagreeable, that they may see the Buddhas.

"May all beings be endowed with the fragrance of virtue, with virtue unbroken, endowed with the Bodhisatva's perfections. May all beings be perfumed with liberality, full of sacrifice and renunciation. May all beings be fragrant with compassion, possessed of unshakable thoughts. May all beings be fragrant with courage, armed with patience for the Path. May all beings be fragrant with meditation, standing face to face with the existing Buddha, possessed of concentration. May all beings be fragrant with the application of a Bodhisatva's merit; may all beings be fragrant with all things that are pure, free from all things that are evil. May all beings have a divine couch for the attainment of high knowledge. May all beings have the couch of holiness. [32] May all beings have a happy couch by dwelling in the thought of wisdom apart from the common herd. May all beings have a peaceful couch, by avoiding the pain which belongs to the realm of transmigration, and be endowed with a feeling for the love of the Law. May all beings be brilliant in the pure field of the Buddha, provided with a dwelling of virtue, from dwelling in a noble palace, not separated from the dwelling of all the incomparable Buddhas. May all beings enjoy the potentiality of becoming a Buddha. May all beings have infinite vision in all the things of the Buddha, may all beings have light unhindered, entirely penetrating all elements of existence. May all beings have bodies free from disease, having received the body of the Tathāgata. May all beings be like Bhaishajyarāja [1] having unshakable qualities. May all beings be like a pillar of healing, infallible, acting for the world's cure. May all beings

[1] A Buddha.

thwart the pangs of disease, possessing the health of the omniscient. May all beings be skilled in the healing of all the world, practising the use of medicine according to their wish. I make my application for all beings to repel all disease. I make my application for all beings in the infinite strength and vigour of the body. I make my application for all beings to have bodily strength not to be crushed, like the mountains that surround the universe. I make my application for all beings in their hunger for all supports of strength. May all beings be vessels of infinite capacity, wide as space, endowed with the sense of memory, not bewildered in memory for words through comprehending all worldly and transcendental language. May all beings be of good and purified meditation, taking pleasure in the perpetuity of wisdom in all Buddhas past, present and to come. May all beings go as they list, attaining the Buddha's field which leads everywhere. May all beings be unhampered in thought about all beings. May all beings without effort enter manifestly upon all the fields of the Buddha, with power to understand all things by instantaneous insight. May all beings enter every sphere unwearied and unexhausted, having a spiritual body never resting. May all beings be free through an easy course, following in the ways of all Bodhisatvas. By this root of good may all beings always be possessed of the thought which does not renounce the good friend, grateful by cherishing benefits. May all beings have one common purpose with good friends by seizing upon the common root of good. May all beings have good resolutions, by approaching the abodes and the common dwellings of good friends. May all beings be purified by the ripening of their deeds through the root of good friends, with one sole aspiration. May all beings attain good delight in the Great Vehicle, with no obstruction to their course which ends in omniscience. May all beings have their root of good hidden,[1] guarding the condition of all Buddhas. May all beings have the knowledge of their virtues hidden, avoiding the wrath and sin of all the world. May all beings be without break or hindrance in goodness, rivers of

[1] *I.e.* not proclaimed abroad.

Buddha's qualities undestroyed. May all beings be like sunshades, forming a canopy for the Daśabala. May all beings attain the seat of infinite wisdom. May all beings attain the throne of Buddha's courage, conspicuous to behold."

And in the holy *Gaganagañja* Sūtra he says: "May there be in me no root of good or knowledge of righteousness or skilfulness [1] that is not useful to all beings."

The resignation [2] of past or future good is described in the holy Akshayamati. Sūtra. "The remembrance of good thoughts or feeling; and after remembering, the application of wisdom: this is skill concerning the past; namely, bringing into vision the conscious consideration of past goods. 'Those good thoughts that shall arise in me, these I shall apply in the infinite and supreme wisdom:' such is skill as regards the future. Thus by mental practice [34] one fulfils the intention of renouncing all; with a bodily practice that is directed by the impulse of renunciation, one relinquishes all acquisitiveness. One who is set free from the pains of existence which are rooted in acquisitiveness, is said to be liberated; and he attains through infinite, immeasurable, countless ages manifold ends, worldly and transcendental, showers of happiness and bliss. By his own person, becoming as it were a baited hook which does not of itself enjoy, he draws others and serves them. Therefore it is said in the *Ratnamegha*: giving is the Bodhisatva's enlightenment."

[1] Read °ज्ञानं.

[2] That is, to others. Quoted in *Bodhic*, iii. 10. Delete ना at beginning of line 14 of text.

CHAPTER II

THE DUTY OF SELF-PRESERVATION

THUS we must duly preserve the self and its belongings, though they are sacrificed to others. How so? Because it is "for the enjoyment of living beings that one's frame and all besides is given."

If unpreserved, how then enjoyed? what gift is given, if unenjoyed? Therefore that creatures may enjoy, guard thine own frame and all beside.[1] For the *Bodhisattva-prātimoksha* tells us: "O Sāriputra, one must preserve one's self when one intends to preserve others. It is armed with that benevolence which takes just this form [of preserving his body for others' good], that a Bodhisatva refuses to do an evil deed, yea, even for dear life." In the *Vīradatta-paripṛicchā*, too, the speaker says: "He who hath a mind for the Law must carry about his body like a cart for the supporting of burdens."[2] So too says the *Akshayamati Sūtra*: "[The righteous man] too is not afflicted by the ills of the flesh, because he hath regard for his fellows."

Accordingly the question arises: how is one to preserve one's self? "By never giving up one's Good Friend."[3]

As in Holy *Gaṇḍa-vyūha* Śrīsambhava[4] says: "Restrained by trusty friends, O noble youth, Bodhisatvas fall not into evil destinies; [35] taken into guidance[5] by them they transgress

[1] Kārikās 5 a, b, 6 a.

[2] *I.e.* of others 'Αλλήλων τὰ βάρη βαστάζετε. The body is a kind of truck to carry loads.

[3] Kārikā 6 b.

[4] A boy who instructed Sudhana, the hero of the work Raj. Mitra, *Nep. B.L.*, p. 92.

[5] See Mhv. I. 564.

not the doctrine of the true Bodhisatvas; shielded by them they become recluses from the world; with their respect Bodhisatvas become men whose acts are free from violent transport in all the actions of the Bodhisatva; through their favour Bodhisatvas become unassailable by the depravities of action. It is our trusty friends that inform us of what should not be done;[1] they it is who keep us from each temptation to indifference;[2] and drive us forth from the City of Re-birth.[3] Accordingly, fair sir, ceasing from such[4] thoughts we must have recourse to our trusty friends.

"With mind like the earth that bends not though it support the burden of all things:[5] like the diamond unswerving in intent; like the Cakravāda sphere unruffled by any ills; like the servant of all the world uncomplaining in undertaking all duties; like a mere sweeper[6] in avoidance of overweening pride; like a vehicle in bearing forth heavy loads; like the dog not easily provoked; like the ship, unwearied in coming and going; [36] like a good son, in ever watching the face of the true friend, thou, my son, must give thine own self the name of the sick man: thy Friend, the name of the physician: his precepts the name of the medicine: thy deeds of merit the name of the smiting of the disease. Again, thou must call thyself the coward, thy Friend the hero, his instructions the weapon, and thy deeds the smiting of the foes."

In the same book, in the passage called *Vācanopāsikā-vimoksha,* it is said: "The Bodhisatva who is possessed of the precepts of the Good Friend propitiates the venerable Buddhas. The Bodhisatva who remains in harmony with the words of the Friend, comes near to the omniscience of a Buddha, and when he never doubts one true Friend's words, all true friends

[1] The reading of our MS. *sañcodakāh,* "inciting to attempt the seemingly impossible," is less probable than that of the gaṇḍa-vyūha MS. adopted.

[2] Cf. Childers, s.v. pamāda.

[3] A Buddhist Bunyan's "City of Destruction."

[4] A good deal has been omitted here in the sūtra quoted.

[5] Mil. P. vii. 3, 4.

[6] I follow the Tib. (*v.* note to text) here.

draw near him. And he who never lacks the Friend's regard, has every object realised.

"Then Sudhana, saluting the feet of the Brother Sāradhvaja with countless sunwise turns, gazing at him and making obeisance, and again gazing at him as he was making his due salute doing him honour and inclining himself; bearing him in mind reflecting, meditating, deeply meditating, making an aspiration and [1] exclaiming in wonder at him, realising and taking in his virtues, and while he stood there, remembering them all, resolute, unremitting in his mind, recounting, taking note of them, composing himself into an aspiration, yearning for the sight of him, receiving the happy omen of the sound of his voice [2] . . . departed from his presence: then beholding the omniscience comprised in the Good Friend, his eyes full of tears, . . he left the presence of Megha."

In the *Bodhisatva-prātimoksha*, too, it is said: "A Bodhisatva in this world has no jewel that he does not give up out of love of the Law. [37] There is no service of his body he does not make: there is no bodily activity [3] on which he does not venture. There is no word or deed on which he does not venture out of respect for his pastors and masters. . . . Wherefore? This duty tends to the cutting of earthly bonds; it tends also to the cutting away of despondency, pain, lamentation, sorrow, death, disease, old age, and birth. With such precious thoughts, with such healing thoughts, assuaging the maladies of all beings, and devotion that takes this form we ought to seek, in that it makes for the assuaging of the maladies of all beings."

In the *Ugradatta-paripṛcchā*, too, it is written: "Moreover, householder, if a Bodhisatva, who sets before him reading and study, in the presence of any one hears or points out or takes to himself a single Versicle of four feet, a verse connected with the Perfections of giving, virtue, patience, energy and meditation, or hears that which is the summary of the equipment

[1] Tib. ṅo mtsar du bya ba daṅ.

[2] Tib. smon lam gyi rjes su *h*jug par bya ba daṅ

[3] Tib. rim *h*gro.

of a Bodhisatva, he must do reverence to the Law in the person of that teacher for so many ages as there are in the stanza syllables, words, and names; if for so many ages he does reverence to that teacher, with sincerity and all manner of offerings, honour, and devotion, even to-day, householder, the teacher's reverence due to the teacher is not fulfilled; how much less the reverence due to the Law!"

And then in the *Ashtasahasrikā Prajñāpāramitā* it is likewise said: "Fair sir, thou must render fervent homage towards thy Good Friends, and must love them too. . . . It came to pass that the great Bodhisatva Sadāprarudita, with feelings such as these, with homage and with deep thought, proceeding on his pilgrimage, came in the course of his journey to another town. There he repaired to the midst of the market-place, and thus he thought, 'What if I sell this my body, and with the price thereof do honour to the Bodhisatva Dharmodgata; for through the long night of the past thousands of bodies of mine have been shattered and wasted and sold in an endless cycle of births, endless have been the pains of hell that I have suffered for the sake and cause of earthly love and not for the honouring of such principles or such persons.' Then Sadāprarudita [38] went to the market-place and lifted up his voice, and made his speech to be heard. 'Who wants a man?' quoth he," and so the tale proceeds.

"Then Māra, the evil one, so disposed the Brahmans and householders that they heard not his voice. When he could not get a buyer for himself he turned aside, wailing and shedding tears. 'Alas!' he cried, 'I have a hard thing to get, in that I cannot get a buyer even for my own body.' Then Śakra, lord of the Gods, in the guise of a disciple . . . addressed Sadāprarudita thus: 'Good sir, why art thou dejected in mind, and wistful, and why standest thou shedding tears?' Sadāprarudita replied, 'Through passionate love of the Law, and with desire to do homage to the Law, I have offered my body for sale, and yet do not find a purchaser.' . . . The disciple replied, 'I do not want a man, but my father has to offer sacrifice. There I require the heart of a man, his blood, his bones, and his marrow. So thou shalt give thy body at a price.' Then Sadāprarudita thought, 'I have easily got what I desired, and I now know that my body is fit for the attainment of all skill in the means [1] of the Perfection of Wisdom, in that I have got a purchaser for my body, for its heart, its blood, its bones and marrow.' Then he spake aloud with calm joy and delight, 'Disciple, I will give my frame to thee, since thou hast need of it.' . . . Then Sadāprarudita drew a sharp sword and pierced his right arm and drew blood, and pierced his right thigh and cut the flesh from it, and strode up to the foot of the wall to break the bone.

[39] "Then another merchant's daughter came to the upper window, and saw Sadāprarudita . . . and came where he was, saying, 'Fair sir, why dost thou give such pain to thy body?' . . . When she heard that it was for purposes of worship, again she said, 'What accumulation of merit will accrue to thee from that?' 'That good man will show forth my Perfection of Wisdom and my skill in the means. Herein I shall be a teacher, herein as I give my teaching I shall become the refuge of all.' . . . 'Marvellous, good sir,' she exclaimed. . . . 'Noble and goodly [2] are these principles that have been proclaimed by thee. Man's bodily frame should be sacrificed for ages innumerable as the sands of the river Ganges for the sake of one principle such as this. Truly, noble and goodly are the principles thou hast proclaimed. Yea, I will give thee gold, jewels, pearls, beryls, as many as thou mayest require, wherewithal thou mayest do honour to the venerable Dharmodgata.'" . . . And so forth, until he tells of the meeting of Dharmodgata with that girl accompanied by five hundred others.

"Then the Bodhisatva Dharmodgata arose from his seat and entered into his own house. . . . For seven years he remained immersed in a single trance of meditation, and Sadāprarudita for seven years conceived no thought of desire

[1] Upāya has perhaps here the semi-technical meaning that afterwards became so common in the Mahāyāna: *v.* Kern.

[2] Praṇītā is not in the Tibetan: *v.* Childers.

nor of taking life, nor of injury, neither [40] elsewhere did he engender the greed that comes of gratification. 'When,' thought he, 'will Dharmodgata arise, that we may duly appoint the pulpit where that worthy man may sit and teach the law, and that we may make that spot of earth, duly sprinkled, anointed, and adorned with varied flowers?' And those five hundred maidens, with the merchant's daughter at their head, passed their time in two postures only, learning from the Bodhisatva Sadāprarudita. Then Sadāprarudita heard a divine voice which said, 'On the seventh day hence Dharmodgata will arise from that his trance, and take his seat in the midst of the town to preach the law.' This when Sadāprarudita heard, transported with joy, gladdened with pleasure and satisfaction aroused within him, went to cleanse that spot of earth with the five hundred maidens; and appointed that pulpit, decking it with sevenfold gems. Then Sadāprarudita desired to sprinkle the ground but could get no water, though he sought it from around, wherewith to sprinkle it. For all the water had been hidden by Māra, the Evil One, and it was done, too, in order that when he failed to find the water his heart might be grieved and dispirited, or that he might change his purpose, and so his roots of merit might disappear and not shine forth.

"Then thought Sadāprarudita, 'What if I pierce my own body, and so water this place with blood? and why? This place is full of rising dust: let not a cloud of dust fall on the body of the Bodhisatva. What can I do with this frame of mine, which is doomed to dissolution? Better surely that my body should perish in an action such as this, and not in an ineffective act. For the reason and sake of mere passion, [41] thousands of frames of mine have again and again gone to dissolution as I wandered without end from birth to birth. If once more they are dissolved, at least let them be dissolved on such a holy place as this.'

"Thus reflecting he drew a sharp sword, and with it pierced his body on every side, and thus watered the spot with his own blood. So, too, did the maidens; and thus neither he nor any of them swerved in their purpose, so that Māra, the Evil One, might gain an occasion thereby."

So, too, in the *Caturdharmaka* Sūtra it is said: "The Bodhisatva, Brethren, must never give up the Good Friend, for his life long. Nay, not even at cost of life."

So, then, we must secure the preservation and all else of our body "by never leaving the Good Friend." [1]

But also he must do it by diligent study of the Scriptures; for it is only in the Scriptures that the teachings of the Bodhisatvas are generally seen. For we are told that in the respective Sūtras the practices and the precepts of Bodhisatvas are laid down. Hence diligence should always be shown on searching the Scriptures, lest if we do not regard them, we should fall into sin and commit some act of intemperance through ignorance. Hence, by this phrase, "Not leaving the Good Friend," and "study of the Scriptures," is implied the whole acceptance of the law.

As the holy *Sāgaramati* Sūtra tells us, "When a man receives, and is taught, the explanation of the syllables whereby the ineffable law is declared, then he is said to receive the good law. Again, my son, the preachers of the law who teach the Sūtras of this kind, to honour, respect, sit near, rise and bow before them, do them homage, show them admiring obedience, guard, receive them, give them robes, bowls, beds, seats, help and medicine for sickness, appurtenances and the like, honorific gifts, to guard them as masters, and have carried it out, to proclaim their praises, and to shield them from dispraise, all this, too, is called receiving the law. . . . [42] Again to be intent on peace from dispute, and rebuke according to the law individuals such as speak of the law unlawfully. Again, giving a pious gift to a neighbour of a heart that is unworldly, a mind that is set on the salvation of the world, whose good tendencies are unchecked, or, when a man so much as changes a step or breathes out and breathes in, so the motives of these acts be only the hearing or teaching of the law. Here, too, he accepts the good law.

[1] Kārikā 6 b.

"Suppose, my son, a mind perverted towards worldly objects. The repelling of this, concentration, restraint, entire quietude and discipline, all this is called receiving the good law. . . . Again the refusal to take and accept the principle by which unprincipled conduct goes on, is called the accepting of the Good Law."

In all this the maxim of "never leaving the Good Friend" is illustrated by such acts as reverence to the preacher: and so, too, we learn the means of recognising him; for without this acceptance of the Law we cannot have the threefold principle of preservation, purification, and increase. And thus without this requisite your Friend is no real Bodhisatva. Hence this acceptance is a matter of necessity.

For in the *Śrīmātāsimhanāda* Sūtra we read, "All the aspirations of the Bodhisatvas, countless as the Ganges sands, are included and comprehended in one great aspiration—namely, the accepting of the Law. This, then, is our great object." In the same work it is said, "Just as we find, Lady, that a small blow inflicted on a mighty man, if it be in a vital part, is painful and harmful, so the acceptance of the Law, even though it be but feeble, causes pain, sorrow, and lamentation to Māra, the Evil One. I cannot regard any other good act so effective against Māra as accepting the Law, be it ever so little." [43] Further, we read, "Just as Sumeru, the King of Mountains, shines forth supreme in loftiness and extent, surpassing all mountains, so when a follower of the Great Vehicle, caring nought for life and limb, with no niggard mind accepts the Law, this action outweighs all the good principles of Mahāyanists who are careful of life and limb, and have newly set forth on the new Vehicle.

So also it is said in the holy *Sāgaramati* Sūtra: "He is received by Jinas, Devas, Nāgas, and Kinnaras, endowed with merit and wisdom,[1] in his holding fast the Law of the Tathāgatas.[2] . . . He verily is not born again in empty worlds,

[1] Tib. theg pa la gsar du (freshly) yaṅ dag par źugs.

[2] In later stanzas, *e.g.* l. 18, *infra*, the unexpressed subject is supplied in Tib. mkhas. pa.

for in every birth he beholds a Jina, and seeing him gains faith in him. He has the nature of the high minded; he remembers previous births, and in birth after birth he joins the Order. Pure in his ways, and full of achievement. . . .

"He becomes a taker of the spells of the wise. Even by a hundred ages what is good in him is not effaced. [44] He becomes endowed with understanding and is free from passion, in holding fast the Law of the Tathāgatas. He is a Śakra, a Brahma, a guardian of the world, a king of men, yea, a world conqueror on the earth with ease, with joyous joy he is enlightened with enlightenment, in holding fast, etc. The two and thirty marks are in his frame, blameless are his limbs, alert his mind; all they that see him are never displeased, in holding fast, etc. His thought of enlightenment is never beclouded,[1] and he walks in the paths of righteousness with self-restraint.[2]

[1] Join bodhicittam pāramita carīṣu. [2] MS. kusalaiḥ ?

CHAPTER III

AVOIDANCE OF EVIL

WE have told in general the means of preservation, etc., with regard to our three topics. Now we have to say what are the preservatives. Our memorial verse says: "Herein how do I guard my frame? It means to shun the way of ill."[1] By "herein" is meant that we are concerned with personal preservation of one who is engaged in the acquisition of the Good Law, in such a way that he should not cause ruin to others. And this avoidance of evil is spoken of in the holy *Gaganagañja Sūtra* by certain Bodhisatvas who are energetic in laying hold of the Good Law.

[45] "We are patient, O Lord, now that the noblest of men has passed away. We will hold fast the Good Law, and be ready to lay down our body with its very life.[2] Leaving all greed and aggrandisement, leaving also all attachment, but never leaving that great Law which sets forth the Buddha's knowledge. With patience we will endure abuse and censure and words of reviling, because we would hold fast to the Good Law. Scoffing, threats, decrying, and defaming, all these we will endure, laying hold the while on the rule of life. In such a time of great terror and disruption for living beings, shaking brethren and kings alike, we hold fast the Good Law. The profound scriptures which are composed for the fruit of salvation shall then not be acceptable to men: they will ponder on all manner of tales instead. . . . Such as abide not in the Law, to them we will show loving-kindness and compassion, the while holding the rule of life. And when we see creatures

[1] Kārikā 7 a.

[2] Read सज्जीवितं.

of evil nature, abiding in desire and greed, we shall shed tears and say, Whither is the blind sinner going ?

[46] So soon as we have beheld the transgressor of the Good Law, from afar we shall show loving-kindness to him that he show not anger towards us.

We will be on our guard as far as in us lies, restrained in word and deed; not too suddenly addressing such as abide in their sin :

Yet with gifts and deference we will here ripen those men, and afterwards exhort them so that they may in very truth be beyond the sphere of sin.[1]

Giving up the society of householders, making our home the wilderness and the forest, we shall become like beasts of the field, with little wealth and little care.

Subdued, restrained, set free, in yon village we will settle and preach the Law to such as strive for it.

Very far, too, will we go when we hear of such as desire the Law, and having ourselves obtained the love of abiding in it, we will work the good of all beings.

Herein seeing face to face the manifold error of all creatures, we will examine ourselves abiding in love for the Law.

Well received or ill received, we must stand forth like Meru, and unspotted by the world we shall become the world's leaders.

And when we observe the reproach of Brethren who have broken their rule of life, we will take heed to our own Action lest their action bear its fruit.[2]

[47] They will employ [3] murderers, saying, 'These qualities belong to those who walk in them : they are not found in us at all.'

Monks we are, but have not monkish ways. When they have heard our full rebuke, they reject this sūtra.

[1] Reading *-āpāpa-* as in note [2] of text. With text, it would be: reading *-āpāya-*, "when they are in very truth in the sphere of perdition."

[2] There is a mark in the MS. which seems to denote an omission in the MS, although no lacuna is marked in the Tibetan.

[3] Tib. apparently "discover." The Tibetan makes the following words a quotation.

A mirror to men docked of nose and ear, how should it please them? But when fully they have heard our rebuke, then they cast away the Good Law.

The monks that will be receivers of the Good Law will thus act, and let no one listen to their doctrine.[1]

Kings will receive it, and the people will be there; as though under Buddha's authority all beings will listen to that doctrine in those days:

At that evil time we will hold fast the Good Law, sacrificing our body with very life for it, for the good of all creatures."

In the *Sūtra of the Good Law* it is also said: " Let him keep to the sphere of duty, living a life apart, and pure: shunning intercourse with princes and with kings.[2]

[48] No converse let him hold with king's servants, with Caṇḍālas, or with gypsies, with drunkards or with heretics at any time.

He should not pay court to those who are puffed up, but defer to such as abide in the discipline. Let him shun monks of evil conduct and such as approve of the Jains:

Also let him always shun the nun of giggling chattering ways; lay sisters, too, that are openly unsteadfast.

Such women as are made barren, let him shun converse with these: he must even shun matrons and maids living in their families.

He must of a surety not address them courteously to ask after their good health. He must shun also intercourse with butchers of swine or sheep; and those who are panders, with dancers, fencers, and wrestlers, and all other persons of that sort.

[49] Let him not pay court to choice singers and all others who live by luxury, let him wholly avoid showing any courtesy to these.

And when the sage has to preach the Law to womankind, he must not enter their room alone, nor stand jesting with them."

Here is another evil to avoid, to wit that mentioned in the

[1] Read °धर्मामिमं शृणोत् ॥

[2] MS. °पृच्छेहि, a Pali ending.

Prajñāpāramitā as a work of Māra. Māra the Evil One will make a special effort against a Bodhisatva who has not long entered in the Way. In the same book it is said: "Again Ānanda at the very time that a mighty Bodhisatva is exercising himself in the Perfection of Wisdom, then do most evil Māras bring hurt to the Bodhisatva and engender fear in him. They send abroad and display fiery meteors in every quarter of the world. Would this mighty Bodhisatva flinch [1] or shudder, whereby even a single aspiration after righteousness should fall away from the unsurpassed full enlightenment?

"Again they will write . . . and study with their minds on other things. 'We have no relish in all this,' say they, and rise from their seats and are gone. So gaping and sneering they will study. All this is the work of Māra. So too there will arise wranglings in village and countryside. Thus they will take anxious thought for teachers, parents, friends, counsellors, relatives, cousins; thus too about thieves, thus too of robes and raiment. Again, the preacher will be desirous to dictate . . . and recite this august *Prajñāpāramitā*, and the pupil will be weary; or the reverse will happen. The preacher will be desirous to go to another country, and the pupil will decline: so we must suppose. The preacher will be full of willingness, the pupil unwilling: so we must suppose. In a word, dissension whatever between teacher and pupil is all the work of Māra; so are we told."

[50] In the *Gaganagañja Sūtra*, too, it is said: "So too . . . busying oneself in things which are evil and abandoning things which are good, all this is the work of Māra."

In the *Sāgaramati Sūtra* also we read: "Again, O Blessed One, the Bodhisatva becomes a dweller in the forest, one who delights in sitting and lying in remote places, with few wants, easily content, a complete recluse, having no intercourse with householders or monks. Because his aims and his objects are few, he dwells at ease, and is not zealous for the pursuit of wide learning. nor for maturing the heart of man: and when there is preaching or discussion of the Law,

[1] Read अवलीयेत ॥

or exposition of its meaning, he does not conceive it his duty to attend. He becomes indifferent to religious dialectic and loses zeal for searching after what is good. And thro' living in the forest, by reason of his delighting in solitude, the passions never come into exercise.

" He is satisfied merely with stopping the uprising of passion, and he does not open the way to the destruction[1] of inclination: living there he is intent neither on his own weal nor his neighbours. This, Blessed One, is the *Seventh Hook* of Māra applied to the Bodhisatva's seclusion in the forest" [omission of Hooks VIII. and IX.].

Temptation by False Friends.—"Again, Blessed One, the Bodhisatva honours, respects, and defers to evil friends who have the semblance of the Good Friend, such as dissuade him from the Four Elements of Conciliation,[2] from the accumulation of merit, from laying hold on the Good Law, and make him apply himself to complete seclusion, apply himself also to be a man without interests and without activity, and constantly preach to him discourses really suited for the Disciples and the Pratyeka Buddhas; and at the time when he would make progress in the Mahāyāna by means of the secluded life, then they overwhelm him with occupations,[3] on the ground that a Bodhisatva must have occupation: and just when the Bodhisatva ought to be occupied, then they bid him meditate. And thus they say to him: 'Enlightenment belongs to the active Bodhisatva, not to the idle; if you cannot gain perfect enlightenment in eight or nine æons, [51] you can never gain it.' [But even] in this case, reverend sir, the Bodhisatva by a supreme effort might after all gain the state which is known to have Nirvāna as its fruit.[4]

" This, reverend sir, is the Tenth Hook of Māra working under the guise of the Good Friend." . . .

Consorting with Backsliders.—" There is another class different

[1] Read *-dgh-* for -dy-.
[2] Dhamasaṃgraha, § 19; Childers, p. 447.
[3] Reading *paligodha* with MS.; see note on **text**.
[4] This line seems to be corrupt.

from the last, who belong to the Bodhisatva's Way, but have been pierced by the Hook of Māra, and walk in evil ways. With these he [the Bodhisatva] finds his pleasure. For they pay him court, but he having connexions with low people, never reaches the highest ideal but goes along the lower way, I mean the way of dulness, the brute deaf and dumb way. . . . This is the Eleventh Hook of Māra."

The way in which the character of a Bodhisatva shapes itself through very weariness when he has made a series of manly efforts is described in the *Ratnamegha*. Here the Bodhisatva makes a manly effort in all the four Attitudes,[1] and he makes his effort so as to produce neither bodily fatigue nor mental fatigue. This is what we define as continuous manly effort. And what is the nature of this?[2] It is this which prevents his having fatigue; which there would be if a man of little strength should undertake a heavy task, or if out of due time, or if a man whose aspirations are immature should undertake a difficult task such as giving his flesh. Certainly the Bodhisatva has given his own person; but the author is guarding against an untimely consummation; for otherwise by the destruction of the seed, the thought of enlightenment, which would result from the Bodhisatva's fatigue, there would be destruction of the whole quantity of the fruits for those beings. That is why in the *Gaganagañja Sūtra* we find the doctrine expressed, that untimely desire is the work of Māra.

He[3] must not refuse to make up his mind to sacrifice his body on the plea that "this is an unseasonable time;" for unless he begin to exercise himself he would never give,

Accordingly, with this principle borne ever in mind, one must guard one's person from all who check the maturing of thought-enlightenment, who from infatuation murder their own welfare, from cannibals, and from all who have their own ends to serve.

[1] *i.e.* Walking, sitting, standing, lying (Childers, "P.D." *s.v.* iriyāpatha).

[2] At end of line 9 add न.

[3] A new paragraph begins here. In line 15, read °*dyam abhyāsa*° with MS.; see note on text.

"Even when one gives the seed of the beauteous tree of healing, meet for man's enjoyment root and branch, it must be preserved from untimely fruition; so must it be with the healing tree of the enlightened sage."

This then in brief is the evil that comes from the works of Māra.

How to avoid Evil.—How to avoid this evil we are told in the *Ratnamegha Sūtra*. "And how, my son, is the Bodhisatva to gain skill in the means for avoiding the works of Māra?

"To begin with, by all means in his power he shuns the bad friend. [52] Living in a country unsuited to the faithful, observing the spells of the Lokāyatas,[1] gain and honour, worship, deference, and excessive respect, all this he will in every way avoid: and all the other lesser sins which obstruct the way of such as choose enlightenment; while the contrary of all these he cherishes."

Avoid Evil Communications.—In the same book, the characteristics of the bad friend are given. "By his abandoning every one who has failed in morality you may know the man who is ready to avoid the evil friend. So too by abandoning every one who has failed in doctrine, failed in behaviour, failed in conduct; by abandoning men who take delight in society,[2] by avoiding the indolent, those who cling to the chain of births, above all such as have their faces turned away from enlightenment. If he abandon all association with householders, you may know, I say, him who is ready to abandon the bad friend. But observe, my son, that while he avoids all these conditions, he must not feel towards these persons an evil, repellent, and a contemptuous feeling. And this is the feeling which he must foster within himself: 'Since the Lord has told me, "Towards the evil principles severally, such as lust and the rest, man's nature flows and ever oozes, and from the association they perish," therefore I will avoid such association.'"

[1] For this sect, see *Athenæum*, 20 June, 1900, p. 811.

[2] *Saṅgaṇikārāma*. Cp. V.P. iii. p. 449, cited at p. 403 of text.

Another evil is discouragement in the thought of enlightenment; how this comes to pass is described in the *Ratnakūṭa*.[1]

"There are four principles, O Kāśyapa, which obscure the thought-enlightenment of the Bodhisat if they are found in him. (1) To break faith with preceptors, teachers, and those worthy of respect; (2) To show scrupulousnessness for oneself[2] and none to others; (3) To speak in depreciation, dispraise, defamation, disparagement of such as have set forth in the Great Way; (4) To approach a neighbour with deceit and guile, and not with good intent."

The same book tells us how to avoid the evil.

"There are four principles which, if they are found in him, bring the Bodhisatva face to face with thought-enlightenment in every birth so soon as he is born, and he does not become confused in the interval until he takes his seat on the Throne of Enlightenment.

"What are the four?

"(1) He never knowingly speaks an untruth, not to save his life, . . . (and so on to) even to raise a laugh; [53] (2) With good intent he walks amongst men, and puts from him deceit and guile, and unto all Bodhisatvas he gives the title of teacher, and unto the four winds of heaven he proclaims their praise; (3) All those whom he brings to maturity in the faith, he excites towards the perfect enlightenment; (4) No longing for an inferior Vehicle.

"These, O Kāśyapa, are the four."

And in the *Siṁhaparipṛcchā* it is said further:

"He who makes no obstacle to teaching the Law, gains thereby speedily communion with the lords of the world."

[1] Tib. has nothing to represent *jāyante samsyandante*, and translates *āsravanti* by *bsten*=stick to. A causal would be expected. *Jāyante* is omitted, as it seems to disturb the metaphor. Compare Cowell, *Sarva-darś. saṅg.* p. 53.

[2] *sva-* must be understood in the text; it is expressed in the Tibetan. Compare *Dh.-Sṇi*, § 1161, and Mrs. Davids, *ad loc.* The text may mean: "to cause others to feel scruples when scruples are not needed."

Again:

"Thus know, O prince, through teaching the Law one gains memory of former births."

So too in the same book:

"Therefore, in all his births he loses not the thought of enlightenment. Even in dreams he has this thought: much more if he be awake."

Again he says:

"Whensoever in pleasure grove, village, or town he incites to wisdom, by this act he loses not the enlightened heart."

Again, in the *Mañjuśrībuddhakshetraguṇavyūhālaṅkāra Sūtra*, he says:

"There are four principles which, when found in the Bodhisatva, keep him from swerving from stedfast purpose . . .; his pride is abased, envy and greed he eschews, when he sees another's success his mind is transported with joy."

The way to avoid the loss above described of the thought of enlightenment [of a duly qualified person],[1] is still more clearly set forth in this same work, the *Ratnakūṭa*: "in every bodily posture[2] to have ready the thought of enlightenment, as a foundation for the action."

So we read in the *Candrapradīpa Sūtra*:[3] "I declare and make known to you: In proportion as a man exercises his mind, [54] so his heart becomes fully engrossed through his reasonings[4] fixt upon their aim."

Despondency is an evil, and we see how to avoid it in the *Ratnamegha*.

Evil of Despondency. See Introd. xxxii.—"Now the Bodhisatva must not let himself think thus: 'Hard to attain is enlightenment while one is but a man; see my energy and small it is; indolent I am, and enlightenment must be sought and won through hundreds and thousands of æons by

[1] Not in Tib.

[2] See p. [518].

[3] The same book as *Samādhirāja*.

[4] Cf. Pali *vitakko* in *Dh. Sṇi.* trans. p. 10.

a saint whose head-dress is radiant with light.[1] I am not equal to bearing such a load.'

" The Bodhisatva then must let himself think in this way: 'The Tathāgata saints of supreme and full enlightenment in the past, present, or future gain it in each case by a way or method such as this, in fact by this selfsame energy they gain it, until they become Tathāgatas and attain to supreme enlightenment. So I too will strive and endeavour by the energy which is the common attribute and the support of all beings to gain the incomparable and perfect enlightenment.' "

Again, another evil is seen in the *Ratnakūṭa*.[2]

Ill-judged Instruction.—" That the Bodhisatva should confide in those who are immature, is a mistake; and that he should explain the exalted doctrine of the Buddha to unworthy vessels, is a mistake: or again, it is a mistake in him to impart the Lesser Way to those whose mind is set upon high things, and it is a mistake with those who have mindfulness and other virtues fully developed and all good qualities besides, to show them a slighting spirit which picks out the qualities which are vicious and evil."

Want of devoted enthusiasm is also an evil, as it is said in the *Rāshṭrapāla Sūtra*: [3]

" In whomsoever is not devotion for Buddha found, he cannot have devotion for his Law and his order; nor has he devotion for rules and discipline; his mind is evil, and his face is set towards the Three Hells. [55] And when he leaves the present birth, fool and blind that he is! he is doomed by the force of Action to find pain, be it amongst men or in hell, amongst brutes or ghosts."

The eschewing of this fault we found laid down in the *Ratnakūṭa*: " If there are depths which his wit cannot sound he does not in this case deny; for he feels, Here the Tathāgata alone is my witness, the Tathāgata knows, I do not

[1] Like the Bodhisatva Amitābha in Buddhist art.

[2] Quoted in *V.C.P. ad* V. 89. See also *Bodhic.* v. 90.

[3] See Fino's text, *Bibl. Buddh.*, II. 20 [5-8]. This reading *Buddhe* is adopted in the present translation.

know: boundless is the enlightenment of the Buddhas. The preaching of the Law is always going on, while the Tathāgatas take account of the variety of dispositions in the audience."

Moreover, it is when one is actively engaged in service that one should be skilful in avoiding all these evils. For in the *Bodhisatvaprātimoksha* we find service enjoined, both in the form of listening to the Law and of worshipping the Tathāgata in the company of fellow-believers.[1]

And what is meant by being thus actively engaged we deduce from the *Ratnarāśi Sūtra*.

"In this case, the monk who does service must win the approval of the whole Order. In cases where monks live in the forest, and have bed and board in remote places, the monk who is engaged in service must not offer every kind of service indiscriminately to them. But if, on the other hand, a disciple's task included in the routine of the Order should fall to the lot of the monk dwelling in the forest, then our serving monk must either do this himself, or must induce yet another monk to do it; but in any case the forest-dwelling monk must not be pressed. Then again: In a case where a monk goes his begging-rounds, then your serving monk must give him a share of any choice food which he may have. Then too, O Kāśyapa, in a case where a monk practises self-discipline, your serving monk must collect means of assistance suitable to the occasion, and also requisites, medicaments, and appurtenances for any bodily failure; and in the place where this monk lives no loud noise must be allowed; but the serving monk must watch over the monk under discipline, must prop up his bed or seat, and must offer him food both hard and soft, pleasant, acceptable, and suited to the character of his disciplinary course . . . Monks who are devoted to the acquirement of knowledge he must inspire with energy," [56] . . . and so on to "they also need his watchful care. For the monks who are preachers he must do duty as doorkeeper;[2] and until the congregation has to

[1] Tib. "in accordance with the Law," "as the Law directs." Query Rh. D. translation of Mahāvagga, 6. 13. 4. See below [94].

[2] Tib. "must make them indefatigable," apparently a different reading.

be dismissed,[1] the assembly-room must be kept in order. In a connected discourse the room must be kept clear until there is the abundant applause which is his due. . . . In no case must he associate with any object the notion of personal ownership. Any transaction, however small, must be done by sanction of his Order, not by his own;" and so on, until these words: "The [property] of his Order must not be confused with that of the œcumenical Order,[2] and *vice versâ*. What belongs to the stūpa in each case must not be made matter for traffic to and fro. But if a deficit should arise in the œcumenical Order, and if the receipts of the local Order should amount to a surplus,[3] then our serving monk, after gaining an unanimous [4] vote of the monks of his Order, may do the business of the œcumenical Order by drawing on the receipts of the local Order. So too when a stūpa is broken down, the same principle holds good: he must beg from givers and generous folk and thus restore it: such is the ordinance. If on the other hand the receipts of the stūpa are somewhat in excess of the ordinary, the serving monk must not hand them over either to his Order or to the œcumenical Order.[5] And why so? Whatever belongs to the stūpa, even unto a single fringe,[6] dedicated by believers rich in devotion, that is in essence a shrine for gods and men: how much more a gem, or object esteemed as such, or the hangings for the sanctuary that are dedicated. Suppose that hanging in that same shrine of the Tathāgata fall into decay by the action of wind, sun, and rain: but a hanging which belongs to the stūpa must not be bartered for gold. For that which belongs

[1] We have followed the usual meaning of *uyyojeti* in Pali, not registered in Skt. Lexx., but apparently applicable in Mhv. iii. 141,[12]. The Tib. *brtson-par-hgyur* seems to imply the keeping of the attention of the congregation.

[2] *Cāturdiśasangha*: See Vin. Pit. ii. 147[22] (Cullavagga, Bk. vi. i. 4); Description, Rh. D. in *India Antiquary*, i. 140; *S.B.E.* xx. 159, note [3]. The masc. noun which we have supplied, probably *lābha*, doubtless occurred in the omitted passage. The Chinese version renders *staupika* by "belonging to Buddha."

[3] *Dele* note [2] in text, as we understand *utsado* in its usual sense of "excrescence," which gives "surplus" naturally enough.

[4] The Chinese adds, "distributing splinters," *i.e.* doubtless *sataka*.

[5] In text 56[10] read *saṅghe na* divisim.

[6] *Dele* note [4], as *ekadaśāpi* stands for *ekāpi daśā*, not *ekādaśāpi*.

to a stūpa has no market price, and a stūpa has no deficit in any respect.[1]

"Any serving monk, Kāçyapa, who in a fit of anger plays the tyrant over virtuous and worshipful men, for that unholy deed is on his way to hell; or if born again in the world of men he becomes a slave, or has to take his orders from others, and to get cuffs and buffetings and violent blows. . . . [57] Suppose he give to a monk an untimely errand or untimely order, with threats putting him in bodily fear of chastisement, the hell to requite that unholy deed is called Bahuśanku, and there he is reborn, until his body is pierced in a thousand places, is burnt and consumed in the flames: his tongue grows out to the measure of a hundred leagues; and there in his tongue-nerves myriads of heated iron spikes are embedded.

"Again, whatsoever serving monk makes a hoard of the corporate revenue as it comes in, and does not produce it punctually when it is due, or produces it with a contemptuous or injurious expression, or withholds it from certain creditors: such an one, as wages for this unholy conduct, is born in the womb of a ghost belonging to the hell of Filth called Jaṅghā. There other ghosts get food and show it to him: the butt of their scoffing, he eyes the food with fixed stare, a prey to hunger and thirst, terrible is the torment he endures, and never does he get the food even in a thousand years; and if by any means he does get it, then it turns into ordure or pus and blood."

In the Tale of *Saṅgharakshita* another evil is recounted. "The beings which you have seen, O Saṅgharakshita, in the form of walls, were once monks. These people defiled walls belonging to the Order with their spittle; by the ripening of that deed they have been brought to the form of walls. Those whom you see as posts, defiled the pillars of the Order with snot, therefore they have been turned into pillars. Those whom you see as trees, leaves, flowers and fruits, were once monks who turned to their individual enjoyment the trees, leaves, flowers and fruits of the community, therefore they have become trees,

[1] Compare 56[6]; *i.e.* a stūpa is not a business concern with surplus and deficit.

leaves, flowers, fruits. Those whom you see as a cord or a besom, turned to their own individual use cords and besoms belonging to the community, therefore they have become cords and besoms. [58] The being whom you see yonder in the form of a platter was once an ascetic: he was once rubbing down a small platter; some stranger monks arrived; they saw him and asked, What is this, O ascetic? Will the Order be supping? In a fit of avarice he replied, Do you not see the platter is clean? the supper is over. Then the time is past, said they, and become hopeless they departed with wretched and dejected mien. By the ripening of this deed, he was made into a platter. The man that you saw in the form of a mortar was once a monk. To him fell the duty of looking after the bowls, and on this occasion a single novice who was arhat had been appointed to take his turn at the stamp. The monk said, Novice, give me a morsel when you have pounded it. He replied, Good Elder, wait a moment, I am busy; afterwards I will pound and give you a piece. His wrath was kindled, and he said, Novice, if it were my pleasure to handle the mortar, I would fling *you* into the mortar and pound you up! to say nothing of the small piece I ask. The novice concluded in his own mind, He has worked himself into a furious state: if I give him an answer, he will only become all the more angry; so he remained silent. When the other's mood had passed, he came round to him and said, Good Elder, do you know who I am? Yes, said he, I know you are a religious novice of Kāśyapa the All-enlightened, and I am a monk and an Elder. The novice replied, Even if that is so, I have done what it was my duty to do as religious person: What have I done? renounced my passions; I have cut away all bonds and am free from all bonds; you have given way to bitter words and deeds. Confess your transgression as being a transgression: perchance so that deed of thine may dwindle, become small, and make an end. [59] But the other did not confess his transgression, and in requital was turned into the shape of a mortar. Those whom you see changed into the form of cauldrons, were servants of the monks to do their behests. Once they were boiling medicaments and were spoken to harshly by the monks; they fell into a rage and broke the cauldrons; and so they were changed into cauldrons. The man whom you saw cut through the middle and held together by thread, was onc a monk greedy and grasping for gain; overcome by avarice, he appropriated the receipts. The receipts which belonged to the rains he accounted for as of the winter season, and the winter receipts he changed over to the rains. By the ripening of this deed he goes about cut through the middle and held together by thread."

CHAPTER IV

AVOIDANCE OF EVIL

THERE are also grave evils detailed in the Sacred Books. As for example in the *Ākāśa-garbha Sūtra*.[1] My son, there are Five Root Sins of the anointed prince; by which Five Root Sins the anointed prince destroys all the roots of merit which he has laid up from of old. Caused to fall by something, and overcome[2] by them, he goes the way to perdition banished[3] from all delights of gods and men.

"And what are the five? When an anointed prince,[4] my son, steals the goods of a stūpa, or of the Order local or œcumenical, or whatsoever is dedicated thereunto, either himself or through another, this is the First Root Sin.

"When, again, one reviles the Law as set forth in the Scheme of Deliverance either of the Disciples, or of the Pratyeka Buddhas, or of the Great Way, reviles I say or causes hindrance to it, that is the Second Root Sin.

"Again, when he, himself or through others, takes away the saffron robes from a monk whether virtuous or not, who for my sake wears tonsure of head and cheek and the saffron robe, [60] whether he observes my teaching or observes it not, or makes him a householder, or inflicts chastisement on his person, or casts him into prison, or deprives him of life: this is the Third Root Sin.

[1] Quoted in *Bodhic.*, p. 159.

[2] See *Vajracchededika* (Anecd. Ox.), p. 32. Compare the text pp. 60[12], 62[5]. The meaning is uncertain

[3] Reading *parājitaḥ* with *Bcp.*, p. 159[13], as in the similar passages 60[13], 61[3] below; compare Tib. The word seems to have been unusual, if not unexampled, and we must suppose the scribe to have written the more familiar word *pārājikaḥ*, "worthy of expulsion (from the Order)."

[4] Reading °क:.

"Again, when a Kshatriya of intent takes (1) his mother's life, or (2) the life of his father, or (3) of an Arhat, being a disciple of the Blessed One, or (4) makes a schism in the uninjured Order, or (5) of intent and with evil mind causes to be shed the blood of a Tathāgata or of an Arhat fully enlightened: when he by these five acts of inevitable result does this or that deed, that is the Fourth Root Sin.

"When a Kshatriya becomes one of those who deny all causes,[1] and cares not for the next world, but is always following the ten Paths of Unrighteousness and incites, leads, induces many others to these Ten Paths of Unrighteousness, and establishes them therein: this is the Fifth Root Sin.

"Other categories of Root Sins are detailed (in the Sūtra), and amongst them the causing division in village, district, town or kingdom. . . .

"There are eight Root Sins which beset young men or young women, when they are inceptors and just entering on the Great Way; which cause them to stumble, which destroy all the roots of merit that they have before fostered. Immersed in objects of sense, they go the way to perdition, banisht from the delights of Gods and Men and of the Great Way; they sink down for many an age into the round of births, bereft of the help of any good friend. And what are these eight?

1. Discouragement of Hearers.[2]—"When any persons have, by reason of previous ill deeds, been born in this wicked world with its five stains, but though their root of merit is but poor they have resorted to a Good Friend, and are taught this excellent and profound Great Way, and so though their wit is but small these youths are turning their hearts toward the excellent and perfect enlightenment, and such among them as are inceptor Bodhisatvas learn, rehearse, and read this[3] scripture excellent and profound joined to the doctrine of the Void; and when

[1] Such as the Ājivakas. Compare *Dh.-Sṇi.*, § 1028, with *Digha-N.*, i. p. 53, *M.N.*, i. 407, quoted by Mrs. Rhys Davids, *ad loc.*

[2] With our title summaries may be compared the summaries of mūlapattis Nos. 2–8 given in *Bcp. ad* V. 102 (p. 161).

[3] The Tib. (43a. 2) implies a reading imam sūtrāntaṃ, not idaṃ (mahāyānam).

they record it as they have learnt it and as they have studied it and publish abroad at length with clear sense and expression in the presence of others who are in a like state of knowledge to what theirs once was,[1] whilst those foolish worldlings not making the effort, as they hear are dismayed, are astonied, and reduced to distraction, [61] and by reason of this distraction turn away their hearts from the Highest Enlightenment and aspire no further than the Disciples' Vehicle; this is the First Root Sin of the Inceptor Bodhisatva. And by this Root Sin, the youth destroys all the Root of Merit that he has already acquired, caused to fall by something, and banished from the joy of heaven and emancipation, and his thought of enlightenment is beguiled, and he goes to perdition. Therefore a Bodhisatva must first know the bent of disposition in his fellowmen, and only then must preach the Law to them according to their dispositions in due order. Thus he conveys them across the mighty sea of existence in due order.

2. Dissuading from following the Perfections—Preaching Ideals that lead to the Hīnayāna.—" Again, the inceptor Bodhisatva may speak thus to some one: You are not capable of practising the Six Perfections. You cannot become enlightened with the perfect Enlightenment. Speedily produce the thought of the Way of the Disciples or the Pratyeka Buddhas; by this means you shall escape from the chain of rebirth. . . . And thus, as aforesaid, this is the Second Root Sin of the Inceptor Bodhisatva.

3. Preaching Mahāyāna as Substitute for Rules and Discipline.—" Again, the inceptor Bodhisatva may speak thus to his neighbour: Good sir, what is the use of monastic rule, the rule of life taught in the Monastic Discipline, or keeping the moral rule?[2] Speedily apply your thought unto full and perfect enlightenment. Study the Great Way; all the demerit which has been accumulated in act, word, and thought by reason of passions is purified and becomes barren by that study. And

[1] *I.e.* as the Skr. gloss (p. 60, n. [5]), " who are in the state of mind which they were in before they took the vow."

[2] Following the Tibetan, the stop is removed to stand after *surakshitena.*

thus as aforesaid this is the Third Root Sin in the Inceptor Bodhisatva.

4. Undue Disparagement of the Śrāvaka Yāna.—"Again, fair sir, the inceptor Bodhisatva may thus speak to certain hearers: 'Avoid, young sirs, the preaching of the Disciples' Way; hear it not, study it not, teach it not to others; hide away this preaching: no great fruit will ye get from it, nor will you be able to make an end of sin as a result of it. Put your trust in the teaching of the Great Way; hear the Great Way, study it, and teach it to others. Thus you will bring to nought all the ways that lead to ruin and perdition, and will quickly become enlightened with perfect enlightenment.' If they do according to his word, then they would be inclining to this wrong view; and both parties are involved in that Root Sin. This is the Fourth Root Sin of the Inceptor Bodhisatva.

5. Self-aggrandisement.—"Again: The inceptor Bodhisatvas may be double-tongued and teach falsely. For purposes of renown and reputation, from motives of gain and aggrandisement, they read that Great Way, study, recite, repeat, [62] and preach it, and teach it to others as far as the ear; and they will use expressions like these: We and no others are the people of the Great Way. They are grudging towards others from motives of greed and aggrandisement; because their neighbours have enjoyment small or great, they make this a ground for displeasure against them, they speak in dispraise of them, treat them spitefully, injuriously, and opprobriously; they exalt themselves and not their neighbours. Next, out of grudge against others, they lay claim to possess supernatural qualities.[1] Then, by this thing they fall, they decline from the bliss of the Great Way, into so great and grievous a sin, that it sets them on the road to perdition. As a man might be going to the treasure island, and to go thither, is for crossing the sea in a ship; but in the midst of the sea should he with his own hand wreck his ship, he would lose his life on the spot; even so when inceptor Bodhisatvas, who desire to cross over the mighty sea of good qualities speak from a grudging heart as we have

[1] See *Pātimokkha.* ‡ 4, and note to trans. in *S. B. E.*, xiii. p. 5.

described, they thereby wreck the ship of faith and lose the life which is Wisdom. Thus it is that these inceptor Bodhisatvas, in their folly, from a grudging mind, by their false speaking, decline into this great and grievous sin. This is the Fifth Root Sin of the Inceptor Bodhisatva.

6. Advertising One's Profound Knowledge.—"Again, young sir, in the future there will arise both householders and houseless folk, inceptor Bodhisatvas, who recite, read and study these scriptures of the Great Way, that are profound, that treat of the doctrine of the Void, that are within the reach of Bodhisatvas full of energy, great sages who are adorned with the patiences and the rapt meditation[1] and the stages of degree; and when they have proclaimed these Scriptures to others, will declare: 'It is I who by my own wit have become wise in these doctrines, and accordingly I am teaching them to you out of pure compassion'; or again, 'You on your part must apply yourself until you shall have discernment in these profound principles; thus you shall one day have insight into knowledge such as I have.' But at this point he does not add, 'It is by reading alone that I myself am teaching you all these profound principles, and not by personal perception.' He sells himself for gain and aggrandisement. For this reason he becomes a transgressor in the sight of the saints fully enlightened, the Bodhisatvas, and the noble ones of time past, present, and to come, and falls into a great and grievous sin: he deceives gods and men by means of the Great Way. Even the Way of the Disciples is not his; [63] much less has he attained to the distinction of having entered upon the Great Way, still less is full and perfect enlightenment his.

"Just as a man who has entered a mighty forest may be oppressed by hunger and thirst, and may climb a great fruit-tree therein; he wants to get food, yet leaving the tree that has excellent fruit, without tasting how full of flavour and fragrance it is, he might ascend a poisonous tree, and eating its deadly fruits, meet his death thereby: such I say is the case of the persons, who have found what is so hard for man to

[1] "well exercised in" Tib.

get, in finding the Good Friend, who have a desire to enter upon the Great Way, yet for the mere sake of glory, gain and aggrandisemen , choose to make display of themselves: they oppress their neighbours, and thereby commit a great and grievous sin, and thus incur the severest censure of all discerning men. Such men are on the way to perdition; they deserve not the respect of any class, whether princes, priests, merchants, or menials. Nay, the man who does honour them is himself a sinner in the esteem of all thinking men. This, young sir, is the Sixth Root Sin.

7. Princes and Advisers who rob the Brotherhood of their Goods.—"Again, young sir, in the future princes will have about them the most degraded of chaplains and ministers and bravos, fools, wise in their own conceit, full of riches and luxury; conspicuous in undertaking of good works that consist in giving, themselves consumed by the pride of almsgiving, alienate the princes [from the ascetics][1] through infatuated vanity, and the ascetics from princes. They will apply to the princes, and cause fines to be put on the ascetics, filching away their money by the fine. By reason of that oppression, the Brethren in question first take from the community of ascetics property belonging to individuals, or the local Order, or the œcumenical Order, or the shrine, and then what is robbed from them they procure to be given to themselves; then again, those degraded persons will offer it to the Prince; these on both parts commit a Root Sin.[2] [This is the Seventh Root Sin.[3]]

"There are degraded Princes who will show malevolence[4] to the ascetics, and declare to them a law in accordance

[1] So Tib.

[2] The problems of this passage are: Who are the sinners? and what is the sin? (1) The gloss in note [1] of the text identifies the Inceptor Bodhisatvas in question with the "degraded chaplains and the rest," and takes the sin as twofold: (*a*) alienation of class from class; (*b*) misappropriation of property. (2) According to the summary in *Bodhicaryāvatāra-pañjikā*, pp. 161–2, the Bohdisatvas are monks (cp. line 14 of our text), who make over the property to certain Kshatriyas, and the sin is double because committed by two parties. With this the Tib. appears to agree.

[3] Added from Tib. 45*a* [6]: compare *B. C. P.*, p. 162, 2

[4] But compare Pali *padussati* and *M. V.*, i. 114[9]. It may mean "show malevolence," and so Tib. apparently *sdañ*, "anger."

therewith ; or abandon the Law and proceed to declare what is contrary to the Law. For they disregard the Scriptures, the Rules and the Discipline, and abandon the great principles and the precepts of casuistry ;[1] they abandon also the precepts of skill and expediency found in the teaching of the Perfection of Wisdon and of universal benevolence ; and the precepts set forth in other scriptures beside : and this done, with intent to injure the Brethren declare to them as their course of conduct the adoption of principles in accordance with all this.[2] And by these courses of action, injury to the Brethren does actually result, [64] and they give up setting their minds upon the systematic practice of spiritual insight and holy tranquillity. The Princes in recklessness become full of malevolence ; and by that course the depraved tendencies of the Brethren, hitherto lulled, are no longer at rest and no longer kept down. Nay, upon occasion the Brethren fall away from their fixt purpose, from virtue, from right conduct and right views ; and for this cause they fall into laxity, busied with many things ; no real ascetics although making professions of asceticism, no true celibates though professing celibacy, giving forth an empty sound like the conch, proclaiming the Law of Sense.[3] Meanwhile they receive all the more honour, esteem, and respect from the Prince and his court ; and they utter reproaches amongst the householders, against Brethren who strenuously keep the rule, and then the Prince and his court use injurious and contemptuous expressions in the presence of Brethren who strenuously keep the rule. All the goods and blessings which are found among the loyal Brethren, all these they transfer to such as delight in meditation. On both counts[4] they fall into a Root Sin. And how is this ? The

[1] Tib. 45a^1 translates *kāla* by *nag. po. bsten. pa*, " precepts of the Black One " apparently.

[2] Tib. *bya-ba-maṅ-bar-gyur-pa* apparently " busybodies," the opposite of *samatha*.

[3] Compare *Jat.*, ii. 127^{16}, 157^{16}, *poṭṭhabbo*, of things sensual. The Tib. *reg-par-bya-bi* implies *sprashṭavya*.

[4] A gloss explains this as (1) evil speaking, (2) corruption of discipline on the part of the renegade Brethren.

meditating Brother is good ground, but not they who abide in study, not they who are devoted to study.[1]

"Those who are fit vessels for the spiritual stages of rapt contemplation, the use of mystic formulæ, or patient endurance, who are worthy of honour and who are fit recipients, these are the lights of the world, who guide the world in the right path: these bring deliverance to beings from the field of action and passion;[2] they stablish them in the way that leads to Nirvāna.

"These, my son, are the Eight Root Sins.

"The means of escape from them is set forth in the same scripture.

"If these Bodhisatvas, when they have heard the name of the Bodhisatva Ākāśagarbha, should long to see him, being desirous of confessing their root sins, for fear lest they fall into perdition; and if they worship Ākāśagarbha and praise his name: then this noble Bodhisatva, as it were, by good fortune appears before them in his own shape, or in guise of a brahman . . . and in other forms, such as a maiden's: he lays before the Inceptor Bodhisatva his sins as they were committed; [65] and teaches him profound skill in finding the Means, his walk, that is, in the Great Way, . . . and he stablishes him on the Ground from which there is no turning back. . . . But if he manifests not himself face to face before the Bodhisatvas, then the inceptor, who is a transgressor and begs for his aid, must in the last watch of the night, arise from his seat, and stand facing the east, and offer incense; and Aruṇa,[3] son of the gods, must be the object of his prayer, and thus he must speak: 'O Aruṇa, Aruṇa, great in mercy, great in fortune, great is thy praise in all India; shield me with thy mercy; quickly make known my prayer unto Ākāśagarbha the merciful. In my sleep show the means whereby I may confess my sin. May I attain to the wisdom in the Means that is found in the

[1] Tib. must have read *adhy* in both compounds without the negative, and made these the subject to the succeeding verb.

[2] Read ०क्षेत्रात्स०.

[3] The Sun.

noble Great Way.' Then for the time he must fall asleep on his couch; and as soon as dawn rises, here in our own India he meets the Bodhisatva Ākāśagarbha, here and in his own form. He standing before the Inceptor Bodhisatva in his sleep, indicates his Root Sin by the means of the Great Path, and lays before him further knowledge of the Means of the same kind. And by this skill in the Means that our inceptor there and then gains for himself, the rapt meditation, whose name is the Never-failing Thought of Enlightenment. And thus he becomes firmly established in the Great Path," and so our scripture continues.

In connexion with the formula of supplication that has just been spoken of, the following ritual must be gone through. "Thus must it be. In the wood or grove, or in the open, agallochum or the tagara [1] powder or something else according to circumstances must be used as incense. Clasping his hands, and offering a benediction on every side, and making obeisance with the five members,[2] he must utter the following formulæ, to wit: '*Sumṛsha* (*bis*), O merciful one, let it pass, let it pass, pass out, pass together, O merciful one; *murara, murara*, O swift one, *namucame, bhujayata*, O merciful one, fill up the mystic gem, O merciful one, establish all my hope, bearing command, [66] *sphugu* (*bis*), eminent in love (*seven times*), eminent in doctrine (*seven times*,) O fulfil, merciful one, my hope, let them fulfil it, and in all ways may there be an advance towards painless bliss. Hail!'" The ritual act must be performed as before, is to be performed for the averting of all pestilence, pain, all fear, all that is against our benefit, and for the perfecting of all that is desirable.

How to deal with Sin in High Places.—If even princes and other persons of rank become Bodhisatvas, how is their sin to be restrained,[3] with all their superiority to others? And then

[1] *Tabernæmontana coronaria.*

[2] Translating *pañcamaṇḍalika*, with the Tibetan, 46*b* [4], as if it were pañcāṅgika.

[3] *Niyamo* is rendered by *ṅes*, and *adhikyam* by the opposite *ma-ṅes* (" certain . . . uncertain "), which appears to be a misapprehension of *niyamo*, and possibly some other word in place of *adhikyaṁ*.

moreover they are bound by no vows.[1] How is their sin to be made manifest? Or how far are those who are bound by vows involved in the other's fault? There is no fault. Whenever this happens to a considerable extent, there the sinners are struck at by their names being known and published, to be a terror to evildoers; the fact is, all must keep clear of all sins by mutual assistance. Or else, in proportion as a man by reason of natural depravity is not even receptive (of admonition), but incapable, and so cuts through his root of good, by so much the more (must) those who are bound by vows (confess to each other). So much for this train of thought.

In the *Upāyakauśalya Sūtra* also another Root Sin is described.

"What, young sir, if a Bodhisatva be regularly instructed in the doctrine of the Confessional Office, and for a hundred thousand æons have been eating roots and fruits, and supporting good report or evil; yet if he dwell with thoughts that are bound up with the spiritual stage of Disciple or Pratyeka Buddha, this is a grave Root Sin in him. And, young sir, just as a follower of the Disciples' Way who has committed a Root Sin is incapable of gaining final Release while his present personality lasts; so also one like yourself, if he have not confessed that Root Sin, and renounced those thoughts of Disciples and Pratyeka Buddhas, is incapable of final Release at the Stage of a Buddha."

And in order easily to acquire and comprehend the abovementioned Root Sins, as well as certain individual opinions,[2] we add these memorial verses by way of summary:

(1) When one steals what belongs to the three precious things to his own use, an offence worthy of expulsion is deemed to arise.

(2) A second like offence is proclaimed by the Sage, if one reject the Good Law.

(3) Another, when one smites a Brother even if of evil life,

[1] Reading *te na* divisim.

[2] Cf. p. 402 of text, *Add. Notes*. The word may possibly mean "unique": B[2] App. The Tib. has *hga-zhig-gi*.

or steals his robes, or casts him into prison, or causes him to leave the Order.

[67] (4) Again, when one commits the five sins of inevitable result, or adopts false views, or causes division in village or other community; each of these is called by the Sage a Root Sin.

(5) When one imparts the doctrine of the void to those whose minds are not fully prepared,[1] or turns away from fullest enlightenment those who have set out on the road to Buddhahood.

(6) When one directs towards the Great Way without keeping up the discipline of the Confessional Office. Or when one maintains that the Disciples' Way does not make for the total abandonment of everything like passion.

(7) When one publishes abroad one's own good qualities while one attacks others, or injures a neighbour, moved by greed and aggrandisement or self-glorification.

(8) Or again, when one says in utter falsehood, "deep-rooted is my patience," or compasses the punishment of the ascetics, or is liberal at the expense of the Master, the Law, and the Order.

(9) If one appropriates what is given to the Order or causes the Brethren to leave their life of tranquillity,[2] or sets before Brethren devoted to their studies the enjoyment of seclusion.

(10) These rooted sins which lead to the great hell, one must confess to the august Ākāśagarbha, standing before him in a vision of sleep.

(11) The same, when one renounces the thought of enlightenment, or refuses charity to him that asks, from keen envy and greed, or from wrath and violence to one's fellow-creatures,

(12) for such an one as has no patience with his fellows even when diligently propitiated by them; and lastly from proclaiming a false semblance of the Good Law out of mere depravity or out of complaisance to a neighbour.

[1] Reading *-ṣva-*, *i.e. akṛ°* with *B. C. P.*, 162[14] and both Tib. versions.

[2] Reading *samatkalyāg°* with *B. C. P.*, 163[5].

In the holy *Kṣhitigarbha* Scripture again it is written:

"O mighty Brahma, he who has been ordained in my name, but has fallen into evil and immoral courses, and though reputed to be a Brother is a man of naught, no true ascetic although making pretensions of asceticism, no celibate though professing celibacy, shattered, fallen, overmastered by many and various sins, nevertheless that wicked and sinful Brother
68] may as on this day become a preacher to gods and men, yea, to all who are vessels of righteousness, may in fact be the Good Friend.

"And all the time he is an unworthy object. Yet by his tonsure of head and chin, by his deportment in wearing the saffron robes, although this be done merely for parade, he may still foster many a root of good in his neighbours and show the way of salvation. Therefore, whosoever has been ordained in my name, whether virtuous or no, in his case I do not allow to emperors and kings even, in that he has been ordained in my name, that even with justice on their side they should inflict on his person stripes, or cast him into prison, or sever him limb from limb, or put him to death; much less unjustly." And how is the dead saint spoken of in this book of the Law? "Now moreover that man is like orpiment and musk," are the words.[1] In the same passage he says: "Whoso shall injure such as have been ordained in my name and are in the Way of Salvation or vessels meet for it, they thereby become exceeding great transgressors in the sight of all Buddhas past, present and to come; their roots of good are cast off and the propagation thereof consumed away; and thus they are on the road to Hell."

In the same passage he says: "This banner of salvation is under the protection of all the Buddhas, namely the red and saffron robe."

And in the same place we are told: "At that time, many myriads of disciples and many myriads of Bodhisatvas were confessing in the presence of the Blessed One a sin of this kind

[1] Apparently the relics of a saint are an ornament to the Church as orpiment to the brow, and of sweet savour.

which they had committed in a previous birth, which formed an obstacle to the acquisition of merit.

" 'We also, venerable Lord, have reviled, have injured, have been wrathful against men who were in the Way of the Disciples of the Blessed Buddhas, whether they were vessels meet or unmeet for the preaching of many Tathāgatas of old time, and have uttered calumny and defamation against them. Through that obstacle to merit, we have each had meted out to us in the three hells suffering varied, keen, fierce, and grievous,' " and so on: " 'All that remains of this obstacle to merit we desire to confess now in the presence of the Blessed One.' Others say: 'We have censured and abused disciples of the Blessed One with our words'; others, 'we have assailed disciples of the Blessed One, both vessels meet and unmeet'; others, 'we have stolen their robes'; others, 'we have diminished the uses and enjoyments of disciples of the Blessed One'; others, 'we have made those who were ordained in the name of the Blessed One to become householders, and thereby placed them in an unseemly position'; others say, 'We, O Blessed One, have cast into common prison disciples of the Blessed Buddhas, whether vessels meet or unmeet, for some transgression of which they were guilty;[1] and by that obstacle to merit for many æons we have each had meted out to us in the three hells suffering varied, keen, fierce, and grievous,' " [69] and so on. " 'Therefore we now confess all that remains of this obstacle to merit in the presence of the Blessed One. For the future we would take the vow. May the Blessed One receive us and show pity, may he raise us up from endless sins.' " And so he proceeds.

In the *Pravrajyāntarāya* Scripture again another evil is described.

"There are four principles, O Mahānāman, which if a householder be addicted to, he is apt to be born at an unseasonable time. Thus he is born blind, or dumb, or tongueless, or a Caṇḍāla, and in no case[2] blessed; he becomes a scandalmonger,

[1] Instead of handing them over to the *Saṅgha*. [2] Read न भाग्.

a hermaphrodite, or a eunuch ; he becomes a permanent slave or a woman ; or again, he becomes a dog, a swine, an ass, a camel or a venomous snake, in each several birth. And what are these four ? In one case, Mahānāman, a householder causes hindrance to the thought of renouncing the world, or of receiving ordination, or following the Holy Way amongst such of his fellow-creatures as have been called by Buddhas in the past. This is the first principle. Again, a householder out of craving for wealth or craving for his son, not believing in the doctrine of the ripening of works, causes a hindrance to the ordination of son, daughter, wife, or the conclave of his kindred, because of his position as head of the house. This is the second principle. There are two besides : reviling the Good Law, and anger against ascetics and Brahmans."

The Ten Bad Paths of action are evil.

In the book *Saddharmasmṛtyupasthāna* we see that they are bitter in their ripening. From this work only a selection of the Scripture is here set down. To begin with, there is the retribution for murder.

The writer says : "There are a sort of birds which can fly into a flame without being burned, but come out with the more alacrity, break the skulls of the victims in hell, and drink their blood. Other birds, which break the head and drink the hot brains. Others tear the tongue piecemeal, and devour it ; and the tongue, when eaten, again grows, more sensitive than the petal of a lotus. [70] Other birds there are, with names answering to their functions.[1] Some tear out the teeth, or rip away the veins of the neck ; some lay bare the lungs ; some devour the stomach ; some twist round the spleen ; some eat into the depths of the intestines ; they feed on back and spine ; others piercing the openings of the joints, and cut away the vital parts, and so enter and consume marrow and pith, amidst their victims' shrieks ; others with beaks like needles

[1] As a matter of fact, each of the above classes of birds has a compound name invented to describe it, for which we refer our readers to the text.

drink their blood, or pierce between the bones devouring all the six skins; some tear with their nails, slicing off the fat and laying the sinews bare; some fill their bellies with hair they have torn out by the roots.

"Now there is a district in the Avīci Hell stretching for three myriads of leagues, called the Quarter of the Dragon Birds, where the guilty one is devoured with the other denizens of hell for many myriads of years, and there is reborn. At last with difficulty he is released from it all, but is still surrounded by the net of misery. There is a second region called the Precipice of the Chasm, whither he goes, in search of protection, refuge, succour, on every side surrounded by eleven masses of flame, unfriended, bound in the bonds of the noose of his actions, girt in on every side by enemies; at last he reaches a wilderness, and so comes to a more terrible pain than any in the whole accumulation of hell, and so he roams over the region of the Śvabhra Precipice, and every time his foot falls [1] it dissolves wholly away, yet as he lifts it it grows again, tenderer and more sensitive, thrilled by keen and bitter pangs. Thus, when his face is distorted with fear, every limb and member is wasting away, this Śvabhra Precipice breaks on his view. Down that place he falls, and he falls down for three thousand leagues: then a wind caused by his actions [2] uplifts him. And as he falls he is the prey of herons, crows, vultures, owls; and this rising and falling goes on for myriads of years. But by some means or other released from this, and wandering round, he falls into the Chasm of the Wheels. Here wheels with a thousand spokes appear before him, with felloes of adamant, fiercely blazing and quickly whirling; as soon as he meets them, they attach themselves to his body and go on moving. . . . [71] Dragging off all his limbs one by one, they burn them, and the soles of his feet are pierced by spikes. So on the Hill Makkoṭaka,[3] when he is devoured by the tribes of animals called Mākkoṭaka even to the uttermost atom within and without. But as he is devoured, so each time he is reborn

[1] Read पतितो.

[2] Cf. *Avadāna-śat.* text 258 (Feer, p. 176 *fin.*).

[3] Tib. *gnad-hjoms-pa*, "vital-tearing."

more sensitive than before, and by reason of his sensitiveness, has an ever-increasing pain to bear over and over again. And each time that he is devoured, his skin and flesh return in larger bulk to see. This is the fruit of the guilt of murder."

He next describes the ripening of the sin of theft.

"The sinner who practises evil deeds sees a great heap of wealth, piles of jewels, clothes, money, and corn, but unreal like a circle made by whirling a firebrand, like a mirage or a castle in the air. Thus he is overcome by greed, and maddened by his past demerit, he imagines, 'Yonder thing is mine.' The deluded wretch leaps over flaming fire-pits in his pursuit of the treasures. He is caught by the servants of Yama produced by his actions, and enmeshed in knives he is torn limb from limb, cut to pieces, and burnt, until nothing but bones is left. And yet that greed, which existed for endless time past never fails to torment him even though he has been reduced to this plight."

And as to sexual passion he says: "The sinner, after passing through that lane of knives and with difficulty crossing the fire-pits, is sent wandering by his past actions, and reaches another region, called the Region of Phantoms.[1] There he sees women [2] produced by his actions, the same whom he saw before when he had sinned; [3] on seeing whom, the fire of lust which has been accumulating for endless time past, arises in him. He runs in their direction; and they by his past actions are turned into women of iron. They catch him, and devour him, so that from his hips onwards he is so devoured that not a piece is left of that body of his so big as a grain of mustard seed. But again the body appears only to be devoured once more. Though he endures keen and bitter pain, he cannot turn away from the fire of his lust, but runs again after the women: and the pain of all this is not so grievous to him as the fire of his lust. [72] Then those women, with limbs of adamant and iron all red-hot, catch the man; and all their

[1] In 71[13] of text, transfer the stop to stand after *nāma*.
[2] So better with Tib.
[3] Lit. "when he had consciousness of transgressing (the Law)."

bodies enwreathed in rising flames, crush the doomed one like a handful of sand. Again he is born as before. . . .

"Women are ever the root of ruin, and of loss of substance; when men are to be controlled by women how can they gain happiness?" And so on, to the words—

"A woman is the destruction of destructions in this world and the next; hence one must ever avoid women if he desires happiness for himself."

As to false speaking, he tells us:

"The Sinner is caught by the servants of Yama, who then rend his mouth open and drag out his tongue from it. And his tongue, through the force of his actions, is stretched to a length of five hundred leagues, as the fruit [1] of his false speaking. And at the moment when it issues forth from his mouth, the servants of Yama pin it to the ground, which is made of red-hot iron; and a thousand ploughs appear, produced by his actions, fitted with red-hot shares, and by the strength of stout bulls they plough deep into his tongue: and in it are rivers flowing with blood, pus, and worms. . . . And the tongue is then as sensitive as the eye of the gods, until from agony he thunders, and roars, and cries, and there is no one to relieve his pain. . . . And while he endures this fierce torment, myriads of years roll by, and the tongue is still being ploughed. Yet this tongue (large as it is) somehow can always go into the mouth of this prisoner in hell. He with his face distorted with fear runs hither and thither, plunging into the fire-pits and is burnt therein. When he is thus maddened by pain, without refuge or retreat, [73] once more Yama's servants appear, with hammer and sword in hand. They grind him to powder from head to foot. . . ."

Again: the ripening of Slander is the same as for Lying; namely, the tongue is three hundred leagues long. But the distinction here is, that the servants of Yama draw swords with red-hot blades and cut it up. And in another region, the tongue is eaten by jackals. Tormented by bitter agony he

[1] Read फलेन, as the Tib. shows: 50 *l.* 7, *hbras-bu*.

cries and wails with indistinguishable sounds because his tongue is gone.

As to the maturing of harshness, he says: "They rip open his mouth and tear out the tongue. They slice it with keen-edged knives, and throw it into his mouth again that he may eat it. He, tormented by starvation, his face all emaciated by hunger, proceeds to devour that very tongue of his, streaming with his own blood and spittle. And the tongue although cut up again takes root by force of his actions. Then smitten by pain he writhes on the ground and struggles and cries. And while he is thus pierced with pain, his eyeballs rolling in agony, prostrate, friendless, and alone (for thus he reaps the fruit of his own deeds), the servants of Yama thus preach to him in an admonitory stanza:

"'The keen shaft of speech, which once was shot from the bow of thy tongue, which was regarded as harshness, behold here is the fruit of it.'"

And so the text continues.

And next he describes the sin of inconsiderate [1] talk. Molten red-hot copper, heated by his actions, burns his tongue. After the tongue it burns the neck, then heart and entrails, then the stomach, then goes out by the lower part. Then too the servants of Yama recite these stanzas.

[74] "The speech which thou usedst inconsiderate, its words unconnected with what went before or after, senseless, and incoherent: now behold its fruit come to thee.

"The tongue that never spoke truth, that cared not to recite the scripture, has never been recognized by the wise as a tongue but merely as a lump of flesh."

He tells of the ripening of the sin of covetousness.

"Next he sees a hollow unsubstantial heap of wealth in the possession of his neighbours, all this the product of his own actions. Then impelled and driven to distraction by his own actions, he thinks, All that must be mine. Thus our prisoner in hell runs where that wealth is. The fruit of this passion

[1] See *Abhidharmakośa*, iv. 76, 77.

called Covetousness, increased and harboured and indulged, is that the sinner sees in hell everything reversed. When his vision is thus distorted, overcome by covetousness, a knife appears in his hand, and he runs with it ; and the other prisoners in hell also have knives appearing in their hands. With the knife he fights with them, until he is hacked to pieces so that not a piece of his flesh as large as a mustard seed remains on his body, and only the bones of his skeleton are left. . . . When he sees his neighbours' blessings,[1] he longs for them to be his. This is the fruit he gets from the poison [2] that arises out of covetousness."

He then describes the fruit of malevolence.

" A crowd of lions, tigers, serpents, generated by his actions, surround him full of fury. Panic-stricken at their approach, he flees this way and that. But how can he fly away from his actions ? They seize him ; and when they have seized him, the front part of his brain is being devoured, while on each side he is gnawed by continual bitings from the serpents' fangs, and behind is devoured by the tigers. His feet too are burned with fire ; the servants of Yama pierce him from afar with their arrows." And so the author continues.

[75] The fruit of Heresy, again, is great beyond words, and we abridge our description of it. " He is overwhelmed in a rain of knives, of javelins, lightnings, thunderbolts, and thunder-stones ; he is constantly being consumed by eleven jets of flame and by the fire of thirst and hunger issuing from his mouth.

" Because desire is the root of all evil, therefore one must fear." As he continues in the same passage. " There is a Hell called Fire-pit. Then what is the action that brings beings to birth therein ? When a man who is no monk but pretends to be one, hearing the sound of the singing, dancing, or the bangles of womankind, listens with mind overcome owing to a wrong judgment to the laughter, sport, and revelry, and becomes

[1] From Tib. *hbyor-ba-mthoṅ-nas* supply *sampadaṁ dṛshṭvā*, or the like.

[2] *Viṣasya* is not in Tib., which has the equivalent of *karmaṇas, las.* The sentence (as reconstructed here) is a śloka in both Sanskrit and Tibetan.

incontinent.[1] . . . Then the prisoners in hell are ground to powder limb from limb beneath a shower of iron, are boiled and burned under a rain of live coals.' Similarly: we read of the Hell called Paduma, the Lotus, as arising from the remembrance of the pleasant flavour of one's former passions, and from their remembrance taking place during sleep. There these prisoners in hell are boiled in cauldrons, and are pounded with pestles of iron in vessels.

Likewise the hell called Mahā-paduma is said to come into existence if by the prayer of a heavenly nymph one brings one's chaste life to an end. There flows the river called Kshāranadī-taraṅginī, the Stream of Brine. All the stones of this river are bones, its weeds are hair, its mud is flesh, its water is molten [2] copper, and its fishes are prisoners in hell, etc. Likewise, endless varieties of punishments are described for the sin of sodomy. Likewise as the result of misconduct with children he beholds boys floating about in the River of Brine. They cry out to him, and he plunges into the river through the impulse of grief and pain arising from his keen affection and attachment to them.

So sexual commerce, evil in its nature, with cows, mares, goats, and sheep is described as bearing especially bitter fruit. The sinner addicted to this bestiality enters by way of the womb into those same animals, who by the power of his action have been fashioned in red-hot iron; and in their belly, which is filled with a heap of red-hot coals, he swelters and is fried for myriads of years. [76] Similar punishments are described at length.

Likewise, we read of men falling into hell who have misconducted themselves with nuns even when these have been already seduced by others. So too of the man who uses his wife against kind. So it is with those who abuse other men's wives forcibly abducted or girls whom they have procured. Terrible punishments in hell are also described for sin with

[1] *Semen emittit.*

[2] Reading *kvathitaṁ*, as suggested by the Tib. *bskol-ba*.

women performing a fast, with wives of preceptors, or with women honoured by the title of kinsfolk.

In the *Saptamaithunasaṁyukta* Scripture it is said :—

" Then a certain one, O Brāhman, avows himself to be chaste. He has no intercourse at all with womankind ; but when with his eye he beholds womankind, he gloats over their shape : he then delights in it, is absorbed in it, abides in that absorption. This, O Brāhman, is said to be a chaste student who is attached to sexual passion, not one detached ; the chastity that he practises is impure. So too when a man sports and romps and dallies with womankind, his chastity is but impure. So too when one delights in dancing attendance upon womankind. So also when one delights in such sounds as those of dance and song that come from womankind through wall or curtain, it is said that he thereby delights in sexual union. So again when one delights in looking at his neighbour who is given over to the five forms of lust. So again, by applying the fruit of his chaste life in the worlds of gods,[1] he is attached to sexual passion, not detached from it."

And how these lusts, although as described merely affecting the province of memory and wish, in that way tend to ill, is expressed by the same speaker in the *Kāmāpavādaka Sūtra*. " Keep your heart, O Brother, from lusts : fearsome and terrible is that road, full of thorns and of precipices, a rough road, a bad road, the path of pain, frequented only by wicked men. Never is that road frequented by good men. You are not wondering, are you, why the Blessed One pronounced desires to be insipid ?[2] Full of pain are they, full of misfortune, full of anguish ; [77] in them distress increases ever more and more. A disease, O Brethren, are lusts, a boil, a thorn in the flesh, sin and a root of sin,[3] a baited hook, mere death ; unstable are lusts, and delusive ; their nature is to deceive and beguile ; they are but as a dream. Nay, these are but wheed-

[1] The Pali *Aṅg. N.* iv. p. 55 explains this by his uttering an aspiration : " By this my virtuous life may I become a god." Tib. *sño.*

[2] Dhp. 186, appassādā dukhā kāmā, iti viññāya paṇḍito. Jāt. ii. 313, Divy. 224[13].

[3] Reading *agha* for *adya*, with Tib. *sdig.*

lings of children.[1] . . . Like a trap for catching deer, a net for birds, or seine for fish, a snare [2] to catch monkeys, a flame of fire to catch moths: even such are lusts. . . . In the case of one who long time goes after the pursuit of passion, there is no limit to what is put into the lion's mouth; (he is insatiable) as butchers or beefeaters, as the appetite of snakes for frogs. There is no end to the number of those who for a long time follow their lusts, and are apprehended for thieves, and their heads are split; they are apprehended for adulterers, highway robbers, plunderers of village or countryside," and so on to "cutpurses, and their heads are split, and there is no end to the examples of this. Lust is a thing grievous, sharp, acrid, sour to the taste, blood shed and oozing, a thing more widely spread than the water in the mighty oceans. . . . In fact this body is full of suffering. It is a framework of bones, bound by sinews, clothed with soft flesh, enclosed in the cuticle and covered with the epidermis, pierced and perforated with pores, swarming with vermin, pernicious for living creatures, the dwelling of sins and evil deeds. In this body many plagues arise: such as disease of the eye, disease of the ear, and so forth, piles, blains, or fistula. . . . The body has torments, the body has pains, it suffers decay, is broken down, is bent double; it is lame, is greyheaded, is full of wrinkles; the senses come to maturity and then decay, [78] the elements of the body grow old and decrepit:" and so on, to the words "one should not at this rate have respect unto the body, crumbling and falling away. . . .

'And what, Brother, is this insatiate quest of passion in thee? [3] and who [4] is it entices thee? How art thou caught, unmanned, attached, fallen into a state of attachment? [5] When I enter Nirvāna, and the Good Law is obscured, and you through your persistently pursued passions will be on the way

[1] *Lal. Vist.*, xv. 258[18] *ed. B.I.* = 212[12] *ed. L.*

[2] So Tib.; the Skr. word *leya* is unknown. Query *lepa?* Chinese has "dung."

[3] Tib. appears to read सन्ति

[4] Tib. understands *kāmah*, "what desire."

[5] Dh. S. 1059. *ajjhōsanaṁ*. M.V. iii. 201[5], *anadhyavasito anadhimūrcito . . . kameṣu vigatamado.*

to perdition, when will you release yourself from old age and death? Enough, O Brother, keep thy heart clear of passions; this is no time for the pursuit of passion, this is the time for the pursuit of the law."

In the *Ugradatta-paripṛcchā* [1] also we read as follows:—

"Therefore a man must cease from the fulfilling of passion and lust, contented with his own wife, free from desire for his neighbour's, beholding her with an eye unbewitched, with distaste in his heart. He must continually apply himself to the reflection, that desires lead to the perfection of pain. And even if in the case of his own wife his mind should come to dwell on passion, then even in the case of his own wife the passions must be regarded as under the dominion of sin; he must regard her with misgiving, regarding her as full of impurity. Thus he must fix his mind. I will strive that even in my intent I may not gratify my passions, much less by sexual union, or by amorous solicitation."

And again in the same work, we read: "The Bodhisatva in presence of his wife must realize three thoughts. And what are the three? She is my companion for passion and dalliance, but not for the next world; my companion at meat and drink, but not for the fruition of the maturing of my acts. She is the companion of my pleasure, not of my pain. . . . Three other thoughts are these: that a wife must be regarded as an obstacle to virtue, to meditation, and to wisdom. And yet three more: she is like a thief, a murderer, or a guardian of hell."

Further, in the *Candrottarādārikāparipṛcchā* it is said: "Then the girl Candrottarā, seeing that mighty crowd as soon as it began to run, [79] went up in the air to the height of a palm tree, and there poised addressed the crowd in the following verses:—

"'Behold this my body, delightsome, radiant as gold, glorious in splendour; this fair form by no means belongs to a man with heart inflamed. But those who renounce passions inflamed like fire-pits, not greedy for things of sense; who live

[1] Chapter II., =fol. 9b of the separate Tibetan translation of the work.

the life of chaste students, held by their vow from the indulgence of the six senses; who when they see a neighbour's wife call her mother or sister: these become full of grace, of beauty, supreme in charm for ever.

"Behold[1] this brilliant city on every side, and the fragrance that comes from every pore of my skin: this I bestow not with heart inflamed, nay this is the fruit of liberality and self-control. No thought of passion rises within me; fix not passion on women in whom passions are dead. Witness is this mighty sage before me, that what I know is truth, and verily not falsehood. Ye once were my parents, and I was once your mother; I have been to you brother, sister, and father: who could fix a heart of passion upon his mother? And yet again before I plotted for all your lives; I once more, I was slain by you; ye were all enemies and murderers of your neighbours: how can there be a thought of passion in you? No true beauty do men gain from passion; hearts that are inflamed with it go not the Way of Bliss; nor do they go the road to Nirvana; therefore passion must be eschewed. [80] Through lust men fall into hell, through passion they become ghosts or beasts; priapean demons and goblins are men whose minds have been narrowed by passion; through passion men are born one-eyed, crippled, with tongue awry, misshapen: every varied blemish is the portion of such as walk the miserable way of lust. When men reach the rank of universal empire, or gods like Indra and the Thirty or Brahma, or such as exercise lordship, they owe it to having followed a long course of continence. Those who are ever agitated by lust are blind from birth, deaf, and idiot; dogs, swine, or camels, asses or boars, elephants or horses, cows, tigers, moths or flies. But those who have followed a long course of continence become proud lords of the earth, great merchants, rulers over houses and ministers—in peace and contentment they wax great. The slaves of lust come to boiling tortures of the skull, suffocation, bonds, stripes and threatenings, cutting in sunder, cutting away of head, ears, hands, eyes, nose or foot."

[1] Tib. *ltos* as for *ikshadhvam* in line 3.

In the *Udayanavatsarāja-paripṛcchā* passions are also described.

" He runs like a fly which has spied a wound, like an ass which has spied something unclean ; as a dog to the shambles for meat : so rush fools in their passion for women.

[81] " Enveloped in ignorance, clad in a mass of darkness, as crows to carrion, so are fools attached to women.

" He is the prey of Māra whosoever has entered on the downward course. The lustful have but the same sort of enjoyment as a worm on a dunghill.

" Like a painted pot of worms [1] wheresoever it be seen, full of urine and ordure, or a skin inflated with wind :

" Mucus, phlegm, spittle, brain liquefied in humour, fetid matter discharges from the body ; like as honey from flowers.[2]

" Like an ulcer, a thing full of bones, with the mouth for its opening, a pile of flesh, skin, and such-like things, is this body, despicable and smelling raw.

" Full of all sorts of life, as an ulcer would be : just so this body is a vessel of impurities such as ordure. The belly is full of the twisted gut, stuffed up with liver and lungs ; there are the kidneys with blood bile, brains, bone, and marrow. The eighty thousand worms which remain within the body, fools cannot see, because they are enveloped in the net of delusion. [82] Men's bodies discharge impure and fetid pus by their nine wound-like openings. Fools take a hint at word or look, but when once filled with desire, thenceforward know not how it is a place despised of all. Fools take to excrement, and feed on humours and phlegm. They cleave to what is abominable, as flies when they have caught sight of a wound ; sweat drips in their armpits and evil odours fly about. Evil deeds they do whereby they go down to hell, cherishing evil desires and evil principles. Foolhardy, they go to the Avīci hell, there to suffer fierce pain. Unsavoury as ordure are women ; so the Buddhas declare. Thus 'tis an evil man that consorts with

[1] Tib. " ordure," which is also a lexical meaning of *kīṭa*.

[2] Tib. joins *kāyād* with *bālānāṁ*, " from the body of fools."

evil women. Who penetrates a body which is but a receptacle for impurity, receives like fruit to that which he does."

And in the same passage the author says:

"Owing to these enjoyments, sought with pain and accumulated as though for dear life, they are not able to give anything to ascetics or Brāhmans or to the deserving poor and suppliants, being brought into the power [1] of women, mastered, enthralled and enslaved by them. As a result of the same passion for women they have no power left even to contribute to the support of the woman herself and to follow the moral law. With his desire set upon them, he bears with the women's chatter and even with their threats, their angry looks, and their reproaches. When threatened by womankind, man though he is he subsides and takes a humble place, and has regard to her good pleasure. To indulge and gratify his passion he becomes her slave. Such, O King, is the evil course of the man who is tormented by lust, occupying himself in pleasure which is but dung, who delights in the unclean, behaving like a senseless fool. . . ."

[83] "When they but hear of fever like this, there is no emancipation for them. All the more they have to do with women, and take delight with them. They make a habit of wretched passion, and are blameworthy in their talk. When they have heard the Law, they speak, they are confused as to its meaning, and so they speak the good word. His mind is set upon a woman as a cat's is upon a mouse. When he has heard a saying of Buddha, bursts out again like deadly poison his fever of passion in a moment. On seeing a bit of filth, like a swine's appetite, it goes on for a moment, then . . . it becomes greedy again. So it is that fools, bent on pleasure, forsake the Buddha's teaching, and make a habit of base passion which leads them to hell. Infatuated and given over to passion, they commit some dire crime and renouncing virtuous ways, go at the last to hell.

"But the man who knows the path of duty in such matters, and carries no favour for womankind, has the path to heaven

[1] Reading *vaśīkṛtaḥ* with Tib. *dbar-du-gyur-ciṅ.*

ever clear before him. The highest enlightenment is not hard for him to gain. . . . The wise man, when he has gained the fitting time, and has listened to teaching such as this, will forsake all lusts in this world, and may enter the Order if intelligent."

In the *Praśāntaviniścayaprātihārya Sūtra* another evil is described.

[84] "If (O Manjuśrī) a young man or woman were to slay all the inhabitants of India and take their goods, and if another should cause hindrance to a Bodhisatva whose mind is wholly set on good, or stunt his root of merit, even when he is born as an animal, if it be but the depriving of a morsel of food: the second commits an immeasurably greater crime than the first. And how is this? The hindrance to roots of merit that might have resulted in the uprising of a Buddha is permanent. Whosoever, O Manjuśrī, behaves with spite or contumely towards a Bodhisatva amongst others has to fear therefore at that time as his reward three terrors, which are: the fear of being born in hell, the fear of being born blind, or the fear of being born at the ends of the earth."

Again he says:

"The man who does him despite, or speaks to his discredit truly or falsely, or in a fit of anger speaks harshly or disturbs his peace: such an ill-disposed person is born in the hells with a vast body, and as a fallen being feels bitter pain. His body is five hundred leagues in length, he is for ever being lacerated and devoured by a hundred thousand dogs.[1]

"The reviler has five thousand heads, and each head five hundred tongues; each tongue has five hundred flaming ploughshares to plough it for the sinful word it spake.

[85] "The unrestrained sinners that oppress Bodhisatvas fry in the Hell Pratāpana, which surges with the fire of bitter pain. All too easily they may find birth in the womb of an animal in hell, to last for a thousand æons. In the next birth they become cruel serpents with fell poison; hunger and thirst overpower them, and make them commit merciless acts, and

[1] *śunā* is therefore collective. So Tib.

even when they get food and drink, it never satisfies them. And if such an one after that birth appears amongst men, he is born blind, or wicked, or malicious and uncontrolled.

"The man who has spoken an injurious word, a speech of contempt for the venerable, when he passes from the world of men again goes to hell, so that in many æons he sees not a Buddha incarnate."

Again he says in the same place :

"As often, O Manjuśrī, as one Bodhisatva cherishes towards another feelings of hatred or contempt, for so many æons he must make up his mind to abide in the nethermost hells.

"A Bodhisatva can be brought to shipwreck by no other act than just the sin of defaming another Bodhisatva : just as the diamond, Manjuśrī, cannot be cut by another hard object, such as stick or clod, but only by a diamond, so a Bodhisatva can only be brought to shipwreck by defaming another Bodhisatva."

[86] In the *Āryaśraddhābalādhānāvatāramudrā Sūtra*, it is said :

"Suppose, Manjuśrī, a man or woman in a fit of wrath were to succeed in shutting up every living being of all the ten quarters and all the worlds in a dark prison ; and suppose another man or woman in a fit of wrath were to stand and look askance at a Bodhisatva, saying, 'I will not look at yonder sinner' : the second would be a sin immeasurably greater than the first." And again, in the same passage : "Whosoever, Manjuśrī, might be supposed to steal all the property of every one in India, commits a sin immeasurably less than one who should revile a Bodhisatva of any standing whatever." Again, in the same book : "The man or woman who should wreck and burn stupas numerous as the sands of the Ganges, commits a sin immeasurably less than one who abuses a Bodhisatva devoted to the Great Way, cherishing a heart of malice and obduracy.[1] The reason is this. It is from the Bodhisatvas that the venerable Buddhas come ; and from the Buddhas

[1] *Khila.* The Tib. *tha-ba* is variously rendered "evil" (adj.) and "anger" (subst.). In Sanskrit, it means "barren soil," and as a derivative meaning "a problem that will not come out," "obduracy." See Pali *khilo.*

come the stūpas and all other depositories of blessing, and all the assemblages of the gods. When one neglects to honour a single Bodhisatva, all the Buddhas are thereby left unhonoured; and when one has honoured a Bodhisatva, all the Buddhas are honoured thereby. Thus he who would show the highest honour to all the Buddhas, must needs honour the Bodhisatvas."

And how the honour done to such persons comes to maturity is shown in the *Praśāntaviniścayaprātihārya Sūtra*.

"But he who gives righteous protection to such as proclaim the Law leaves behind all forms of perdition and becomes an Indra, yea a Brahma, a Yāma, a Tushita, a Vaśavartin, in successive births. And when he is born amongst men he becomes a universal emperor, [87] or a flourishing and wealthy merchant or householder armed with wisdom and mindfulness, blessed and free from ill."

But why speak of helping or hindering a Bodhisatva? It is the same just with an ordinary person; as is said in the *Śraddhābalādhārāvatāramudrā Sūtra*.

"If a man or woman, Mañjuśri, should give[1] day by day to all the beings in all the world, numberless as motes in a sunbeam, fine food of a hundred flavours and fine raiment likewise, and continue for the space of ages countless as the sands of the Ganges; and if another should give but for one day food to but a single lay Brother whose only master is the Master, and follows the Ten Paths of Virtue, because he says, This man is taught in the teaching of the Blessed One; then this person lays up immeasurably greater store of merit than the first. And if a man or woman likewise gives these countless gifts to as many myriads of lay Brethren, for as many ages, and if another gives food but for one day to a Brother; this last giver lays up stores of merit immeasurably greater than the other."

In the *Niyatāniyatāvatāramudrā Sūtra* we read:

"If all beings in all the worlds, Mañjuśrī, should have their

[1] dadaṅ here and below (87. 11) is a misprint for dadad.

eyes torn out (to put an imaginary case) and any man or woman out of a benevolent heart should restore their sight (to put an imaginary case); yet if another man were to look with kindly heart upon a Bodhisatva who is an enthusiast for the Great Way; the last lays up stores of merit, immeasurably greater than the first. If a man or woman, Mañjuśrī, should set free from prison countless prisoners who are in prison in all the worlds, and set them in the bliss of emperors or the estate of a god; and if another merely desire to behold with kindly heart the enthusiast for the Great Way, and tell forth his praises: the second lays up stores of merit immeasurably greater than the first."

[88] So too we read in the *Kshitigarbha Sūtra*:

"Suppose again, reverend sir, a noble prince, minister, soldier, ascetic, or brāhman, shall have a care for his neighbour, himself, and the world to come, who shows care, deference, and honour to every man (be he meet or unmeet to receive the gospel of the Blessed One, be he a shaven monk or the friar clad in tatteis of the yellow robe) and likewise shall listen with due respect to the word of the Disciples, and the Pratyeka Buddhas; honouring of course the word of the Great Way and those who have set forth on the Great Way, when holy, rich in virtue, ready with fit speech,[1] with such he takes pleasure and delight, consults them and interrogates them, thinks he must listen to them and act accordingly. . . . How much sin, O Blessed One, shall he thereby cancel? The Blessed One replied: Well, fair sir, suppose a man arise who fills all India with the seven precious things, makes gifts to venerable Buddhas when they are there, and does the like at noontide and at even, and so for the space of a hundred thousand years, what think you, would he lay up great store of merit? The disciple replied, He would indeed accumulate a mass of merit immeasurable and vast; insomuch that it could be estimated by none but a Tathāgata.

[1] Tib. 59, l. 3 appears to have read *muktān* (*grol-pa*) as a separate word, which is followed by *rig-pai* (translating an uncertain Sanskrit equivalent) *spobs-ba-can* (=*pratibhānān*).

'The Lord replied: But the noble prince who acts as aforesaid lays up a greater store of merit, in measure far greater and more vast. He who in the last five hundred years of the present dispensation preserves the leading [1] of the Good Law, he preserves himself, his neighbours, the next world, preserves my gospel, preserves also the disciples whether apt or inapt [89] . . . (yea, all the Church), whether tonsured monks or friars clad in the yellow robe. He causes no hurt. Yea, he increases his own realm and the realm of his neighbour; he diminishes the states of suffering and brings men to the abode of the gods and prolongs their life; he destroys the depravities of himself and others; he gives support to the Six Perfections in the way towards full enlightenment. He leaves behind all states of perdition. He has not long to traverse the round of Birth. He always associates with Good Friends and Venerable Buddhas, with Bodhisatvas and Great Beings. He is destined at once without separation from his Good Friends to attain full and perfect enlightenment at no distant time in Buddha-fields according to his wish. Then all spiritual beings from the gods and their attendants down to the goblins with their attendants arose from their seats and did reverence to the Buddha, and said: Whatsoever followers, O Blessed One, thou shalt have down to the last five hundred years, be he noble prince, or householder, or others as aforesaid, so they be preservers of the Good Law who shed lustre upon the traditions of Buddha, the Law, and the Order: . . . these, each and all, we and ours will preserve, protect, and give them increase in ten ways. And what are the ten ways? We will prolong the life of each, and we will duly avert any obstacle to his life, we will give them increase in health, state, wealth, use and enjoyment, lordship, fame, Good Friends, and achievement of wisdom: these are the ten ways." And so he proceeds.

And so with those who have not entered the Stages this course of ripening may be observed.

[1] See *Add. Notes* to p. 88 in text.

In the *Avalokanā Sūtra* moreover it is said:

"He who makes solemn procession round the stūpa of the Lord of the World, when he has aroused the thought of enlightenment for the weal of all that breathe:"

[90] Thus the poet goes on to describe the reward, and tells of further benefits; and then proceeds:

"But he who works malice upon these sons of the Buddha, shall leave the worlds of gods and of men with hell in his sight."

And so he proceeds in the description. And in what has just been said no cause of superiority can be seen; and when we have said this we may pass on.

In the *Karmāvaraṇaviśuddhi Sūtra*, an evil is meant by the term hindrance. "Passion, hatred, delusion are called hindrances, and also giving, and the group of virtues, good conduct, patience, manliness, meditation, wisdom. . . . How so? Fools and worldlings, Manjuśrī, when they give a gift, cause ill feeling amongst the envious, and from this ill feeling they feel malice; and through the sin of malice and obstinacy they are reborn in the hells. Such men, when they practise good conduct, blame and gird at the ill conducted and speak in their dispraise; and when they hear of their faults excite ill feeling against them in society at large; and as the result of this ill feeling they are on the road to perdition. Such men when they practise patience, in their pride therefore exalt themselves and become heedless. 'We are they,' say they, 'who are entitled to speak of patience, while the rest of these are malevolent.' These persons, intoxicated with pride of patience, fall into the pains which have their root in heedlessness. When such men begin to practice manliness, they exalt themselves and oppress others. 'These men,' say they, 'live but the life of lazy monks, enjoying the offerings of the faithful without any personal devotion. They do not deserve even a cup of cold water.' Thus their practice of manliness turns to self-glorification and the oppression of others. I call them mere fools. When they reach the stage of meditation, on reaching it because of this attainment they allow arrogance [1]

[1] So Tib. *sñems*, although this meaning is not recorded for Sanskrit *spṛhā*.

to spring up within them That is what they think. 'We,' say they, 'are they who abide in meditation; the rest are persons of dissipated intelligence: How can they ever become Buddhas?'" In this strain he continues.

In the *Sarvadharmāpravṛttinirdeśa Sūtra* moreover it is said:

"The Bodhisatva exhorts sinfully: enlightenment is far off; [91] and he gets an obstacle to his merit. He exhorts enviously [1]: enlightenment is far off. He exhorts with ceremonial posturing: enlightenment is far off. If he conceives a mean idea of a Bodhisatva, and a lofty idea of himself, he injures himself and gets an obstacle to his merit. Now when a Bodhisatva has to apply admonition or instruction to another Bodhisatva, it is only after he has caused the other to regard him as a Teacher that he may admonish or instruct him. A Bodhisatva must not engender a feeling of contempt for another Bodhisatva, so long as the latter has not lost his enlightenment. My son, there is no way in which a Bodhisatva can so easily cut his roots of good as when he has to do with another Bodhisatva." Thus he says.

The fact is, that even when the thought of enlightenment has not been produced, contempt for a being capable of enlightenment [2] is forbidden: how much more when that thought has been produced.

As it is said in the *Śūraṅgamasamādhi Sūtra*. "Here, Dṛḍhamati, we inquire what is meant by a declaration as to the thought of enlightenment when not yet developed. Now such a man is born in the five divisions of successive existence,[3] whether it be in hell, the brute creation, in the world of Yama, amongst gods, or amongst men; suppose this man to be keen in his faculties and noble in his enthusiasm: of him a Tathāgata has foreknowledge. That man will develop the thought of the highest enlightenment in so many ages, and in ages untold will

[1] Reading *īrshayā*.

[2] Reading, with the MS., *bodhibhavye*.

[3] *Dh.-Sang.* 57 gives six states of existence: nirayo, tiracchānuyoni, petavisayo, manussa, deva, asura.

arrive at full enlightenment. This is what we mean by a declaration as to the thought of enlightenment, when not yet developed, for a Bodhisatva. On the same occasion the Venerable Kāçyapa addressed the Blessed One thus : From this day forth, my lord we must give the title of Teacher to all creatures ; and why ? Because we have not your knowledge. How many Bodhisatvas can be credited with faculties that will mature enlightenment, and how many cannot ? We in our ignorance, O Blessed One, might meanly regard such and thereby we might be injured.[1]

[92] "The Blessed One said : Well spoken, Kāśyapa ; it was because I fully saw that this was the force of my teaching, that I preached to you in this strain, 'Brethren, let not a man take upon him the duty of discerning between men. For a man is quickly injured in discriminating between his fellows, thinking he or one like him might do an injury to a fellow-man.' On this principle, Kāśyapa, a Bodhisatva and a Disciple also will give the title of Teacher to all fellow-creatures, saying to him, 'May not such a man prove a follower of Bodhisatvas' Way ?' Hence one must be on one's guard in this matter. But in a case where a man unmistakably shows a sign of the attainment of Enlightenment ; here one must be most carefully on one's guard against showing contempt."

As we read in the *Saddharma-puṇḍarīka Sūtra* :

"Men joyfully make stūpas to the Jina of brick or clay piled up : who erect even heaps of dust in forests or mountain fastnesses in devotion.

"Children playing here and there have made mounds of sand as stūpas in devotion to the Jinas. All these have become partakers of enlightenment. . .

[93] "Such as on painted walls make a figure [of the Sugatas] with every limb and their hundred sacred marks : when one so paints, himself or by another, all such become partakers of enlightenment.

"Such again as when they were receiving instruction there

[1] Cf. 15. 18, *supra.*

and then were amusing themselves in sport, and made with nail or wood figures on the wall, whether men or boys they all became partakers of enlightenment.

"Such as sounded iron cymbals or drums or water-drums or sang a sweet and lovely song in homage to the Sugatas: all these became Buddhas in the world.

"And all the manifold worship done to relics, be it even but a tittle [1] to the relics of Sugatas, or if one have sounded no more than a single musical instrument, or done worship with but one flower, [94] they shall behold myriads of Buddhas according to their works

"Such too as have made homage of the hands before a stūpa, be it complete, or but a single joining [2] of the palms, or have bowed the head, be it but for a moment, or bowed the body but once, or have but once made the salutation 'Glory to Buddha' there and then before the relic shrines, yea even but once and with distracted thoughts; all these have attained the highest enlightenment.

"Such beings as in that ancient day heard only the name of the Law from the Sugatas, whether entered into rest or then living, all these became partakers of Enlightenment."

In the *Mahākaruṇā Sūtra* again it is said:

"Just as an angler by a large pond throws out his baited hook to catch fish, and as soon as he has thrown it finds it swallowed by a fish; the fish swims about in the water, and yet it is to be considered caught by the line which holds it fast and is tied to a staff on the shore. Then up comes the fisherman, and knows that a fish is caught by the tautness [3] of the line. Accordingly he lands him, and takes him off the line, and uses him as he will. [95] Just so there are, who amongst the Blessed Buddhas, bring their hearts to confidence, and establish a root of merit, even by one such act. Yet such men have often been born at an unfavourable time [4] owing to the

[1] *pī* for *pi* with Tib., which does not support *-kampī* from *kamp* as in text:
[2] *śakti* MS. for *sakti*.
[3] *sūtralāghavena*: Tib. thaṅ, explained by S. C. D. as "tenseness."
[4] See *Dh. S.*, p. 66.

obstructive power of their evil actions; and then the Blessed Buddhas catch them as with a line by the Conciliations,[1] by reason of the knowledge of a Buddha. Then they draw them out of the waters of the Lake of Transient Existence and land them upon the dry ground of Nirvāna."

And this is why one must give to such men the title of Teacher, and when we honour them, must do the honour in heart. For even a novice is worthy of honour by virtue of the thought of enlightenment; just as Megha the Dravidian, though himself a great Bodhisatva, honoured the novice the Reverend Sudhuna, bowing his whole body low before him. And this is a matter of certain interpretation. Just in matters like exhortations towards thought for higher things, reverence was to be permitted to every member, all and several, of such as follow the Bodhisatva's Way.[2] And how can we avoid the contradiction of the same person receiving and giving honour? Because we rely on their being mutually entitled to honour. Hence too we infer that there is no true holiness without giving credit for the same.[3] And the same is expected[4] in the case of a Buddha: we must not fall into the logical fault of *regressus ad infinitum*. Though alone, he must not fall short in this.

In the holy *Sarvadharmavaipulyasaṁgraha Sūtra* yet another evil is described.

"Subtile, O Mañjuśrī, is the hindrance to good merit that comes from the rejection of the Good Law. In case of a man who speaks in praise of a principle set forth by the Tathāgata, while in another case he speaks in dispraise: he rejects the Good Law. In so rejecting he denies the Tathāgata, and rejects the

[1] *Dh. S.* § 19 and p. 39.

[2] "And by the expression all, we must understand oneself." *Gloss, not in Tib.*

[3] We can make nothing of the Tib. *ñam(s)-su-blaṅs-pa.* We assume a strict causal sense in *āsvādana*, for which however we cannot quote examples. But compare the use of *svādayati* in the entire language, and Ved. *svādana*, "one who prepares a savoury mess."

[4] That he must give as well as receive honour; because if we give honour only to our superiors we should have an indefinite series of persons above the Buddha.

Law, and traduces the Order. The man who says of the Law] 'This provision is fitting, that unfitting,' is really rejecting the Law. I have never preached the Law in separate portions, one for the Disciples' Way, one for the Pratyeka Buddhas' Way, one for the Great Way. Therefore are they children of confusion who make divisions in this my Law: saying, 'This belongs to the Disciples, that to the Pratvekas, and that to the Bodhisatvas. He who says this rejects the Good Law by describing it as being divided. So does he who says, This point of the Law belongs to the discipline of a Bodhisatva, and the next does not. He rejects the Good Law who says, The Preacher of the Law has inspiration, has not inspiration. He rejects the Good Law, who represents a principle of the Law as not a principle.[1] [96] He rejects the Law, who says, Although a Buddha no longer appears in the world it is unlawful to have recourse to spells.[2] He also rejects the Law, who defames the conduct of the preacher, or says that he is not endowed with religious grace,[3] or rebukes him heedlessly, or finds fault with his deportment, or rebukes him for following the letter rather than the spirit, and falling away from morality; or says that he is not[4] effective with his intuitive wit; that in him the light of true principles is not clearly seen. So too he who says that he sets spell against spell without enlightenment; or does not sound the depths of the Buddha's teaching, because he cleaves to the letter; or that he sets scripture against scripture, or sacred verse against verse; or uses the letter of the Law as a test to make out this man to be devoted, that man not; or who wrests the preacher's words into another meaning than they have; or who attributes to him the action of one whe

[1] So with Tib. 64*a* 1, chos-ni-chos-ma-yin-par-ston-te. The Sanskrit text as explained by the gloss (96, note 1) appears to mean: "He who represents a thing (*dharmaṁ*) as really a thing rejects the Law," which, according to one sect at least, teaches that things do not exist but are really void.

[2] We omit the next sentence of the Sanskrit, with Tib.

[3] Tib. phun-sum-tshogs-pa, which contains the word for "three," and is explained by Sarat Chandra as "grace, glory and wealth." Cp. *Mah. V.* ii. 357[10].

[4] MS. *na* added in margin of MS. which, as the sense as well as the Tib. shows, must be restored at this point.

sees crooked[1]; or accuses him of frivolous speaking; or of inconsistency, attributing to him moral conduct in this and not in that, saying that this is well said and that ill said[2]; or says that part of his preaching agrees with the Buddha's doctrine, and part does not:—Thus, Mañjuśrī, as far as he wrongs the preacher in any point, so far he rejects the Law. If the preacher is said or thought to be like this by Brother or Sister, by lay disciple male or female, each one of them rejects the Good Law."

In the same work we read:

"Whenever, good sir, it comes into any man's mind to preach to beings, according to their devotion, a precept of the Tathāgata, who has entered into Nirvāna; if then in that congregation only one hearer feels one thrill of joy or lets fall but a single tear: in each case it comes by power of the Tathāgata. At this point there will be sons of delusion, Bodhisatvas in profession but not in practice, who disparage the Bodhisatvas, hypocrites,[3] who will say to the preachers of the Law, 'Who are these? they know nothing.' . . . . [97] When men thus throw contempt on Bodhisatvas, I cannot say that hell has any limit for them. And why do I say this? The Bodhisatva who reviles the preacher, is abusing Buddha, is rejecting the Law, is reviling the Order. He who flouts the preacher, flouts Buddha. He who does not desire to see a preacher, does not desire to see a Buddha. He who speaks in dispraise of a preacher, speaks in dispraise of the Buddha. He abandons Buddha, who cherishes a thought of anger against a Bodhisatva, even if he be one who is only just begetting in his own mind the first thought that leads to enlightenment. . . . As regards the full knowledge, O Maitreya, of the six Perfections for the enlightenment

[1] The Tib. here is unintelligible. On further consideration we have restored *vicaksuḥkarma* as a compound.

[2] The next sentence is not in Tib. and appears to be a mistake of the copyist, whose eye caught the line above.

[3] "Men who deceive by a show of religion": Tib. chos-rku-ba-thsul. Compare Sarat Chandra Das, Dict. 76, col. 1, "*chos-rku-ba*; 'stealing by (imposing on another in the name of) religion,'" with Tib. authority cited.

of Bodhisatvas, this is how those sons of delusion will speak: 'A Bodhisatva's instructions need only be in Wisdom; what has he to do with the other Perfections?' They think that any other Perfection is to be disparaged. What thinkest thou, Ajita: Was the King of Kāśi foolish, who gave his flesh to the hawk to save the dove? Maitreya answered, He was not, my Lord. The Blessed One answered, When I was living as a Bodhisatva, and accumulated the roots of merit that are bound up with all six Perfections, did I aught amiss in respect of these roots of merit? Maitreya replied: You did not, my lord. The Blessed One said: You at least, Ajita, attained full understanding in the Perfections of Liberality, Morality, Patience, Manliness, Meditation, Wisdom, in the course of your transmigrations, sixty æons for each Perfection. Now these sons of delusion will say, 'It is only by one rule that enlightenment is attained, namely by the doctrine of the Void.' Now I ask you, Can such men be pure of heart in matters of conduct?"[1]

[1] The Tib. expresses this rhetorical question by a negative. The gloss (see note [3] in text) implies that a negative answer is implied. The delusion here seems to be the supposition that the higher teaching, *e.g.* that of the Void, can be got directly without previous practice of the various aspects of morality.

CHAPTER V

AVOIDANCE OF EVIL

We have given a summary description of Evil. The avoidance of it may be exemplified by a passage like that in the *Adhyāśayasaṁcodana Sūtra*.

Commencing Bodhisatvas who are afraid at hearing evils such as these, must act in accordance with what they have taken upon them to do. [98] This is what they say: "We who are here present, O Lord, from this day forth, in the presence of the Tathāgata do make this solemn undertaking. We shall have broken faith with the Tathāgata, the Saint, the fully Enlightened, O Lord, if hereafter we reproach with a sin, whether truly or falsely, any man, householder or one who has taken the vows, who walks in the Bodhisatva's Way; if we contemn or speak in dispraise of such an one; yea on seeing such an one gratifying or indulging himself with the Five Pleasures of the Senses, if we treat him unkindly, or upset his mind, or show him disrespect, or then refuse him the title of Teacher; if to please friends or dole-givers [1] we inflict pain of mind or body to men who walk in the Bodhisatva's Way; if when we see such an one we address him with but one ugly word; if we should fail in one threefold reverence by night or day to such an one; if we fail to sacrifice the acquisition of Kingship or of wealth, or life itself for the motive of the vow we have taken upon us; if we show contempt to one who walks

[1] With Tib. sloṅs-mo-ster-ba, "givers of alms," "patrons of the dole," we regard *-āda* as causal. Thus *bhikṣāda* has not the sense of the later word *bhikṣāsin*, "beggar, rogue." We abbreviate the verbiage in the following passage.

in the Way of the Disciples or the Pratyeka-Buddhas, saying, We are more distinguished than they; if we fail to live with humble mind, with mind like that of the lowly pariah; if we exalt ourselves, or oppress our neighbour; if we refuse to go a league, or a hundred leagues, to avoid wranglings and quarrels, as soon as we are urged to do so; if we profess ourselves to be virtuous, or learned, or pre-eminent in the ascetic practices, or exalt ourselves in respect of one or other virtue; if we fail to live with our good points concealed and our faults confessed; then I say, we shall have broken faith with the Tathāgata, the Saint, the fully enlightened. . . . Then the Blessed One said to Maitreya the Great Being: [99] 'Maitreya, the disciple of either sex who desires to diminish the Hindrance [1] arising from action, must take a vow as these disciples did.'"

Again, in the *Sarvadharmāpravṛttinirdeça* it is said:

"Thrice by night and by day as often, he should do reverence to the Bodhisatvas: he should not spy out for any slip of theirs; let him ever follow his duty according as he has chosen.

"When he sees one [2] indulging in pleasures of the senses, he is not to spy out a slip in him; that man also in time will attain [3] the good path, the best path towards enlightenment, with its endless stores of virtue.

"By graduations of fitness [4] and by graduations of acts he will become a Conqueror, and not all at once: 'tis countless ages since he has set forth in the panoply of righteousness without a change of character."

In the same book he says:

"All [Bodhisatvas], young sir, who are in evil case, through the obstacle to good action just described, must see that they

[1] See note to abstr. *Bodhisattvabhūmi*, I.

[2] Gloss: "A Bodhisatva."

[3] Restoring the MS. reading; see note [4] in text.

[4] Tib. *rigs*, implying the doctrine of *gotra*, as to which see *Bodhisattvabhūmi*, I. 1.

fall not into error respecting any of the conduct of a fellow-Bodhisatva. All his actions must be left alone.[1] Thus he must think: 'I know not the thoughts of my neighbour; men's motives are hard to discern.' Seeing the real meaning of this, the Tathāgatava thus declares the Law: [100] 'One man must not measure another. It is I, or one like unto me, that can measure a man. Whoso desireth to preserve himself in safety, must never sift the conduct of any man; nor must be censorious about his neighbours, assigning one character to this and one to that. He must be devoted to the Buddha's Law; day and night he must have a longing desire for service to the Law."

Then in the *Kṣitigarbha Sūtra* it is written:

"Then the myriads of sages rose from their seats, and did obeisance to the Blessed One in these words. 'Thus, Sire, in the presence of the Blessed One, we make our solemn vow. As long as we remain in the circle of rebirths, so long, since we possess the desire for the virtue of Patience, we will never possess the estate of a King, nor of a minister, nor of chief in town, village, or market, nor the chief estate amongst chaplains or soldiers, or even caravan-leaders; nor yet amongst teachers, ascetics, householders, landowners; yea, in all ways we renounce leadership over our fellow-creatures, until we are fully possessed of patience. Otherwise we should be casting discredit upon a profound principle of action, such as we have described, the gospel of the Buddhas." And so it goes on.

In the Candrapradīpa *Sūtra* again, the avoidance of evil is thus described:

"Suppose any persons have [2] this idea, that no sin is not allowable, with such hold no intercourse in this late age. But if you must speak to them in ordinary talk, show them due

[1] A sense not easy to parallel; but Tib. 66, l. 6 has bya-ba-la mos-par-byas, "acquiesce."

[2] The MS. is corrupt, and the Tib. gives little help. Query: *iti bhūteshu* for *kumārā teshu*, which may help to explain (1) the gloss *rājakumārāṇām*, *i.e.* "he means princes," and (2) Tib. gzhon-nur-gyur-ba=*kumārabhūta*. *Rājabhūteshu* would scan, but *iti* is needed.

civility. Do not hesitate to show them honour, for the sake of the higher enlightenment.

[101] "When one is elder, ask his age, then do him honour, bowing your head, and reverencing his feet.

"Let him not look for a slip in them; for they also look unto the Throne of Enlightenment. Let him conceive no malice, but let the thought of friendship be in him.

"When one sees a slip in any of them, one must not proclaim it as a fault: for whatsoever act a man shall do, he shall reap the fruit of it.

"With clear and smiling face to young and to old alike, be the first to say a kindly word, and ever be free from pride.

"Receiving them with gifts of raiment and alms, thus you may do them a service,[1] and all will be leaders."

And if one does not show outward respect or favour to one who has begun to cherish the thought of enlightenment, he should impute to him all the virtues of one who has begun to cherish thoughts of enlightenment, as we read in the *Gaṇḍavyūha* that the Venerable Maitreya did to his teacher Sudhana, and this for the following reasons: to guard himself against the danger of falling headlong into perdition, for the enjoyment of all pleasures seen and unseen, for the purifying of all that is turbid in the heart, for attaining goodness and activity of heart.

"When [the good man] beholds mortals oppressed by old age and disease, attacked by a hundred pains, tortured by sorrow and fear from birth to death, moved by pity he directs his conduct for their weal: when he beholds a world oppressed by instruments of pain in the region of hell, he seeks for the thunderbolt of knowledge which surely breaks these instruments of pain in that region.

[102] "He seeks for the strong plow of knowledge in order to clear the field of the world, which is covered with the scrub,

[1] There is nothing in the Tib. to represent *cittam*; the translation of the pāda being: *de-dag-la ni phan gdags śiṅ*, "by doing them a service," which suggests *hitaṁ*.

thorns, and weeds of passion and hate, and all tangled with thick undergrowth of heretical doctrine.[1]

"The world is sunk in delusion, ignorance, and greed, with the eye of wisdom blinded, and its guide lost. He will lead the world like a caravan, well able to show it safe places.

"Riding upon the chariot, and clad in the armour of patience, drawing the sword of knowledge against sin his foe, son of heroes, giver of peace, he will be the guide of the world.[2]

"As a well-trained captain he guides the ship of the Law on its voyage on the sea of knowledge: holding the helm, he steers it to the isle of the priceless treasure of peace over the ocean of threefold existence.

"He is a sun whose disc is resolution, whose rays are knowledge, illumining all the world of beings, rising over the world of being as the sun in the sky, he is pointed out [3] as the Buddha sun.

"Cooling with meditation on brotherly love as with sandalwood, shining fair on all beings alike, in his purity like the moon at the full, he is pointed out as the Buddha moon.

"He will stand upon the firm ground of resolution, and walk in the path of a Buddha's conduct: he will be the shrine of all the jewels of the law, the chief ocean of knowledge.[4]

"Having the power of the lord of snakes [5] for the enlightenment of the heart, as the rain falls from the clouds upon corn and fruit, [103] so he will send into the world of being increase of every noble act.

"He is as the lamp-wick of purity which drives away the darkness of the threefold defilement; he is the sure vessel of benevolence, affection, and mindfulness; as the lamp of the

[1] The two accusative adjectives agree with the noun implied in the compound *satva°*. For *dosha* the Tib. has *sdaṅ*, "hatred" = *dvesha*; as in Pali *doso*, and the list of five *saṅgas* in Childers, of which *rāga* and *dosha* are the first two and *ditthi* the last.

[2] Read *°varma°* with Tib. and Chinese versions.

[3] There seems to be a confusion between *samuddeśyate* and *samudeshyati*: Tib. has "rises."

[4] Read *°sāgara°*.

[5] *I.e.* power to bring rain.

Law, he will enkindle on every side the radiant and pure fire of the enlightened heart.

"The thought of enlightenment is the germ; in the second stage of growth is compassion; the third is brotherly love, firm, steadfast in resolve; then the limbs duly grow forth, which are enlightenment; and so it finally develops into the embryo Buddha.[1]

"In so far as he is born with the embryo of resolution, in so far he will develop the embryo of holiness and of prudence, and will be manifested as the embryo of knowledge.

"As those rare men in this world, endowed with mercy and brotherly love, with minds bent upon good and the salvation of beings: so is he pure in heart.

"As a tree which stands being well rooted in resolution and grows through firm unswerving practice to give shade to the three classes of beings, a tree most rare that gives the fruit of knowledge.

"He being desirous to perfect all good qualities, eager to question on all things, and to cut away every doubt, he uses every friend assiduously.[2]

[104] "He cleanses the sin and depravity which come from Māra, he purifies the defilement and desire[3] that come from heresy, he is active for the salvation of all the world, he is ever wise in searching for excellent things.

"In whatever path of virtue he stands, he makes hell empty and shows the way to heaven, and will lead the way to final release.

"He releases from misery in all the kinds of existence, he gives happiness in all the kinds of existence, he cuts all the bonds of existence, he will become the illuminator of the states of existence."

By thinking of this the avoidance of evil becomes easy.

Then in the *Adhyāśanasañcodana Sūtra* the avoidance of

[1] Technical terms of Indian embryology are used. See Jolly, *Medizin*, § 41.

[2] "Good friends," gloss.

[3] Reading °*tṛshṇa*°; see p. 103, note [10], to which the note [1] p. 104 refers.

evil is described. "There are four qualities, Maitreya, wherewith if the follower of the Bodhisatva's Way be armed he will be happily saved even when the destruction of the Good Law is going on in the five hundred [1] latter years. And what are the four?

"Heedfulness intent upon his own failings; charity for the sins of his brother Bodhisatvas; not excessively to regard the opinions even of the tribes of one's friends and fellow-monks; abstaining from senseless talk. With these four, Maitreya," as before. "There are four others: and what are these? Avoidance of ignorant men; having no addiction to company; keeping bed and board in remote places; the practice of self-control and quietism. With these four," and so forth.

Again in the same work we read:

"The commencing Bodhisatva, Maitreya, who has attained to wisdom, must eschew greed of gain and honour, but must regard such greed as a sin. . . .[2] [105] He must eschew taking pleasure in society, but must regard it as a sin; he must eschew taking pleasure in talk, or slumber, or action of all kinds, or useless activity [3] but must regard each as a sin. . . . In this connexion, Maitreya, the Bodhisatva, the Great Being, must regard greed of gain and honour as begetting passion, as causing the failure of watchfulness, as causing pride or despondency according as one gets or does not get, as making delusion arise, as tending towards selfishness in the family, as giving rise to cunning by promoting one's personal interest, as causing shamelessness by avoiding the society of the four castes; [4] likewise greed of gain and glory must be regarded as having the disapproval of all the Buddhas, and as giving rise to pride and infatuation. This greed despises its teachers, is of the host of Māra, has its root in utter heedlessness, cuts off the root of good, is like to a wheel of lightning and the thunderbolt;

[1] The Tib. again supports the correction of 50 to 500.

[2] Cp. *Aṅg.-Nik.*, iii. p. 449.

[3] See below, 115.

[4] *I.e.* apparently, if it tempts him to live amongst degraded people for greed's sake.

it is full of longings and cravings, it has excessive regard for the opinions of the tribes of friends and fellow-monks, produces dejected melancholy and distraction of wit, makes one partaker of pain by giving him beloved objects, robs him of the four forms of mindfulness, weakens his moral quality, makes him eschew the four kinds of quietism,[1] destroys transcendent knowledge and the supernatural faculties, makes him now do honour, now dishonour, honour his enemy and desert his friend, like a courtezan seduces him, makes him abstain from meditation and the perfect exercise of virtue,[2] causes him to fall into hell, the womb of a beast, or the world of Yama, makes him like Devadatta and Udraka [3] in conduct. So he must regard the greed of gain and honour.

[106] "These are the evil results, Maitreya, which the Bodhisatva must regard as inherent in the greed of gain and honour. With this view, he must rejoice in having modest wants, and must not torment himself. And why so? For the man of modest wants, Maitreya, has no faults of this kind, nor anything to hinder his becoming a Buddha. He is not moody with householders or members of the Order; he is worthy of the protection of gods and men, as abiding in his pure principles; whatever calamity may befall, he is undismayed; he is not overcome when assailed by threats [4]; not to be caught, being released from Māra's domain; not to be tempted by any vice; beloved both by gods and men; [5] ever abiding in the practice of ecstatic meditation, he becomes pure; devoid of all guile and cunning, perceiving the mischief of the

[1] The four *prahānas* embody the ideal of avoiding all kinds of *Karma*. See *M. Vyut.* § 39, which gives them; where the expression *pradadhāti* is used indeed, but is not confused with *pra-hā-*, as is done first by Childers 435*a*, after him by Wenzel, *Dh. Sgr.* 44, Sarat Ch., *Tib. Dict.* 1127, and Senart, *M. Vst.* ii. 519.

[2] See *M. Vyut.* § 69, Childers, *s.v. appamaññā:* friendliness, compassion, goodwill, equanimity.

[3] *M. Vyut.* 178[1], a heresiarch.

[4] Reading *tarjanādhigataḥ*, *dh* and *v* being practically indistinguishable in MS.

[5] The Tibetan arrangement places a stop after *bhavati* in line 7, which is preferable to that of the MS.

five pleasures of sense, he is vigilant ; a man of his word, by living in a good caste ; [1] beloved by the wise and the chaste. Such, Maitreya, are the blessings which the Bodhisatva who is wise must recognize, and therefore must take delight in a resolution towards moderation in his wants. Therefore one must cherish moderation so as to put an end to the greed of gain and honour."

As touching the delight in society, it is thus written.

" Avoiding passion, avoiding fault, the devotee does not mix in society : bent and devoted he is to this end ; so he would not take delight in that fault.

" Pride, laughter, and also wrangling, all these are found in society : wicked and unrestrained is the life of him who frequent vain society.

" The fools delight in worldly talk ; the fools renounce converse on higher things in this life ; [107] strife and superfluity of wranglings increase ; on account of that fault [the Bodhisatva] is not to be found amongst them.

" And the Brother also does not thrive by learning when once he has set his affection on improper talk : therefore eschew improper talk, and take your delight in the Law continually.

" A thousand times did I give up my members,[3] because each time I longed for enlightenment ; never did I get my fill in hearing the Law ; but they will be wearied in listening to the Law.

" Altogether to be eschewed is talk improper and unhallowed : thus set your affection upon the precious Law, which is hard to attain in many a hundred ages.

" He who lives in the forest, virtue his quest, must not pry about for a neighbour's fault, nor must he allow the thought to rise, that he alone is the elect, he best alone.

[108] " Such infatuation is the root of all heedlessness :

[1] Cp. 105[1] above (trans., p. 106).

[2] Tib. uses here and hereafter the word *smra* (used 108[5] for *bhāshya*) for *mantra*, apparently in the sense of " talk," which suits the context better ; but we can find no exact Sanskrit authority for it, although the word means " counsel."

[3] *aṣṭāni* is a misprint for *aṅgāni*.

even lowly Brethren are not to be despised: this is the regular course [1] of the gospel in the world, in one birth [2] none can obtain enlightenment."

In the same place he discusses delight in talk.

"These are the faults of the man who delights in talk. Intoxicated with learning he loses respect, and becomes immersed in contentious talk. He becomes forgetful and undiscerning.

"He is far from thought centred on the inner self,[3] neither thought nor body is tranquil; he falls into pride or despondency; these are the faults of one who delights in talk.

"The fool is ready to fall away from thought on the Good Law; he is harsh and unkindly in heart, far from insight and holy calm; these are the faults of one who delights in talk.

"He ever lacks respect for teachers, [109] having conceived an affection for talk [4] about worldly desires; abides in that which is naught, is bereft of wisdom: such are the faults of one who delights in talk.

"He receives no honour from the gods [5]; they conceive no affection for him in that respect; he is devoid of discernment: such are the faults of one who delights in talk.

"He is reproved also by wise men, such as are eyewitnesses [6] from time to time, his life is aimless: such are the faults of one who delights in talk.

"Suppose the fool has to die, he grieves: 'I have achieved nothing,[7] what am I to do this day?' He is plunged in an abyss of sorrow. Such are the faults of one who delights in talk.

"He is unstable as grass waving in the wind; so wavers he, be sure; never is his mind firmly fixed: such are the faults of one who delights in talk.

[1] *anupubbo* seems to be a subst., cp. Pali *anupubbam*.
[2] Tib. reads *kalpena*.
[3] Tib. *nan-gi-sems*.
[4] Tib. *gtam*.
[5] *guṇaiḥ* is a misprint for *gaṇaiḥ*.
[6] Cp. Jat. 5, 424[12], *kāyasakkhi*.
[7] *I.e.* no karma.

[110] " He is like an actor[1] who stands on the stage and recites the virtues of other heroes, and yet has no achievements of his own to tell : such are the faults of one who delights in talk.

" A hypocrite he is, frivolous, hopeless, wrangles again and again, far is he from the true religion : such are the faults of one who delights in talk.

" When he is well treated he is thrilled with delight, lacking steadfastness ; being ignorant, when ill treated, he cowers ; for like an ape, his mind is fickle : such are the faults of one who delights in talk. . . .

" When for a long time he has enjoyed his spell of talk, he finds no satisfaction or inward joy ; now to think of one subject is better, in which he may find lasting joy.

" Not in the husk of the sugar-cane is any sweetness ; in the middle its sweetness is, which is so delightful ; it is not possible in this world for what is best in the sugar-cane to be enjoyed if only one chew the husk.

[111] " What the husk is, in this world is talk ; what is the juice, that is meditation on a good thing ; therefore ye must eschew all delight in talk, and think of what is good with unceasing vigilance."

Of delight in sloth it is written :

" He wraps him in a great and increasing net of error ; he becomes a doubter, and falls into heresy ; many an act of his is done in heresy, when a man delights in sloth.

" Their judgment becomes weak ; a man's wit leaves him, nay is absent altogether ; wisdom he loses for ever, when he delights in sloth.

" He is lazy, idle, without judgment ; goblins find their occasion against him, and wound him as he lives alone in the forest, when a man delights in sloth.

" He has no desire for a wholesome mind ; he cares not for the Law, nay his love is generally for the unlawful,[2] when a man delights in sloth.

" He is distracted and bereft of all desire for the true Law ;

[1] Read in text *naṭo*.

[2] Read -kāmas-.

the fool is lacking in every virtue; he obstructs light and himself falls into darkness, when a man delights in sloth.

[112] " He lacks readiness, he becomes desponding at heart, his joy is not unbroken, swallowed up he is in sleep, his limbs are slack, when a man delights in sloth.

" Himself unconsciously [1] becoming a prey to laziness, he grudges at those who are endued with manly strength, he speaks ill of those that have manly strength, when a man delights in sloth." . . .[2]

" That which is the destruction of all pain and darkness, the principle which leads us to avoid perdition, the virtue that has ever been praised by all Buddhas, that noble virtue manliness ever keep in thy grasp."

As touching devotion to works, he says :

" He is unruly wnen exhorted by his teachers; he does not accept their instruction respectfully, and soon he falls away from good conduct. These are the faults of the man who is devoted to works.

" He is always full of regrets,[3] since he is for ever brooding over the works of a householder's life; meditation and abstraction are nothing to him: these are the faults of one who is devoted to works.

" His passion becomes keen, and infatuated amidst things which are sweet or loathsome, [113] and takes no delight in anything. These are the faults of one who is devoted to works.

" He is pleased with a great company, he is annoyed when he is deprived of it; he is confused like an ass [4]: these are the faults of one who is devoted to works.

" Day and night his heart is set on nothing but food and

[1] Tib. *mi-śes*, which suggests *tv ajñātvā*, the reading of the text correctly reproduces the MS.; but it is probable that the scribe had before him *ātmān na jñātvā* (cf. similar form of *nn* in line 15 below=59*a* 3). If so, *ātmān* is accusative by analogy, Pali *attam*

[2] Cp. Jat. No. 381, line 2 and *passim*.

[3] The gloss explains this, " he desires all other kinds of works."

[4] The reading is confirmed by Tib., de-ni boṅ bu-bžin-du hdre-bar-hgyur, but the point of the simile is obscure.

raiment continually ; very poor is he in virtues always : these are the faults of one who is devoted to works.

" He asks of worldly doings ; he finds his pleasure in improper talk ; in proper talk he finds no pleasure : these are the faults of one who is devoted to works." . . .

" Then Maitreya the Bodhisatva, the Great Being, thus spake to the Blessed One. ' Limited in wisdom, Blessed One, nay devoid of wisdom, will be the Bodhisatvas who will renounce their high principles of action to busy themselves in works of insignificance.' At these words the Blessed One thus replied to the Bodhisatva Maitreya, the Great Being : ' Yea verily, Maitreya ; true is it that thou hast said : limited in wisdom will be those Bodhisatvas who will renounce their high principles of action to busy themselves in works of insignificance ; and thus I declare and announce to thee.

[114] " ' They are not true Bodhisatvas ordained in the gospel of the Tathāgata, who have no application, no power of meditation ecstatic and concentrated, no studiousness, no eager pursuit of learning. Moreover, Maitreya, the gospel of the Tathāgata arises from meditation ecstatic and concentrated, it is fitly framed and compact of knowledge, it arises from earnest application : it does not arise from subservience to the usual ends of the householder's actions. For such action belongs to those whose application is misapplied, who delight in the chain of existence, by the way of subservience which is longing desire for worldly objects. Not on such an object a true Bodhisatva must set his heart. If, Maitreya, a Bodhisatva devoted to such subservience were to fill a myriad worlds with stūpas each composed of the seven precious things : such an one would do me no homage, no honour, no respect. . . . . Then suppose India to be filled with Bodhisatvas doing such subservience : a single Bodhisatva devoted to his prescribed duty and his portion of study is worthy to receive from all of them homage and respect. And if India be full of these latter, one Bodhisatva devoted to profound and secluded meditation is worthy to receive from them all homage and respect. . . . And why is

this? A difficult thing is this to get, the getting of wisdom. High, higher than all, exalted above all the three worlds, exceeding marvellous: therefore, O Maitreya, the Bodhisatva whose aim is self-discipline, whose longing is manly effort, must earnestly strive for wisdom.'"

About delight in useless activities, it is said:

"The eight unlucky moments are not far from him, the best moments of success are not for him; these evils are ever with him; these are his faults who practises the useless activities. . . .

"The wise man should fully understand these faults, and avoid all useless activities; evils come all too easily to one who practises these: therefore he must not abide in useless activities.

[115] "Let him far rather walk an hundred leagues than stay where there may be useless activity or strife. Let him not make his dwelling, nor abode, where even for a moment there is passion.

"The truly ordained make virtue their object, not wealth; do not make strife with anger at heart: you have no fields, no husbandry, no commerce, for which cause there might be such activities.

"No son nor daughter has he [the true Bodhisatva], nor no wife; no friend has he, no troop of kinsmen; he has neither manservant nor maidservant nor any to exercise lordship over: therefore make no strife when once ye have forsaken the world.

"When once the red robes with faith have been taken, they are cherished in peace and quiet; in stillness, peace and quiet rest, avoid useless activity and beget patience.

"Be on your guard against serpents of cruel heart; hell and the region of Yama's beasts [1] are not far from him who practises useless activity: therefore to patience one should add manliness. . . ."

"By this devotion lay hold on purity; bring to naught all hindrance that comes from action: that man who firmly gets

[1] Compare the "hellbirds" at p. 70 of the text.

in his grasp Māra with all his hosts and chariots, he produces patience."

[116] And our whole topic of the Avoidance of Evil is thus summarily discussed in the same book:

"Therefore, O Maitreya, a disciple of the Bodhisatva's Way, of either sex, in the last five hundred years of the world, when the break-up of the Good Law is in progress, if he desires release with full and unimpaired salvation, and if he desires to bring to nought all hindrances of action, he must delight in the absence of society, living in the remote parts of the forest, must avoid all persons that lack devotion, must keep watch for his own failings and not for those of others, must delight in silence and abiding in wisdom."

In the *Ratnamegha* also the Avoidance of Evil is thus described:

"He tramps for alms so long as there is gain in so doing: only wherever there are fierce dogs, or cows with young calves, or naturally vicious beings who have passed into the womb of beasts, or men or women, young be they or old, who are bent on mischief, or in fact all places of reprobation, he is to shun by all means in his power."

By this the following is proved: "that when one does not avoid an instrument of mischief, altho' he see it, sin accrues to him."

Now the avoidance of evil that is spoken of in the line, "And that how must I well secure? By ever shunning fruitless waste," [1] in this the fruit is for others' good; and any waste of power that does not tend to others' good, must be avoided, because it cannot result in fruit.

Similarly we read in the *Candrapradīpa Sūtra*, in discussing the topic of bodily vows, "he is not destructive [2] in hand, nor in foot, because he has restraint both in hand and foot."

Then in the *Daśadharmaka Sūtra* also it is pointed out:

"Flourishing of hand and flourishing of foot, running

[1] *Kārikā 7b.*

[2] So with Tib. *mi-rgod*, a meaning allowed in M.W. Dict.,[2] without however quoting authority.

up[1] and down, leaping and swimming, all these are called the depravities of the body."

[117] Now in the holy *Dharma-saṁgīti Sūtra*, the point is clearly illustrated how no other activity is fitting for Bodhisatvas, except working in another's interest. "Every case of the Bodhisatva's bodily action, O Blessed one, or verbal action, or mental, as it goes on, is regarded from the point of view of his fellow-creatures, is under the constraining power of mighty compassion, has as its object to establish the weal of all creatures, as the result of taking thought for the weal and happiness of all beings. Then it is called 'Thoughts for others' weal.' This is the attainment that I must attain, bringing as it does weal and happiness to all beings. . . . Looking on the bodily faculties as a collection of emptiness is also[2] an attainment; and accordingly the Bodhisatva does not desire to relinquish his faculties altogether."

So too in the holy *Gaganagañja Sutra* we read:

"Just as the wind enters through a chink, so Māra takes his opportunity from any point where there is a chink in the heart. Therefore the Bodhisatva's heart must be whole and without chink. This is what we mean by whole-heartedness; namely full realization of the doctrine of the Void, which implies a knowledge of all kinds.[3]

But what is this doctrine of the Void "implying a knowledge of the best of all kinds?"[4] Why, it means the Doctrine of the emptiness of all existences, realized in the present and in the past, without giving up the practical morality of the Bodhisatva.

And this is explained fully in the *Ratnacūḍa Sūtra*. A similar point is set forth in the *Akshayamati Sūtra*:

"Suppose a man conceive a desire to renounce sinful and

[1] Delete the *avagraha* with Tib.; it is, however, in the MS.

[2] This word is expressed in the Tib. Cp. Kārikā, 21, 23. This is the speculative side, the other was the practical.

[3] Tib.

[4] For a definition of this scholastic phrase (which Tib. records in line 9 in place of *sarvākārajñatāyāḥ* of our text) see line 11 below, and 272[11]. The printed text reads as the MS.

wicked principles. In this connexion, anything whatsoever which tends to perplex the mind, whatsoever also is hostile to the aggregate of his meditative faculty, this is called the opposing principle of meditation. Therefore are these called sinful and wicked principles."

CHAPTER VI

PRESERVATON OF THE PERSON

[118] THE avoidance of fruitless waste has been described; the writer now proceeds to describe how this is to be secured: "this aye complete by mindfulness." [1]

These are the twelve forms of mindfulness which conduce to the avoidance of fruitless waste, namely: (1) Mindfulness of the respect due to the Law of Ripening, by observing and not transgressing the commands of the Tathāgata. (2) Mindfulness of the abiding character of the immovable essence of each body. (3) Mindfulness of the abiding nature of the essential quality of each body.[2] (4) On the part of a novice,[3] mindfulness to move the limbs when there is a commotion [4] connected with such events as fear, joy, or the like. (5) Mindfulness in consideration of the question of assuming the four Postures. (6) From time to time mindfulness to consider perfection in the matter of postures with a view to guarding against disorder in these postures. (7) At time of speaking, mindfulness of restraint as to any contortion of face, head, foot or hand which would be excessively disagreeable, under the influence of partizanship, contentiousness, pride, or carelessness. (8) A person who is to be addressed as a pupil, recognizes his

[1] Kārikā 8*a*.

[2] That is, from the point of view of *saṁmiti*, "conventional truth." Really they are neither stable not unstable, because they are *sūnya*, "void." (The rest of this line is unintelligible to us both in the Sanskrit and the Tibetan.)

[3] Reading *navakasya* with Tib. *gsar-bu*. He is not to remain immovable.

[4] In the comment on the passage quoted in note [3] of the text, a burning house is given as an example of alarm, and *ratnapūja* as an explanation of *utsada*. The Tib. translates *sambhrame* as "to show respect by things like fear, joy, etc., by means of a connexion"; whatever that may mean.

object by a tone which is moderate; so we must be mindful not to use accents which are excessively high, because otherwise we should fall into the fault of intimidating our neighbours.[1] (9) In presence of a gathering of uneducated persons, one must be mindful of a steady aim to propitiate their intelligence by one's own. (10) Mindfulness that the mad elephant of the heart should be firmly bound to the post of quietism. (11) Every moment mindfulness to examine the state of one's heart. (12) In a great assembly of people mindfulness of a steady aim to maintain all these forms of mindfulness as they have been detailed, even at the cost of relinquishing all other actions." [2]

[119] By these kinds of mindfulness the avoidance of fruitless waste is secured. And what is meant by "devotion keen gives mindfulness"? [3] There "devotion" is essentially the main thing, and the opposite to wilful disregard. And this "devotion wisely bred of zeal is the great soul of inward peace" by steady aim.[4]

What is this "inward peace"? The "peace" which in the *Akshayamati Sūtra* is thus described: "What do we mean by the indestructible nature of peace? It means the calm and the tranquillizing of the thought, the control of the senses which lose their power to perplex: not being puffed up; not making too free, not fickle, not wavering, courteous, well guarded, ready for action, noble,[5] single in purpose, single in delight, avoiding society, rejoicing in solitude, apart in body and undistracted in heart, with the mind set upon the woodland life, craving little . . ., watchful in regard to bodily postures, knowing the right time, the occasion, the just mean, and deliverance; frugal, easy to support, and so forth."

What again is the great soul of this "inward peace"? The power of engendering the knowledge of things as they are.

[1] Tib. omits *anyatra*, but combines *parā*° with what follows. We translate it "otherwise," *i.e.* if not mindful.

[2] In place of *anyakāryatyāgena* Tib. has *ma śor-du.*

[3] Kār. 8*a*.

[4] Kār. 8*b*; *tātparyena*, which breaks the metre, is not in the Tib.

[5] So with Pali, see notes to text, pp. 26, 119; or with Tib. "wise."

For "'Whoso hath fixed mind, knows well all as it is:' thus saith the sage.'[1] As it is said in the *Dharma-saṅgīti*: "The man whose mind is wrapt in meditation sees things as they are. The Bodhisatva who thus sees things as they are feels profound pity towards all beings; and thus he thinks: 'This meditation, the means, with the power of seeing all things as they are, I must put within the reach of all beings.' He[2] being impelled by that profound pity towards lofty virtue, lofty thought, lofty wisdom—a discipline fine[3] in its fullness—attains full and perfect enlightenment. 'Therefore,' quoth he, 'I must be well established in virtue, unswerving, unrelaxing.'"

When one has grasped the fact, that this "great soul of inward peace," for oneself as for one's neighbours, has as its essence the avoidance of pain (such as perdition in its endless forms) and the full attainment of joy in this world and in others, likewise endless: one must cherish zeal through a longing for it; even as a man shut up in a burning house longs for cool water. Therefore he is keen in his attention to his studies, and therefore also mindfulness is ever at hand; and with mindfulness at hand he avoids all that is fruitless. [120] And he who avoids fruitless waste, in him wicked things do not arise. Therefore he who desires to protect his person, must reach the root of mindfulness and must ever have mindfulness at hand.

It is just on this point we find in the *Ugraparipṛcchā*[4] the following passage in reference to a Bodhisatva who is still a householder: "Therefore one must shun the intoxication that comes from spirits, arrack, and other liquors, and thus sober, one must be neither frenzied nor fickle, wavering nor confused, garrulous nor savage, not puffed up, with mindfulness at hand and awakened consciousness."[5] In the same book in reference

[1] See *Add. Notes to Text*, p. 403. The saying is quoted in Milinda 39[3] as a saying of Buddha. It is a prose saying forced into verse. *Kārikā*, 9*a*.

[2] If *sa* can be the person just mentioned, the speech will go on here. Otherwise *sa* means the person who thinks, and is said by the author.

[3] This adjective *caturām* is unconfirmed by the Tib.

[4] From chap. ii. fol. 10*a* 6 of the Tib. version of this work.

[5] Reading with Bc-p. v. 54 *smṛtinā sasamprajanyana*. So the Tib.

to the Bodhisatva who has renounced the world, it is said: "There must be no disturbing of the mindfulness and the awakened consciousness."

On this matter, mindfulness is mentioned in the holy *Ratnacūḍa Sūtra*: "That mindfulness which keeps all sin from arising; that mindfulness which gives no occasion for the works of Māra; that mindfulness which keeps from being wrecked on a wrong path or a bad road; that mindfulness which is the doorkeeper, and gives no entrance to any of the unwholesome principles of heart or thought: this is the perfect mindfulness."

Of the awakened consciousness it is said in the *Prājñā-pāramita*: "When he walks, he is conscious that he walks; standing, he is conscious that he stands; lying, sitting, or howsoever his body is placed, he is conscious that so it is. . . . Whether he pass on or step back, his movement is done with full consciousness. Whether he look this way or that, whether he contract or expand his limbs; whether he have on him wristband, cloth, band and robes; in eating, drinking, chewing; in slumbering or resting, in coming or going, in standing or sitting, in sleeping or waking, in speech or in silence or absorption, of every act he is fully conscious."

[121] For virtuous conduct is conducive to meditation.[1]

As it is said in the *Candrapradīpa Sūtra*: "He quickly gains meditation free from sin. These are the blessings of one whose virtue is pure."

Hence we understand that all outward acts that lead to meditation are included under virtue. Therefore if you want meditation, you must have the virtue of awakened consciousness; so also if you want virtue, you must make an effort for meditation. As we learn from another passage in this book.

For we read there[2] amongst the blessings of ecstatic meditation: "Not devoid of good conduct but well established

[1] Cp. *J.R.A.S.* 1898, pp. 191, 461; but Sarat Chandra, *Tib. Dict.* 490[1], gives the traditional interpretation of the Tib. as sinless, *nishkleśa* and *anaṅgana* being added as synonyms.

[2] See p. 404[4] of text.

therein, the devotee keeps to his proper sphere and avoids a sphere which is not his. He lives in freedom from all distress, guarded, his sense restrained."

By these two, virtue and meditation, interacting one on the other, comes the complete perfection of the action of the mind; the Bodhisatva's doctrine amounts to this, the cultivation of the mind, because all things [1] have their root in the mind.

For it is written in the holy *Ratnamegha*: [2]

"All principles of things have their origin in mind: when mind is exactly known, all principles are known. Moreover, 'By mind the world is led; mind beholds not mind; [3] mind is the mine of action, whether merit or demerit.' Mind is like a circling firebrand: mind is like a heaving wave: mind is like a blazing forest fire: [122] mind is like a rushing mighty flood. The Bodhisatva [4] by full examination, living with ever-present watchfulness directed to mind, goes not into the power of mind, nay it is mind that comes into his power; and when mind is come into his power, all principles of things come into his power."

Likewise in the holy *Dharmasaṅgīti Sūtra* we read as follows: "The Bodhisatva Mativikrama said: 'Whatever thing is called a thing has no local existence general or particular, but only in dependence upon one's own mind. Hence I must strive to make my own mind well-ordered, well-established, well under control,[5] well-trained, well-subdued. And why so? Where mind is there is virtue and vice. Where is no mind is no virtue or vice.[6] Then the Bodhisatva diverts his mind from

[1] So with Tib. *hdi-ni chos-thams-cad-kyi rtsa-ba yin-te*, which ignores *satta*. For the doctrine see the saying of Buddha quoted twice by Nāgārjuna: *Subh.-Saṅg.* 20^{10}, note 2.

[2] MS. *tur°*, but Tib. *rlabs*; see p. 404.

[3] Apparently the author connects *cittam* with *cīyate* etymologically; lit. "*Karma* is heaped up." Cp. *Laṅkāv.* ii. 109.

[4] Skr. *sa*, "he," meaning the ideal Bodhisatva or sage, spoken of in the Sūtra from which the passage comes.

[5] Adding the word *suparijitaṁ* from Bṭ. *ad* V. 18, which is confirmed by our Tibetan *śin-tu yul-ba*.

[6] The MS. *dharmasamādānaḥ* may stand as a compound; cp. *micchā-diṭṭhisamādāno*, Childers, p. 423[b], and *vissaṁ dhammaṁ samādīyati*, Childers, 244[b].

vices and turns it towards virtues. (Thus it is said: Things depend on mind, and enlightenment depends on things.) He, O Blessed One, takes upon him the Law of things,[1] and he is on the road to the easy attainment of perfect Enlightenment.' "

Again, in the *Gaṇḍavyūha Sūtra*, the matter is further described. " Dependence upon his own mind is the whole discipline of the Bodhisatva; this is the training which brings all beings to maturity. . . . This, my son, is my opinion, mind and mind alone must be supported by all the roots of merit. As the clouds water the earth, so the mind must be by the Law of Things. It is the mind that must be cleansed from the Things that lead to obscuration. The mind must be fortified by manly energy."

In the same book, when the Venerable Sudhana was perturbed because he could not find Māyādevī, here is Ratnanetrī, patron deity of the city, giving him the following admonition with a view to finding her: " You must take care, young sir, to protect the City of the Mind by not abiding with the lust for the objects of sense in the chain of existence. [123] You must be earnest to beautify the City of the Mind by attainment of the Ten Powers of the Tathāgatas. You must be earnest to cleanse the City of the Mind by sending into the draught envy, covetousness, and guile.[2] You must be earnest in developing the City of the Mind by increasing your own power of heroic endeavour to prepare for knowledge in all things. You must be earnest in aspiration to make the City of the Mind strong against storm and siege by keeping yourself invincible against sins, and bad friends who are Māra's bodyguard, and against all the hosts of Māra. You must be earnest for the expansion of the City of the Mind by the diffusion of boundless benevolence throughout the world. You must be earnest for the defence of the City of the Mind by aspiration for the wide shelter of the Law and for hostility to every principle of evil.

[1] In the original the same Protean word *dharma* is used for " things " above and " Law " here, which we have therefore paraphrased " Law of things."

[2] The Tib. here, and elsewhere, inserts four passages which are not in our text.

You must be earnest to throw open the gates [1] of the City of the Mind, by putting the whole world in possession of the reality of things, personal and external. You must be earnest in aspiration to make strong and firm the City of the Mind by the conviction of the essential impermanence of all principles of evil." [2] And so on, until the following: "By being earnest in cleansing the City of the Mind, the Bodhisatva can attain to the perfection of all the roots of good. And why so? For such a Bodhisatva as has the City of his Mind thus cleansed cannot be confronted by any of these obstacles: be it the obstacle to the vision of Buddha or to hearing of the Law [3]" . . .

From this we conclude as follows. The doctrine of the Bodhisatvas simply amounts to the preparation of the mind: and that is a mind not unstable. "From inward peace move not thy heart, turning away from outward acts." [4] The mind of one who is robbed of his watchfulness, under the influence of some unintelligent neighbour, is unstable, because it is always being led in a direction other than the desired object. But when the man is intelligent and watchful and has succeeded in keeping off outward activities, [124] then his mind by virtue of these qualities can remain fixed as long as desired on a single object. And then as before there follows a full statement of blessings. And moreover, at this present, he becomes capable of ministering to the needs of all beings, because he has won their confidence. How? "Steadfast in all, with loving speech gently win over worthy folk: for this the Bodhisat becomes unto all men acceptable." [5] This then is a duty of the Bodhisatva, the winning over of all beings; which is made clear in the *Dharma-saṅgīti Sūtra*, by the Bodhisatva the Venerable Priyadarśana. "Thus, reverend sir, the Bodhisatva must in every way make it his object that all may feel confidence as soon as they see him. And why? For

[1] Tib. agrees with H. in inserting "door."

[2] Following H. and Tib., which implies that "one cannot suppose a continuity in evil."

[3] See 309[16] of text; and *Bodhisattvabhūmi* 7*a* in *Muséon N.S.* vi. 46.

[4] Kār. 9*b*.

[5] Kār. 10.

this is the whole duty of the Bodhisatva, reverend sir, to win over all beings. It is the ripening of all beings to maturity, reverend sir, which is the Bodhisatva's true Rehearsal of the Law." [1]

On the other hand, the guilt in neglecting this course is set forth thus:

"The worldling who the scion spurns of Jina, and accepts him not, shall burn alive in all the hells like fire that smoulders under ash." [2] As it has been shown above.[3]

That which causes this contempt for him is an Evil. "Therefore the essence of the Vow Jina in *Ratnamegha* tells: all that destroys men's confidence, that one should strenuously eschew." [4]

As it is said: "What are these practices of the Bodhisatva? In this world the Bodhisatva does not abide in a wrong spot, nor at a wrong time; speaks not out of season, is not ignorant of time or place: which might give his neighbours an excuse to want confidence in him. He by watchful care for his fellows, and to attain the fulness of the perfect Buddha, shows himself one that has all the excellences of deportment, speaks gently and deliberately, frequents not often society, but rather turns his face towards solitude, yet is of a cheerful countenance."

[125] Therefore it has been declared in the *Dharmasangīti Sūtra*: "He that preserves living beings preserves virtue." In this way the world would be preserved with the womankind in secret and in public. This is why in places watery or dry meant for use one should not emit urine, excrement, spittle, pus, or such vile matters secretly or openly, for the protection of the multitudes of gods and men.

In the *Saddharmasmṛtyupasthāna* is described how a man who has thrown away the leavings secretly without giving any of that which is not left shall become a Preta.

[1] Here the title *Dharmasangīti* is taken in its etymological sense.
[2] Kār. 11.
[3] Above, Chapter IV. pp. 69 73 of text.
[4] Kārikā 12.

Then again in the *Bodhisatvaprātimokṣa* we are told to avoid want of respect: "Do not use a toothstick before them; do not drop phlegm before them. This rule of respect and decency is to be always observed, not amongst the religious students only." In the same Sūtra is a paragraph for the religious, to show them the danger of more serious offence: so he says in that place, "Do not speak loud." This too is an absolute rule. So also it is said in the *Brahmaparipṛcchā:* "The Bodhisatva must not be like one who takes life." So from the *Prātimoksa* also one must avoid carefully what is objectionable to people.

For instance: [1] "Do not fill the mouth in eating, or make a noise, and stuff the cheeks; sit not with dangling leg; chafe not the surface of the arm."

Thus one should observe for himself, should see and hear, and avoid what is objectionable to people. But it is easy [2] to avoid offence in word, therefore this avoiding is explained only to refresh the memory.

[126] In the holy *Sāgaramati Sūtra* it is laid down as follows: "He has no despondent talk, no disconnected talk, no misrepresentation,[3] nothing inflammatory or provocative of passion, no vulgar talk or unrestrained, none to excite malice, no wavering or unstable talk, nothing fictitious, nothing to discredit an eye-witness."

In the holy *Tathāgata-guhya Sūtra* again it is said: "Indeed, sir, the Bodhisatva's speech is not passionate, or malignant, or foolish, or tortuous; confused in details, partial to his own side, or unfair to the other side; no encouraging his own praise, or discouraging the praise of others; no shirking a promise, no show of self-conceit."

Again, in the holy *Daśabhūmaka Sūtra* it is said: "Whatever speech is unpleasant, whatever hurts one's own nature or others, that speech he avoids; but the speech that is kindly, gentle, pleasant, sweet, agreeable, winning, gracious, welcome

[1] Reading तत्र, Tib. de-la.

[2] Tib. omits न.

[3] Cp. Digha, i. p. 247. Tib. *nog-nog*, "obscure."

to the ear, reaching the heart, affectionate, clear to the ear and the understanding, worth hearing, independent, agreeable, welcome, and pleasing to many, commendable and wise, bringing good and happiness to all creatures, making the heart leap for joy, causing delight to one's own and others' nature, allaying passion, hatred, delusion, and all faults—this kind of speech he uses." . . . and so on, to the words, "he utterly abandons the gossiping manner of speech."

In the holy *Gaganagañja Sūtra*, moreover, it is said: "By not violating the teacher's words, by not disregarding the words of others, he is born as one whose words are received and be accepted."

[127] And in the *Dharmasaṅgīti Sūtra* it is said: "Gaganagañja the Bodhisatva said: A Bodhisatva must not use that speech which would irritate another, or which would annoy another, such as to inform an enemy,[1] nor that by which purposes are thwarted; he must not say that by which he would not convey knowledge, nor what does not go to people's hearts, what is not understood of the people, not pleasant to the ear: that kind of speech also must not be used."

How to avoid offence to others is concisely shown in the holy *Sāgaramati Sūtra*: "Another rule serves to sum up the Great Vehicle: By taking heed to one's own stumbling, one would take care of all."

This is the care of oneself, that one should not be injured by others, and that one should not injure others. This essence of a world of texts must be always kept in the heart of the Bodhisatva:

"All unmovable, all gracious, firm, respectful and reverent, modest, cautious, calm, intent upon conciliating others, at the service of self and all creatures always in blameless things, like the model bodies created by the will of a magician,[2] without pride: such is the mind I keep."

[1] The Tib. seems to mean "what another would not understand." It translates *apara* and *para*, gzhan.

[2] Bodies created by the will of the Buddha, and so without selfishness.

Is that the whole guarding of one's nature? Not so, but it is also protected by medicines, dress, and so forth. Here medicine is of two kinds: one for permanent use, one necessary for sick persons.

Taking first the permanent medicines, this class is set forth in the holy *Ratnamegha*: "So he puts forth one morsel from the dish for the pious, a second for the afflicted, a third for the ruined; a fourth he partakes of himself. This he takes without appetite, but detached, not greedy, without setting his mind on it:[1] only just so far as to support the body and to maintain it. He eats in order not to become too emaciated, and not too stout. [128] And why is that? Too emaciated, he fails in health; too stout, he is confirmed in sloth. Therefore, in partaking of the food he must have health in view."

In the holy *Ratnarāśi* it is also said: "Therefore before you go a-begging through village, or town, or city, you must buckle on the armour of righteousness. And what is this armour? If you see unpleasant shapes, you should not repel them; if you see pleasant shapes you should not attract them. Thus with things pleasant or unpleasant, sound, smell, taste, touch, when discerned, you should neither repel nor attract. With senses carefully guarded, the eye not being raised from the ground, and looking ahead no more than a yoke's length; with mind noble and disciplined, that forgets not the doctrine it has learnt, with nature not bent on desire, you should go a-begging; it should be done district by district;[2] where alms is given, there should be no attraction, and where none is given, no repulsion. Alms is not taken by entering in at ten households and leaving the eleventh. Nevertheless you should not worry, but you should think such thoughts as these: 'Those persons are busy (ascetics,[3] Brahmans, or householders); they are not obliged to give me anything; it is a

[1] Compare M.V. i. 139^{11}, anadhyavasito anadhimūrcito ānupaliptacitto.

[2] In M.V. i. 301^{9} and note 595 this word is discussed. It appears to mean dividing the town into districts, and each keeping his own, not choosing the district or house.

[3] Om. Tib.

wonder that they notice me. How much more that they give alms!' Thus one should go a-begging without worrying. All the beings that come within his view, men, women, boys or girls, and even the lower animals, for these friendship and pity should be felt. 'I will so behave that I shall make those creatures attain bliss that come into my sight or give me alms. This is the way I will set about it. Whether the alms gotten be poor[1] or good, we must look round all the four quarters of the world, and ask: [129] 'What poor creature is there in this village, or town, or city, to whom I may give a share of this my alms?' If he sees a poor creature, he must give him a share of the alms. It he sees no poor creature, he must ask, 'Are there any unseen that have not come into my sight? For them I set apart a first share of this alms: I hope they may accept and enjoy it.' Then let him take the alms of these persons and go up into his place in the forest, and wash his hands, in decent fashion, and with the ascetic's proper customs and ceremonies,[2] seated upon the proper place with legs crossed beneath him, let him eat his doles. . . . As you eat, you must ponder thus: 'In my body are eighty thousand worms; by this same energy may they dwell happy and at ease; Now I will partake of this food for them. And when I attain wisdom again, I will feed on the Law.' But if he has a poor dole, he must think thus to himself: 'By the poorness of food my body will become light and fit for meditation, the quantity of my excretions will become small; and the offerings of the faithful will become small: lightness of body and lightness of thought will be mine; weak and little will the sloth be in me.' But when he has an abundant dole, even then he must be moderate in eating and must abstain. Then as from his receipt of alms he moves away from one or other doorpost he must say to himself: 'Whatsoever company of birds or beasts may wish for food, let them accept the gift and enjoy it.' "

[1] For *lūha* see MV. Index and ii. 509, note.

[2] Reading with Tib. न्व for त्व.

Again he says: "He must not notice the flavour at all. [130] . . . 'I must be like a young Caṇḍāla; clean in mind and body, not ceremonially clean in food. For this reason however nice be the food eaten, all becomes putrid excretion in the end, stinking, offensive. Therefore I must not desire nice food. So I must not think, It is a man gives me alms, not a woman; it is a woman, not a man; it is a boy, not a girl; it is a girl, not a boy; it is nice, not poor food I receive; it is hospitably given, not inhospitably; given at once, not after delay, and may they welcome me as soon as I enter, and may there be no neglect of me; I would take food that has been carefully kept, nice food of many kinds, but inferior poor food I would not take; whether all should come out to meet me, men and women, lasses and lads.' All these thoughts are bad: one should avoid them. . . . For as a rule beings that are greedy of fine flavours do evil deeds for the sake of food, and go to the hells; but those who are content, not greedy, not covetous, careless of flavour, contented as to the sense of taste, and support their life [1] on even the poorest food, these when they leave the body and die, attain heaven; they come to happiness among men and gods; they share the nectar of the gods. Thus, Kāśyapa, when a Brother goes on his begging rounds, he shall put away the lust of the palate, with contemplative thought he should eat the cooked sour gruel without being annoyed; and this is the reason why: 'I must eat food for the purpose of supporting the body and keeping to the Road.' . . . But if, Kāśyapa, the Brother on his rounds is unable to proceed in a storm of rain, he may spend two or three nights provided with the food of friendship and fixed in the contemplation of the Law, without eating. And he must think: There are ghosts of the world of Yama that have done evil deeds, who in a hundred years do not receive so much as a clot of phlegm for food. Therefore I must be fixed in true and exact meditation upon the Law, and I must not encourage weakness in body or weakness in mind. I will endure hunger and thirst. Nor again will I relax my

[1] Reading *jāpayanti*, line 11.

resolution by meditating upon the holy Road. . . In whatever family he shall make the food pure food, [131] there let him sit down and discourse on the Law. When the food is not wholesome, let him take his dole, and arise from his seat and go further. A Brother on his rounds, Kāśyapa, should not give broad hints; there should be no gossip, no hypocrisy.

"Now what is a hint? When he says to other people: 'My dole was poor, my dole was disagreeable; what I ate was not what I ought to have had. I had to share my dole with a number of people. I had little to eat and I am hungry.' Anything of this kind said for the sake of hinting, is called hypocrisy of mind. All this must be eschewed by the mendicant on his rounds. He should be indifferent. Whatever drops in the bowl, be it poor or nice, good or bad, that he should eat, without annoyance, with simplicity of heart, intently meditating on the Law: 'This dole is to be eaten for the purpose of supporting the body and of keeping on the holy Road.'"

So in the *Ugra-paripṛcchā* it is said: "If he is able[1] to complete his own aim or another's by eating of his dole at the house of any woman, I authorise the mendicant Bodhisatva to accept the invitation."

Just so must he support himself by the physic that is always useful: but even then not with fish or flesh, because it is forbidden in the *Laṅkāvatāra Sūtra*. [132] For thus it is said: "No flesh must be eaten; so I say to the pitiful Bodhisatva. . . . Because of kinship, because of its wrong, because it is produced by semen and uterine blood, the devotee should avoid flesh as improper for living creatures. The devotee should always avoid flesh, onions, intoxicants of different kinds, garlic of all sorts. He should avoid oil for anointing; he should not sleep on beds with hollow posts or holes or where there is danger for living creatures.[2] . . . For gain a living creature is killed, for meat money is given; both these sinners are burnt in the Raurava Hell and other hells." . . . And so on to this: "He that eats flesh in transgression of the words

[1] Tib. नु.   [2] Something like this the Tib. seems to mean.

of the sage, the man of evil mind, for the destruction of the two worlds, after being dedicated under the gospel of Śākya, those sinners go to the most awful hell; the flesh-eaters are burnt in terrible hells like Raurava. Flesh free from the three objections,[1] not prepared, unasked, unsolicited, there is none: therefore one should not eat flesh. A devotee should not eat flesh, which is blamed by me and by the Buddhas: members of a family that eats carrion flesh, devour each other." . . . And so on to this:[2] "Ill-smelling and abominable, mad, [133] he is born in a Caṇḍāla or Pukkasa[3] family, amongst low-caste dancers, again and again. He is born to one sprung of a female imp, in a flesh-eating family, he is born to a she-bear or a cat, the vile wretch. In the *Hastikakshya*, the *Mahāmegha*, the *Nirvāṇa*, the *Angulimālika*, and the *Laṅkāvatāra Sūtra*, I have reproved the eating of flesh. By Buddhas and by Bodhisatvas and by religious persons it has been reprehended; if one eats it, he is always born shameless and mad. But by avoiding those who eat flesh men are born among brahmins or in a family of devotees, and one is intelligent and wealthy. In suspicion touching things seen and heard one should avoid all meat; philosophers understand nothing if members of a family that eats carrion flesh. As passion would be an obstacle to deliverance, so would be such things as flesh, or intoxicants. In future time, the eaters of flesh, speakers of delusion, will say that flesh is proper, blameless, praised by the Buddhas. [134] But the pious should take his morsel in moderation, against the grain, like a useful physic, as though it were the flesh of his own son. I who abide in kindliness have always reprehended this food; [such an one] should keep company with lions and tigers and other beasts. Therefore one should not eat flesh, which disturbs men's natures because it hinders deliverance and righteousness: this is the work of the noble."

But the eating of flesh described in the *Jñānaravī-parivarta*

[1] In 132[14] the reading should be °ग्रहं.

[2] Lines 10–17 are wanting in the Chinese version.

[3] MV. ii. 487[2], caṇḍālo vā pukkaso vā: iii. 264[9] = Pulkasa.

is harmless, because it is useful for a great end. Accordingly it is thus said :

" If [1] this Brother should die, the very name of tranquillity in Jambudvīpa would be ever destroyed for all creatures ; if he is cured, he obtains tranquillity."

He was endowed with great mercifulness ; there was no question that kindliness was in him ; thus there is no fault in the statement. [135] Even if this is said in the holy *Ratnamegha*, "one who lives in a cemetery [2] should eat no meat."

This is said elsewhere for the sake of teaching beings of this kind. " Even in the Discipline, what is said to authorise the use of things free from the three objections [3] is no hindrance to renunciation."

This is for the purpose of casting out the over-pride of those who believe that purity is to be obtained by this renunciation. This is also said to put aside the idea that those who are capable of entering salvation cannot enter because they are attached to that sort of meat.[4]

And thus it is said in the *Laṅkāvatāra Sūtra* : " In different places there is in the scripture a succession of rules like putting down the foot on the steps of a staircase. First there is the exception of what is pure in three kinds : [5] but then concerning acts forbidden, in the end even animals that have died a natural death are forbidden."

Now we have dealt with permanent medicine ; we must also use medicine suitable for sick persons.

In the *Śrāvakavinaya* also one may sell even one's bowl

[1] Prof. Bendall's conjecture *yadi* is confirmed by the identification of the passage : *Samādhi-rāja*, ch. 34. R. A. S. MS. fol. 158, b. 2. Below the reading is °*shyan tikinnite smin sa*, which although very corrupt suggests a good reading, *cikitsite 'smin sa sam*°.

[2] Ascetics often lived there to keep death ever in mind.

[3] Not killed by oneself, not seen by one to die, not killed on purpose.

[4] Reading तद्गृद्धतया, de la chags pas.

[5] This is conjectured from the context. First, it is allowed, then it is forbidden.

and robe for one's own sake or the sake of virtuous life to support the body: how much more for the body of a Bodhisatva, for the sake of preserving an infinity of persons! And it is difficult to obtain favourable circumstances for so blessed a consummation. Therefore the Blessed One himself made use of medicine in that place, for the purpose of explaining this matter.

It is also said in the holy *Ratnamegha Sūtra*: "When this is their practice, if they cannot get to eat supports of the body or remedies such as these, whether at the right or the wrong time, that is, ghee or oil, choice roots and raw sugar [1] and fruits, if one sees others eating he does not cherish an angry thought But if one who will not eat what is not permitted,[2] or a Bodhisatva, be ill, with such a disease as is a danger to life or a hindrance to good, then without remorse and without hesitation he may put the idea of a remedy upon these things, and eat them.

[136] The occasion for use of clothes is laid down in the *Ugraparipṛcchā Sūtra*. "The loin-cloth, because of shame and the fear of sin; but to protect from (mosquitoes, gnats, and wind, sun-heat and serpents),[3] and to exhibit the marks of an ascetic, those yellow garments are (in essence) a shrine for the three worlds, gods and men and demons;[4] for the purpose of a shrine they are properly to be worn: those robes are not dyed in the stains of dye, but in stainlessness and emancipation[5]; they induce calm, not attachment and excitement; by those reddish garments our sins will be made manifest. Those who do good deeds are not intent on the ornamentation of their monk's robes. By thinking that those garments are a help on the holy Road, we shall so behave

[1] See Pali *khalupaccābhattiko*, Dict. p. 310. b. If he has once cause to refuse any food he must eat no more.

[2] Tib. *bu ram*; the word *gaṇḍa* is not known in this sense.

[3] The words in brackets come from the Tibetan, the first three from the Chinese also; they are omitted in the Sanskrit.

[4] See 56[11] above.

[5] *rāga*=dye or passion.

as never to be stained with sin as we wear them,[1] no not for a moment."

The cause of this is laid down in the *Ratnarāśi Sūtra*. "But, Kāśyapa, those who from slackness being without self-control, and hence free from the rule of the ascetic's virtue, wear the yellow clothes on their body but do not show respect to them: then, Kāśyapa, there is a special hell, named Śramaṇavarṇapratirūpaka, and in that special hell pains are inflicted in mimicry of the ascetic's life: blazing clothes, blazing heads, blazing bowls, blazing seats, blazing pallets to lie on. He who has had part or lot in these things, he all blazing burns in flames all over. By these things they feel pain and agony in mimicry of the ascetic's life."

[137] Now in the holy *Ratnamegha* it is said: "If a Bodhisatva who lives in the open fall sick or feeble in body, he should dwell in the monastery and think as follows: 'The ascetic's rules have been ordained by the Tathāgata to combat the passions, so I will take care so to behave in the monastery as to work for the cure of passions. But I will not set my desire upon the monastery nor make it my home.' And he thinks: 'We must benefit the munificent, and we must not think only how to support ourselves.'"

Again he says in the same work: "When they arrange their lying down, they arrange it on the right side. Placing foot on foot, their bodies covered up with their robes,[2] remembering, in full knowledge, conscious of uprising, conscious of looking, they arrange their lying; they take no pleasure in sleep; no pleasure in lying on the side, except so far as to keep and support the great elements."[3] Thus by that precept all things must be used for the sake of all beings. But to indulge one's own desire leads to or fall into sin.[4]

[1] A pun on *Kāshāya* and *Kashāya*.

[2] Correct text to सुसंवृत°, 137[6] (so MS.).

[3] *I.e.* to maintain life.

[4] Kārikā 13, p. xliii. of text.

As it is said in the *Candrapradīpa Sūtra*, "They receiving sweet-flavoured food as offered enjoy it without meditation; this food tends to their destruction, as lotus roots not washed do for young elephants." [1]

And in the holy *Ratnarāśi Sūtra*, when the Blessed One enjoins the acceptance and use of the offerings of the faithful: "Then in that assembly, two hundred brethren devoted to meditation heard the teaching of the Law, and wept aloud, and this is what they said: 'Better die, Blessed One! rather than to eat even one mouthful given by the faithful until we have attained the Fruit.' [138] The Blessed One said: 'Softly, sirs, softly; your answer, when you are so full of repentance through shame, having before you fear of blame in the other world, is indeed noble. No; in two cases, Kāśyapa, I permit the offerings of the faithful; and what are these two? The devotee and the emancipated.

"'If, Brethren, a Brother who is meditative, devoted to meditation, familiar with my teaching, aware that all sentient conditions are transitory; if he knows the pain of all the conditions of sense, has confidence in the theory [2] that all states are unreal, if he longs for peace and final deliverance, he may enjoy the gifts of the faithful in portions as large as Mount Sumeru. Very pure is the gift he gets. And whenever the offering is enjoyed by the gift of any munificent givers, most rich and splendid for them is the ripening of merit therefrom. This is the reason Chief of those fundamental good works is the mystic state of benevolence.[3] Then, Kāśyapa, when a Brother after receiving garments and alms from a generous benefactor attains infinite peace of mind, infinite ripening of merit is to be expected for that generous benefactor. If the great oceans in a thousand myriad worlds were to waste

[1] Read बिसा as in Bodhic. p. 141. The Tib. is a literal version of this. The stanza occurs in the *Candrapr.* (Samādhiro), chap. ix.

[2] For the anātmika theory see M.V iii. 446[16] ff., *e.g.* rūpam anātme 'ti samanupaśyanto

[3] See Aṅg. Nik. ii. 54, § 51, 1

away, there would be no wasting for the stream of his merit.' "

That is why, in beginning to seek for alms or beginning to eat, the memory must dwell on three things: benefit for benefactors, the collection of worms in the body, and the understanding of the Law which causes the good of all beings.

Moreover, in all acts the memory must dwell on the accomplishing of the Tathāgata's commands; and to begin with, one should recite the spell set forth in the *Trisamayarāja*, for the purpose of keeping the practice of the sacred circles. [139] 'Glory to all Buddhas and Bodhisatvas, Om Viraji, omnipotent Viraji! Sata, Sārata, Trapi, Vidhamani, Sabhajani, Sambhajani, Taramati, triumphant in the highest, hail!'

With that he enters into any sacred circle. Or let him recite eight thousand times the 'Heart of the Tathāgata,' then he enters the mundane or supermundane circle. And what is that Heart? 'Glory to the Tathāgatas of the three times, past, present and future, everywhere irresistible in might, who have attained righteousness. Om! without peer, wholly and for ever lord! Hara, smara, smarana, in holiness and righteousness! Sara, samabalā, hasa, traya. O sky, O protector of mountains, blaze, O blazing one, in the ocean, Hail!' "[1]

This is the essence of all the Tathāgatas: highest honour is to be paid to it. By this, even the beginners may achieve for all beings the immeasurable activity of a Buddha. It is this that makes the best protection against Māra and all other such malignant powers. With hand-clapping, ashes, white mustard,[2] water, whether with sight or mind, he makes his magic circle sīmabandha around him.

In diseases, medicine and water should be applied with a charm recited. Or let him offer woodland flowers upon a shrine, or to the image of Buddha, or the book of the Good Law, his mind intent. By doing this every fortnight he gets

[1] All these charms are transliterated in Tib. Some of the words have no meaning.

[2] This sarshapa figures several times in the charms of the Bower MS. (see Index). Compare *Lotus*, chap. xxi.

rid of the great diseases. By dependence upon Buddhas and Bodhisatvas, and a mind that yearns after the good of all beings, the charms must be said after the rites of the Bhadracari [1]: this rite is to be taken at the end of the ceremony. If one murmurs it thrice there is no fault in the recital. There is no fault if some recite it even when impure. Things in the shape of parched grain [2] are not to be eaten or treated contemptuously. There must be no mounting on a platform. Intoxicants must not be drunk. The preliminary stage will be achieved if one stand immovable in the moral precepts without doubting, even if one were ill-behaved formerly: always assured for wise or simple.

[140] Thus it is said in the same place: "He whose thought of enlightenment is firm, and his mind free from attachment, he need have no doubt, and his aim is always accomplished." The firmness of the thought of enlightenment is here mentioned to make an exception of ordinary men because they waver in thought, not with reference to one who has entered the Stages of Perfection.

For which cause it is there said: "Success may be attained by one who desires to get the state of investiture and illumination, to come from great darkness into light, yea, even by one who has fallen into sin.[3] The text means to condemn the despondent spirit who says, How can I, so weak in merit, succeed? But that aforesaid fault does not exist in one who has escaped the states of punishment, who has an abundant flood of fortitude and a heap of accumulated merit, having entered the Stages of Perfection. Then there is no fault in the recital from ignorance, if there be too many syllables, nor if too few, nor if they deviate from the ritual. On the contrary, following the power of faith, the power of the thought of enlightenment, the power of all-renunciation, one must unhesitatingly proceed; necessarily he attains the state of a Buddha or a

[1] A charm, Bhadracaripraṇidhānarāja: see Bendall, Cat. Camb. MSS. p. 14, etc., ed. by K. Watanaba, Leipzig, 1912.

[2] Used in Tāntrik ceremonial.

[3] See MV. Index. It applies to the four unhappy kinds of birth.

Bodhisatva,[1] and even in this world he gets all the success he could wish."

Or he should guard himself by the charm, which "holds all the thunderbolts": "Glory to the Tathāgatas of the three times, who wield all thunderbolts, O Caṇḍāla! Cala,[2] vajra, śāntana, phalana, cara, māraṇa, vajra dāla phaṭa. O thou that thunderest everywhere! blaze! glory be to thee, O delight of the high and mighty rulers! Ha! blow, burst, Hail to the invincible thunderbolt!"

When this is only recited, all troubles and hindrances keep away; gods and nāgas and the like are no match for him; it would protect you in all acts of eating and drinking, lying down and sitting, and worship by the consecrated water, whether seen or thought upon. All this one should do with heart unmoved. Or this also:

[141] "Glory to those who thunder everywhere: Protector![3] Unfailing, violent and wrathful, burst it asunder. Ho! drive away, ho! save us, ho! mām! om! I give strength; O garlanded with glory, hail!"

This should be chanted eight times to consecrate the first morsel, in remembering that the Buddhas and Bodhisatvas have supreme power in medicine.

And a charm against poison, namely: "Ilimitte tilimitte ilitilimitte, dumbe, duhse, duhsālīye dumbālīye, takke tarkaraṇe, marmme marmaraṇe, kaśmīra kaśmīramukte, adhane adhanadhane, ilimilīye, akhāpye akhāpye, śveta śvetatuṇḍe, anānurakshe, hail!"[4]

He that hears this spell once, is proof against snake-bite

[1] Reading by conjecture °सत्वत्वम°.

[2] Among the objects named appear to be thunderbolt, death, honey, cobra's head. The translations are uncertain.

[3] If *trāṭa* can be a modification of *trātar*

[4] Most of these words are jingles, but they contain some glimmerings of sense; *e.g. tilitsa* a kind of snake, *marman* vital spot, *maraṇam* death, *kaśmira* Kashmir, *śveta* white, *tuṇḍam* point, *raksh* protect. Similar jingles in the Bower MS. pt. vi. p. 228, show the same liking for cerebrals and liquids: idi viḍi hiviḍi, niḍe aḍe yāḍe drgaḍe . . . elẹ. mele, etc. . . . iṭṭi miṭṭi . . . duma dumba . . . mili mili tili tili . . . chulu chulu mulu mulu . . . huhu (5 times) babā (5), jala (4). So p. 236.

for seven years, and no poison will enter his body. If any snake bites him, its head would burst into seven pieces like a spray of flowers.[1]

He that knows this spell is free for life from snake-bite, and no poison will enter his body. These magical charms which make the snake die must not be recited in the presence of the snake.

To wit:[2] "Illā cillā, cakko bakko, koḍā koḍā, nikuruḍā nikuruḍā, pāḍā pāḍā, māḍā māḍā, puruḍā puruḍā, cobra hood avaunt, top of cobra hood avaunt, snake avaunt, snake's tooth avaunt, serpent avaunt, serpent's tooth avaunt, come, traitor with sharp poison, cold and venomous, halale halale, taṇḍi taḍa tāḍi, mala, sphuṭa phuṭu, hail!"

[142] "So, Brethren, when the snake charmer[3] recites this spell against poison in all the assemblies of all creatures all is real, exact, very truth, unassailable, incontrovertible: 'Let this poison be no poison; let it go back to the giver, let it go back to the biter, let it go to fire and water, mound or pillar or wall, let it pass over the earth; let it go into peace! hail!'"

As protection against thieves and suchlike, let him murmur the *Mārīcī* charm,[4] as follows: "Parākramasi, udayamasi, vairamasi, arkamasi, markamasi, vanamasi, antarddhānamasi. On my path guard me, on the wrong path guard me; from man and from thief guard me, from king and from lion, from tiger, from snake, and from serpent, guard me from all; guard me and all beings from all fears, and from all troubles in every event; hail! Umvaḍili: I praise the knot for all enemies. Glory to the Three Jewels![5] Glory to the divine Mārīcī! I will

[1] *arjaka* ocimum gratissimum.

[2] As before, some words have sense. Pali *cakko*=*cakra* wheel, *bakko*=*vakra* crooked, *koḍā* is a musical term, *rah*=abandon, *accha*=come, *chala* traitor, *śāta* either sharp or decayed, *śīta* cold, *tālaka* a venomous insect; the translation is uncertain.

[3] Reading with Tib. jāṅgulyā.

[4] See R. Mitra, *Skr. Buddh. Lit.* p. 174. The Sanskrit formulæ as usual are transliterated in Tib. (88, 2). *Parākramasi*, "you advance," sets the type for the following jingles, which by their stems imply to go up, to attack, light and darkness, forest, concealment.

[5] Buddha, the Law, the Order.

turn my heart to the divine Mārīcī, thus: Battāli badāli badāli barāli varāhamuchi. Protect from all enemies: close the mouth: hail!"

The following spell he should add, remembering the infinity of births; a spell most mighty, with fifty-seven syllables, written in the *Vidyādharapiṭaka*, with the purpose of guarding against all dangers; thus: "Aṭṭe baṭṭe naṭṭe kunaṭṭe, ṭake ṭhake ṭharake, urumati rurumati, turu, hili mili, sarvajnodupadagga, Glory to all supreme Buddhas, may my spell be effective: hail!"

[143] "*Thus duly to preserve one's frame by raiment and by medicine comes,*" etc.:[1] this must be said with remembrance of the good of all; "*but to indulge one's own desires leads to the fall of sinful men.*"

The Bodhisatva has renounced all things to all beings. Therefore if he forgetful consumes another's property for his own sake, he falls into a bad sin; if he consumes it without desire, without attachment, remembering that it is for the benefit of other beings, he does not fall into a bad sin. If recognizing it for another's property, he consumes it for his own sake, he is guilty of the sin of theft. At the full penalty, in the Prātimoksha he is liable to expulsion. But if he thinks that the body is the servant of all creatures, and it is protected by using that which belongs to all creatures, there is no fault. For a servant always busy about his master's business does not always own that which he is busy with.

It is said also in the *Dharmasaṅgīti Sūtra*: "A Bodhisatva should be like a servant, asking himself what needs to be done for all beings."

And when a servant is wholly devoted to his master's interest, and he is distressed with disease or the like, there is no fault if he eat even without asking his master's leave. Nor is disapproval justified in case of a Bodhisatva who does so,

[1] Kārikā 13.

by one who knows the nature of the action, by failing to distinguish selfishness and renunciation. Nor is there any doubt in the rule: for the whole precept has been set forth already in detail by the Blessed One. And thus the protection of the body has been explained as for the good of all creatures. The precept is laid down to produce clear knowledge of this, not with a view to one's own interest.

CHAPTER VII

CARE OF ENJOYMENTS

So much for the care of the person; now we come to the care of enjoyments. Here one must remember the verse:[1]

"*Put still thy hand to noble deeds, and know withal the golden mean:*
This precept should not make it hard to guard the power well to enjoy."

[144] Now in the *Ugraparipṛcchā* the rule is given: "The quality of acting with careful circumspection and the quality of doing good. This forbids evil use, excessive care, and disrespect with regard to enjoyments.[2] By the description of tranquillity right measure and propriety are enjoined. Then all goes well. By this is discovered the proper aim, that is even by one who has a small or mean share, and there is no need to trouble about the lack of a large share by oneself or others."

Therefore it is said also in the *Ugraparipṛcchā*: "'With due provision for son, wife, servant and handmaid, assistant, labourer.' Thus renunciation or not-renunciation must not be made so as to cause hindrances to the true enlightenment or knowledge of self or others. 'When a Bodhisatva has power equal or superior for the good of all creatures, he must not make givings or not-givings which would be hindrances to a merit equal or superior:' then all is well."

In connexion with this, it is declared in the *Bodhisatva-Prātimoksha*: "But, Śāriputra, when a Bodhisatva has gone out to be an anchoret, and is intent upon the things necessary for attaining enlightenment,[3] how must he give, and what

[1] Kārikā 14.

[2] Read प्र° for प्रे.

[3] Seven *bodhyaṅgāni*: see Childers, p. 93*b*.

gifts, and how great? . . . He must give a knowledge of the Law, a generous giver. If a Bodhisatva, being a householder, Śāriputra, filling the Buddha's fields [1] with the seven jewels like the sands of Ganges' banks, should give gifts to the noble Tathāgatas supreme in enlightenment; and if a Bodhisatva that is numbered among the anchorets should recite one stanza containing four lines, from this he extracts greater merit. The Tathāgata, Śāriputra, does not allow the gift of flesh to an ordained anchoret. . . . But he indeed, Śāriputra, who has received a portion in the bowl, laid in the bowl, a proper portion properly gotten, he must partake of it in common with his fellow-pious. But if any one should go and ask for bowl or robe, he would have something in excess of the three robes authorized by the Buddha; as he casts off one, another may be given him. But if there should be a robe lacking to him on which the dress of a religious man depends, [145] that must not be given up. And why so? The three robes are not to be given up, says the Tathāgata. But if, Śāriputra, the Bodhisatva, having cast the three robes, thinks a great deal of the asker,[2] he would not be practising moderation in his wishes. And, Śāriputra, if a Bodhisatva has left the life of a householder, he must practise righteousness. He must be intent on that."[3]

Otherwise, for the sake of conciliating one person [4] there is great loss of advantage to a great multitude of beings and to that being, by the hindrance of the means by which a Bodhisatva attains purity of motive.[5] Therefore to waste things which might bring great good is called "throwing away."[6] So much for the prohibition of renunciation or not-renunciation.

As it is declared in the holy *Sāgaramati Sūtra*, that receiving much is among the hindrances to the Great Vehicle. The same

[1] When a Buddha appears.

[2] The meaning of the word is clear, but not the sentence. Perhaps "thinks a great deal of asking for new ones."

[3] Read तत्र for तत्व with Tib. and Bodhic., p. 144.

[4] *sattvasaṅgraha*, see Dh. Saṅg. xix.: *dānam* is the first of the four saṅgraha vastūni; see *Lotus*, pp. 4, 5.

[5] *āśayaviśuddhi*, one of the three roots of virtue, Dh.S. xv.

[6] Pali *khalayati*, Jat. 2, 205[13], etc.=cast out.

rule that is applied to oneself is also to be applied in respect of another Bodhisatva. How is that ascertained? Because it is explained in the holy *Ugra-paripṛcchā*: "For the sake of others' interest we renounce our own profit."

So in the *Vimalakīrti-nirdeśa* too it is said: "What must one foster who is in fear of transmigration? He spake: A Bodhisatva, Mañjuśrī, who is in fear of transmigration, must foster the great soul of a Buddha. He spake: He that desires to foster the great soul of a Buddha, where must he abide? He spake: He that desires to abide in the great soul of a Buddha must abide in impartial benevolence towards all beings. He spake: He that desires to abide in benevolence towards all beings, where must he abide? He spake: He that desires to abide in benevolence towards all beings should work for the deliverance of all beings."

So also in the *Dharmasaṅgīti*, Bodhisatva Sārthavāha said: "A Bodhisatva, O Blessed One, desires enlightenment first for all beings, not for himself;" . . . and so on to "this is the Dharmasaṅgīti."

Only from renunciation comes the success of one's own acts. "Moreover, he does not place his own [1] burden on one who is unfit from fear of the loss of the interests of all beings. But where he sees no loss in the interests of all beings, what difference is there whether that which is good for the world be done by himself or another? [146] owing to which he does not renounce his own good for the success of the good of another Bodhisatva; but let us suppose that he fears the suffering of a bad re-birth for himself. Well, that very thing would be the suffering of another. But he would say, the suffering of this 'other' does not harm me, and therefore he would take no account of it. In that case, by the Sūtras already mentioned, he commits sin."

As it is in the *Ratnakūṭa Sūtra*. It begins: "There are four counterfeit Bodhisatvas, Kāśyapa. One aims at his own happiness, not at doing away with the unhappiness of all beings." Therefore, as before by the rule of the *Ugraparipṛcchā*. self must be neglected; this is the doctrine of the

[1] Tib. raṅ-gi khur स्वभारं.

Bodhisatvas, as was explained in the *Dharmasaṅgīti Sūtra* by the holy Nirārambha: "How, sirs, are we to recognize those who are established in the Path? He spake: When they have not a false opinion about other creatures. He spake: And how does that come about? He spake: When they do not reject charity and great pitifulness. Subhūti said: What is the Bodhisatva's great charity? He spake: When they give to all beings body and life and all the roots of good, and expect no return. He spake: What is the great pitifulness of the Bodhisatvas? In that they desire first enlightenment for all beings, and not for themselves."

In the same place he says: "The doctrine of all the Bodhisatvas has as its root great pitifulness. We come necessarily to the conclusion, that a thing is not to be prohibited by the Blessed One, when such a thing is desired for the sake of another Bodhisatva. On the contrary he certainly enjoins it,[1] because a precious gift of a giver, to a man really worthy, gains a wide ocean of great merit. . . . But otherwise, for him who does damage only death would follow."

But as it is declared in the *Praśāntaviniścaya-prātihārya Sūtra*: "The expense that you have incurred here, Great King, in a hundred thousand years, all lumped together would make the support for one brother; so with each of all the Brethren. And when a Bodhisatva, engaged upon reciting the ordinances, dignified, loving the Law, takes the food given by the faithful, thus he must think: By this, I will enter on the inquiry into the Law. The expenditure of that offering does not come within the hundredth part of this good." It is said with reference to the purifying of the happiness of his house. But there is no harm by the rule already given.

The Protection of Enjoyment has been briefly described; it remains to describe the Protection of Merit. Here "thy merit guard by towering thirst for seeing fruit of thine own acts mature." [2]

[147] As it is said in the *Nārāyaṇa-paripṛcchā*: "He does

[1] Sense dubious; the Tib. does not clear it up.

[2] Kārikā 15*a*.

not guard virtue for his own sake, nor for heaven's sake, nor to become Śakra, or for enjoyment, or majesty, form, colour, or glory . . . not through fear of hell. . . . Thus he guards virtue not for fear of being born as an animal: only he does it to get the Buddha's vision . . ." as far as "for the sake of the good, happiness, and welfare of all beings. The Bodhisatva who has this condition of virtue does not lose the ten good qualities. And what are these? That is: he does not lose the power of universal monarch; then he is diligent and desirous of enlightenment, craving for a Buddha's perception; thus he does not lose brahmahood, the getting of the uninterrupted vision of a Buddha, and pious learning," . . . as far as "he does not lose the acquiring of a Bodhisatva's restraint for the purpose of gaining piety according to precedent; he does not lose unbroken clear intelligence, the rapt desire for all things that are good. Thus the Bodhisatva, established in the conditions of virtue, becomes a great being always honoured by the gods, always praised by the nāgas, always honoured by the yakshas, always worshipped by the gandharvas, always respected by the Kings of nāgas and asuras, always well revered by brahmans, Kshatriyas, persons of rank, householders, always to be sought by the wise, always to be noticed by the Buddhas, a teacher approved for all beings, in sympathy with gods and with men. The four ways of birth he follows not, which are these: he does not go the way of misfortune [1] except by the ripening of life; he does not go to a Buddha's field empty of a Buddha; he does not go to be born in a family of heretics; he does not go the way of any of the unhappy births." [2]

Thus care must be taken even of merit abandoned before by oneself, which he might take upon himself again by the power of passion. If merit arise from the resigning of merit, from that same no ripening is to be expected except for another's

[1] See M.V. i. 405, note; Childers, s.v. *akkhaṇo*. It means those lives (as of animals) in which there is no opportunity for the holy life.

[2] These would be the four apāyas (Childers): niraya, tiracchāna, petaloka, asuraloka. See also Dh. Sgr. 57, which differs.

sake. However one may wish to preserve merit, he should "ne'er repent." [1]

As it is said in the *Ugraparipṛcchā*: "And after giving, one should not feel regret." [148] From weakness of completion comes weakness of the act itself; [2] from regret comes also destruction of merit, as well as of sin, that is the meaning. And do not "blaze abroad thy goodly deed." [3] For in many ways the Lord declares that merit must be hidden and that sin is to be revealed; for then what is revealed dwindles away; sin dwindles just by the remorse, and merit by the satisfaction. There is no offence [4] when a disinterested person proclaims it for the sake of all beings; as in the *Ratnamegha* the instance of the physician explains the harmlessness of self-exultation. Again, if one desires to guard his merit,

> "From honour and from gain recoil,
> Exalted thoughts for ever shun;
> The Bodhisat steadfast in faith
> In the good law must have no doubt." [5]

This is also said in the *Ratnakūṭa*: "Four things there are, Kāśyapa, which possessed by the Bodhisatva make the good not yet produced not to grow and the good already produced to disappear. [6] And what are these four? To be proud by searching after casuistical controversies; to be concerned with gain and honour by paying attention to families; by calumny and hatred of a Bodhisatva; by rejecting all scriptures except those which one has heard and been taught."

And in the books of the *Sarvāstivādins* it is laid down: "See, Brethren, that Brother falling prostrate with his whole body on a hair-and-nail shrine; bringing his mind into a reverent frame.

[1] Kārikā 15*b*.

[2] An act is regarded as consisting of preparative, action proper, and completion (prayoga-, maula-, pṛṣṭha-karman).

[3] Kārikā 15*b*.

[4] Reading with Tib. in 148[a]: सौमनस्येन । स्वनाप°.

[5] Kārikā 16.

[6] Reading doubtful: we follow the Chinese version. (See note on text.)

Yes, sir. The ground covered by that Brother, 80,000 leagues downward down to the golden circle,[1] as many as the grains of sand between those so many thousands of imperial kingships are to be enjoyed by that Brother." . . . (as far as) " Then the Reverend Upāli, making obeisance to the Blessed One, thus addressed him: According to what the Blessed One has said, that Brother has great roots of good. How do these roots of good dwindle, decay, disappear? I do not see, Upāli, [149] any such damage or loss, as when one fellow-student encourages evil thoughts in the presence of another; then, Upāli, these great roots of good dwindle, decay, disappear. Therefore in that case the rule must be laid down: That even against the red-hot pillar[2] we will not be angry, much less against a creature endowed with consciousness."

In the holy *Mañjuśrī-vikrīḍita Sūtra* also he says: "Anger indulged again and again destroys a root of good heaped up through a hundred ages; therefore it is said, Anger," etc. And in the holy *Gaṇḍavyūha Sūtra* they give an old story told by the deity of the night to Samantasatvaparitrāṇyojas. These people by a root of mischief created by contempt of one another, fell from the full measure of life, family, and strength. Then pride must never be indulged. This is always said by way of admonition.

But gifts and honour are sometimes sought also. As it is said in the holy *Ratnamaegha*: "Here, sir, a Bodhisatva receiving even a heap of precious things high as Mount Sumeru, accepts it, and so also even when he receives a humbler thing. And why is that? This is what he thinks. 'Those envious creatures, covetous, possessed with greed, miserly, therefore, for that cause, for that reason, dip up and down in the ocean of transient existence as though they were floating in a great water. [150] This will happen to them during a long period for good, for benefit, for happiness: what he accepts he never makes his own. He does not encourage the thought of greed; only along with all beings he praises the Buddha, the Law.

[1] There are circles of earth, gold, water, space, one below another.

[2] Used for torturing criminals to death by impalement or embracing.

and the Order, just as he does service to all unhappy beings. And the generous giver he encourages and gladdens."

So in the same place it is said: "And by this gift he is not uplifted." Again in the same place he says: "But if therefore and for this cause and reason, there is praise, fame, or talk nothing is caused in the nature of exaltation or pride or intoxication; and this is what occurs to his mind: 'Before very long he for whom is this praise, fame, or talk, and they who made it, and the praise, fame, or talk itself, all three will no longer exist at all. What wise man then would crave or would be uplifted or proud of a thing impermanent, not enduring, not lasting, unsatisfying?' Thus then the Bodhisatva lives ever carefully mindful in the matter of gain and glory, fame, praise, and talk."

Again he says: "They dwell in the world like young Caṇḍālas, with mind wholly debased; they are filled with pride, intoxication, and arrogance, by the continual manifestation of the signs of malice."

And again it is said: "In this world, sir, when a Bodhisatva has left his house and become a hermit, he keeps down his pride by thinking, 'I am like a dead man amongst my friends and counsellors, kith and kin. Ugliness has come over me, I am clothed in discoloured garments and a different garb is upon me. Shaven, bowl in hand, I go from family to family, for the sake of begging and of alms. With lowly and humble heart like a young Caṇḍāla's I walk for alms. I live on charity, aloof; my life depends on others; I receive what is despised or cast away; I have to pay respect to teachers and preceptors and those worthy of offerings;[1] I have to please my fellow-students, that is to say, by appropriate conduct, objects, or offerings; [151] I shall obtain the qualities of the Buddha which I do not possess;[2] I shall dwell full of patience in the midst of persons cruel and of corrupt mind.' These thoughts keep down his pride."

In the holy *Sāgaramati Sūtra* it is said: "He has a pure

[1] See *Mahāvastu*, Index, and Pali *dakkhiṇeyyo*.

[2] Place virāma after आन्.

body,[1] his limbs all decorated with lucky marks, hands and feet tender and delicate, his symmetrical limbs are pervaded with merit, his senses unimpaired, perfect in every limb and member; yet he is not intoxicated with pride of form, nor devoted to the use of bodily ornaments; yet he bows and shows respect to beings however low, even if devoid of beauty, having perceived that they are capable of apprehending righteousness."

Again it is said in the same place: "Just as it might be, Blessed One, when a great water collects, it collects in a sunken place of the earth; and because it is sunken, all the rivers and all the streams run easily into it; just so, Blessed One, in a Bodhisatva without pride, a teacher, one worthy of gifts, one reverend, all those deep doctrines [2] of righteousness come to manifestation streaming into the ear and settle in the memory. Therefore in that case, Blessed One, the Bodhisatva who is uplifted and puffed up with pride, who does not bow and do reverence before teachers and those worthy of gifts, it must be understood, Blessed One, that this Bodhisatva is pierced by the hook of Māra."

In the holy *Lokottaraparivarta* it is said: "These are the ten deeds of Māra [3] in the Bodhisatvas, O Jinaputra, to wit: Lack of respect to teachers, those worthy of gifts, preceptors, mother and father, ascetics, brahmans, holy persons and those who do well, is a deed of Māra. He shows no respect to preachers, those who have studied the excellent Law, those who discourse on the exalted Law, those who have mounted in the Great Vehicle, those who know the rules of the path to Nirvāṇa, those who understand the chiefest charms and scriptures. He is proud and arrogant. He shows no honour to the preacher, he gives him neither attention nor regard. This is a deed of Māra. When seated at a hearing or discussion of the Law, when the influence of the Sublime Law is felt, [152] he does not applaud the preacher lest some one should praise him for

[1] Tib. de lus, etc.=स कायº and सु for स in line 4.

[2] Tib. read मुखानि.

[3] The Tib. has all through this passage na-rgyal, pride, i.e. मानº for मारº.

it: this is a deed of Māra. He encourages self-conceit and approves himself but not others; he does not attain to self-knowledge; he does not cultivate philosophical reflection: this is a deed of Māra. With a high conceit, not knowing, not awake, he conceals the praise of men worthy of praise, and speaks dispraise. He is not transported with the praise of another's quality. This is a deed of Māra. He knows that this is the Law, this is the Discipline and the very word of Buddha, yet by dislike of persons he shows dislike of the Law, and casts away the Good Law, and makes others quarrel with it. This is a deed of Māra. He desires a high seat [1]; he seeks for contradiction [2]; he is subservient to others, and applauds them. When men are old and ancient or old in the practice of virtue he does not wait on them or welcome them. This is a deed of Māra. Aye, and he has a frowning face and smiles not; nor is he sweet of voice; always hard-hearted and fault-finding, seeking for weak points. This is a deed of Māra. Falling into self-conceit he does not approach the wise, nor wait upon them, nor resort to them, nor attend them, nor question them, nor ask them what is good and what bad, what is to be done, what if done makes for lasting good, profit, happiness; or what if not done makes for the contrary; he is senseless and more than senseless; deluded in reasoning, sulky, knowing not salvation. This is a deed of Māra. Full of pride, he does not wish for the appearance of a Buddha; he throws away the root of former good, and does not cultivate a new one; he gives instructions that are nought; he begins quarrels, is full of disputes; this is the way [3] for one vainly to fall with a mighty fall who abides in such conduct. But then again, if it happens that he does obtain sovereignty owing [4] the power of the thought of enlightenment, in that case through hundreds of thousands of ages he does not meet the apparition of

[1] Tib. stan mthon-po, *i.e.* उच्चासनं.

[2] So parihāraṃ karoti in Jat. i. 186. But Tib. has las su mi bsko baḥi choṣ tsol, "seeks activities to which he has not been appointed."

[3] See Childers, p. 503*b*, *s.v.* ṭhānaṃ.

[4] Tib. stobs skyed-pas, *i.e.* बधान°.

a Buddha, how much less the nearing of the Law? This is the tenth work of Māra. These, Jinaputra, are the ten works of Māra; which avoiding, the Bodhisatvas attain the ten Deeds of the higher knowledge, and then in these deeds is ripened freedom from pride towards all beings."

[153] In the holy *Rāshṭrapāla Sūtra* it is said: "Opportunity for destruction, the path amid misfortunes,[1] poverty, birth in a low family, blindness and weakness of nature, lack of power: these are what they get, deluded by the powers of pride."

And in the *Dharmasaṅgīti Sūtra* it is said: "'The whole world of creation is the Buddha's field for the Bodhisatva; and I ought not to sin against these creatures, since from this Buddha's field comes the opportunity for me to become a Buddha.' And this is what he thinks: 'Every good or evil act concerns living creatures. In consequence of doing ill calamities result; in consequence of doing well they become gods or men.'"

Therefore it is said also in the holy *Ratnolkādhāranī:* "Here, O Jinaputras, the Bodhisatva who first cultivates his mind, cultivates it from the very beginning in ten ways towards living creatures. And what are these ten ways? To wit: A mind of friendship, of happiness, of pity, of affection, of kindness, of help, of protection, of justice, the teacher's mind, the instructor's mind. These are the ten ways in which he cultivates his mind."

And in the *Śraddhābalādhānāvatāramudrā Sūtra* it is said: "'I am fixed in the purpose to instruct all beings; I will lead others to the purpose of instructing all beings:' this thought gives him confidence. . . ." And so on to "I am firmly fixed in showing respect and courtesy to all beings," as before.

Here in the showing of respect and courtesy to all beings is the absence of pride.

Then in the holy *Vimalakīrtinirdeśa:* "For the production of the pure field of a Buddha, affection is prescribed towards all beings as if they were the teacher. But to safeguard the serenity of the world, even in washing of mouth or feet the

[1] See above, p. [147], note [1].

Bodhisatva must use affection and respect in mind towards women or those in misfortune or calamity."

[154] For it is said in the *Gaṇḍavyūha*, that "as soon as he was seated among the Samantaras on that throne, all the assemblage stood looking towards him in a respectful attitude, doing obeisance to the king. . . . And the king Sarvadharmanirnādacchatramaṇḍalanirghosha was more transported with the sight of these suitors, than by the king's having received the rule of three thousand empires as far as the limit of infinite ages. . . ." And so on to ". . . than the happy life in tranquillity and salvation of gods that dwell in a pure region of the sky, dwelling there for unnumbered ages. In fact, young sir, in a man whose life is all full of craving, who has been long separated from mother, father, brother, sister, friend, counsellor, kith and kin, son, daughter, wife, when he has been lost in forest and wilderness, who desires to see their sight; at meeting with these great love would arise because he cannot have enough of that sight. Just so, young sir, in that King Sarvadharmanirnādacchatramaṇḍalanirghosha at the sight of these suitors impulses of great love arose. Joy and happiness of mind descended upon him, a great impulse of heart-uplifting was made manifest, until towards all these suitors he should feel as to an only son, or to father and mother, or those who are worthy of gifts, or the Good Friend, persons highly esteemed or bestowing highest success, a great help, a supporter of others, teachers of the way of wisdom, a teacher or preceptor."

So if there is not another way, when people show him respect and serve him in various ways, he must remember that he has wholly given himself to others. "This my body belongs to them: therefore let them do as they like with it for their own benefit, as in the cleaning or smearing of the ground." Or through fear of the Master's displeasure and a desire to please him, they must resolve to accomplish his commands. For a Brother being ill once accepted even the service of the Blessed One, when there was no other way.

As it is said in the *Bhikshuprakīrṇaka*: "The Blessed One

said : 'Fear not, Brother, fear not, Brother ; I will serve you, Brother. Give me your robes while I wash them.' When he had thus spoken, the Elder Ānanda said to the Blessed One, 'Let not the Blessed One wash the dirt-smeared robes of this sick man ; I will wash them, Blessed One.' The Blessed One said, 'Well, Ānanda, you wash the robes of this Brother ; the Tathāgata will pour the water.' Then [155] indeed Elder Ānanda washed the robes of that sick man, and the Blessed One poured the water. . . . Then indeed Elder Ānanda would take the sick Brother outside with all care, and wash him, and the Blessed One poured the water. And he said : 'Is it not usual to gratify, even at the cost of one's life, those from whom one receives advancement if they are pleased, and if displeased, terrible misfortune ? And indeed those beings by pleasing whom many have come to happiness—there is no other sphere of happiness for creatures in the world. These are magic jewels, lucky bowls, wishing-cows, and therefore they are to be propitiated like a teacher or a deity. Moreover, what better repayment could there be for sincere friends and incomparable helpers if you relinquish the propitiation of creatures ? Of old the lord bore on his head, as they desired, the people fixed in his hair, having become a mountain by his effort : for their sake the Buddhas break their bodies, and enter hell ; acting for these we should really act for the Buddha ; therefore we must do all good, even to those who do great harm. How can I show pride to just those my masters, and not be their servant, for whose sake the Masters are heedless of their own selves ? [1]

[156] "Those in whose happiness great sages take joy, at whose pain they fall into distress—by pleasing of them comes the pleasure of all great sages, in harming them harm is done to the sages. As there is no satisfaction, even by fulfilling all desires, for one whose body is all ablaze, just so when living creatures are in pain there is no means of pleasure for men of great pity. Therefore I declare this day this sin, that harm done to the world is done to those of great mercy, with which

[1] See Barnett, *Path of Life*, p. 71.

afflicted let the sages have compassion. This day for the propitiation of the Tathāgatas, I undertake service to the world with my whole being. Let the multitudes put their foot on my head, or let them kill me; let the lord of the world be pleased. They have identified themselves with all the world, these beings of mercy, there is no doubt of that; indeed, they are seen in the form of beings: these are the only lords: why show disrespect to them? Just this is the propitiation of the Tathāgatas, just this is the accomplishment of one's own good, just this is the removal of the world's trouble; therefore let me do just this. As one King's man handles a great multitude roughly, but the multitude seeing afar dares not show hostile feeling,[1] because he is not alone, the King's strength is his: so one should not contemn one who does wrong because he is weak, since the guardians of hell and the men of pity are his strong army. Therefore one should propitiate living beings, as a servant does a cruel king. What could an angry king do to cause such pain as hell can cause, which is attained by unkindness done to living creatures? [157] What could a gratified king give that should be equal to Buddhahood, which is attained by kindness done to living creatures? Without mentioning Buddhahood, which should be produced from propitiation of living beings, do you not see that even in this life there is happiness, glory, and comfort? Amiability, health, gladsomeness, long life, the bliss of imperial rule, prosperity, these the merciful man gets in his transmigrations. To be a venerable refuge for friends is the dignity of living creatures; the merit that comes from pleasing the Buddhas is the Buddha's dignity."

For this reason in the *Candrapradīpa Sūtra* the fruit of friendliness is made clear. "All the various and infinite worship [2] in a thousand millions of universes, if all this worship be done to the incomparable lords, it is not equal to a merciful heart."

Therefore one should always eschew pride towards such persons, worthy of the greatest gifts: and that pride arises from inaccurate thinking.

[1] Reading as in note.

[2] Read पूजा in line 10.

Effort must be made to avoid the occurrence of this. As it is said in the *Ratnamegha:* " And how, young sir, does a Bodhisatva avoid inaccurate thinking? In this case it never even comes into the mind of the Bodhisatva when alone, in secret, in solitude, to think, 'I am not in a crowd, I am in solitude, I live in conformity with the Tathāgata's Discipline of the Law; but other ascetics or brahmans all live in a crowd; they mix with many people, and they are without the Discipline of the Tathāgata's Law.' [158] Thus the Bodhisatva avoids inaccurate thinking."

Again in the same place it is said: " In this case the Bodhisatva while attaining strength does not take relish in that mighty strength, and does not uplift himself by that strength, nor treat others injuriously. And this is his thought: 'Who would blame others, being wise of nature and devoted to his own business?' Thus the Bodhisatva is not uplifted by his strength."

The essence of the Preservation of Merit is the application of merit to Enlightenment.

For thus it is said in the holy *Akshayamati Sūtra:* " When merit has been applied to enlightenment, there is no interruption in the root of good till he be seated under the Bo-tree: that is to say, friend Śāradvatīputra, when the water-drop has fallen into the mighty ocean, there is nothing in the way to hinder it before the end of the age."

CHAPTER VIII

PURIFICATION FROM SIN

So much for the protection of the person and what follows:[1] our subject is now Purification, for this reason:

"When once the frame is purified
It will be wholesome to enjoy
For beings, if 'tis fully good,
Like rice without or speck or taint."[2]

As it is said in the holy *Tathāgataguhya Sūtra*: "The great cemeteries that are found in large cities, filled with many hundreds of thousands of living creatures—even there the Bodhisatva, the Great Being, shows his mighty person when dead and his day done. [159] There those who are born as animals, after eating his flesh as long as it suited them, at the end of their lives dead and gone, enter into happiness in heaven amongst the gods. And he alone is the cause of this to them, even unto Nirvāṇa: that is, by the purification coming from his former devotion. He who for long time should pray for those who should eat his flesh after death, he would be to them a cause of being born in heaven until the Nirvāṇa of this virtuous person. His intention is accomplished, his petition is fulfilled, his prayer is heard."

Again it is said in the same: "When he is penetrated by the Law-Body,[3] just by showing it he works good to living beings, just by hearing and touch he works their good; just as, O Śāntamati, when Vaidyarāja was alive after perfecting all

[1] *Atmabhāva*, ch. 6; *bhoga* and *puṇya*, ch. 7. [2] Kārikā 17.

[3] One of the three bodies of the Buddha.

medicines, he made the shape of a girl [1] composed of a collection of all medicinal trees, pleasant, beautiful, well made and put together, well completed; she went to and fro, stood, sat down, slept. All sick persons who came, mighty kings or those in authority, men of rank, householders, courtiers, feudal princes, Vaidyarāja when alive used to unite with this medicine-girl: and no sooner was their union consummated with her, than all their infirmities oozed out of them, and they became whole and happy and without blemish. See, Śāntamati, how Vaidyarāja in life had knowledge to cure all the ills of the world, and see if other physicians have the like. Just so, Śāntamati, when the Bodhisatva has the Law-Body, all beings—women, men, boys, girls—distressed by passions, faults, delusion, who touch his body, no sooner do they touch it than all their passions are calmed and they feel that the distress has left their bodies; that is, by the purity that comes from this Bodhisatva's former devotion. For this reason the person must be purified."

Moreover, he described the fault that is in impurity.

> " Even as a crop that's choked by weeds,
> Perishes, never flourishing,
> So choked by sin, to increase due
> A Buddha-scion reaches not." [2]

[160] The sense is, by the removal of what is antagonistic for the sake of improvement.

> " What means, to purify the frame?
> The purging it from ill and sin
> Following all Buddha's word implies,
> Strenuously, else to hell we go." [3]

Here the purging from sin is set forth in the *Caturdharmaka Sūtra*: "There are four practices, Maitreya which the Bodhisatva, the Great Being, must use to overcome the accumulation

[1] This is the opposite of the poison girl familiar in Sanskrit literature.

[2] Kārikā 18.

[3] Kārikā 19.

of sin. And what are these four? To wit: The practice of self-reproach,[1] the practice of the opposite, the power of amendment, the power of a refuge. Here he who practises self-reproach does an evil deed and at once is full of penitence. He who practises the opposite [2] even after doing an evil deed is exceedingly persevering in good. The power of amendment: by a resolve to abstain he succeeds in abstaining. The power of a refuge: the taking refuge with Buddha, the Law, and the Order, not neglecting the thought of enlightenment; through this very strong support he cannot be overcome by sin. These, Maitreya, are the four practices which the Bodhisatva must have, that Great Being, to overcome the accumulation of sin."

Now how is the practice of self-reproach to be cultivated? As it is said in the *Suvarṇaprabhāsottama Sūtra:* "May the Buddhas take notice of me, their hearts full of pity and compassion, and all the best of men that stand in the ten regions of the earth. [161] Whatever deeds I have done before, sinful and cruel, all I will now disclose standing in the presence of the Daśabala: whatever sin I have done through not knowing my parents, through not knowing the Buddhas,[3] through not knowing the Good; all the sins I have done mad and intoxicate with superhuman power, mad with family and wealth, mad and intoxicate with youth; all the sins I have done by evil thought and evil word, by evil acts accomplished, by not seeing the calamities that follow; all the sin I have done by a fool's intelligence, with mind void of knowledge, with mind confused by passion through the power of the Bad Friend, by reason of vexation and trouble, by reason of dalliance or lust, by offences due to inordinate wealth; all the sins I have done, by the deceitful offences of poverty caused by envy and jealousy through association with worthless men; all the sins I have done at the approach of calamity when weak because of fear for my desires; all the sins I have done when tormented with hunger and thirst by reason of fickle mind or love and anger; [162] all the sins I have done for drink or food or clothes, for

[1] Or detestation of sin. [2] Tib. has gñen-po, "antidote."

[3] Confirmed by Tib., but the syntax remains obscure.

women's sake, with manifold fires of wickedness; all the sins, the accumulated evil doing, in the three ways of body, word, and thought, in these fashions, I now declare; any disrespect I may have shown to Buddhas, laws, ascetics, in the same way, all this I now declare; again, any disrespect shown to Pratyeka Buddhas and Bodhisatvas, all this I now declare; any disrespect shown to those who uttered the Good Law and to other virtuous persons, all this I now declare; the Good Law rejected, and therefore ignorance always mine,[1] disrespect shown to parents, all this I now declare; all done in stupidity and folly, in pride and insolence, in passion and hatred, all this I now declare; let the Buddhas behold me with attentive minds, let them understand my vice, their minds pierced with pity. [163] For all the sins that I have done in hundreds of ages, I am heartily sorry, I am to be pitied, I am troubled with fear; I am always distressed in mind for my evil deeds, wherever I go I am weak as water. May all the pitiful Buddhas, who take away fear in the world, understand my fault and free me from fear. May the Tathāgatas annul the fruit of my evil deeds for me; may the Buddhas wash me clean in the flowing waters of mercy. I now declare all the sins I have done before, and all the sin I have now, I now declare. For the future I undertake to cease all my evil deeds; I do not conceal the sin that I may have done. Threefold are the deeds of the body, fourfold of speech, with mind of three kinds: I declare all. What is done with body or voice and thought with the mind, ten kinds in all, I now declare it; [164] and all the sin I have done, that brings undesired fruit, I will now declare standing in the presence of the Buddhas.

"The terrible sins I have done in my foolishness in the series of my existences, all these I declare standing before the Daśabala; and I declare the sins accumulated in the series of my births, with my various embodiments, in the series of existences, the evils done through fickleness of mind and all kinds of folly or unwisdom: by association with the Bad Friend, in fear or in passion, by fault, delusion, or darkness,

[1] "Owing to my always ignorance," Tib. bdag-gis rtag-tu mi śes pas.

by chance of opportunity or of time, in the acquiring of merit, in every possible situation: all this sin I do declare."

Especially the exposition of the Bodhisatva's offences, great and small, is to be found in the holy *Upāli-paripṛcchā.* But what is a great root-sin? In general it is there stated: "If, Upāli, the Bodhisatva, the Great Being, standing in the Great Vehicle, fall into sins of passion many as the sands of the river Ganges, and if once he should fall into a sin of hatred, by the standard of the Bodhisatva's Vehicle, . . . that sin which is connected with hate is more serious than these. And why so? Since hatred, Upāli, makes for the abandonment of people, but passion makes for their winning, therefore, Upāli, there is no wickedness or danger for the Bodhisatva in that sin which makes for the winning of people. . . . Therefore I tell thee, Upāli, that the errors due to passion are no errors. And what is the meaning of this? As the excellence of the winning of people has already been pointed out, this text refers to one whose inclinations are merciful." Wherefore he says immediately: "In this case, Upāli, the Bodhisatvas who are not fertile in resource are afraid of the sins of passion: but those who are fertile in resource, [165] they fear sins of hatred, not sins of passion."

And who are those fertile in resource? Those who are held back from deserting people by knowledge and pity both. For this desertion comes in either way: by knowledge alone, through the perception of pain and void; and by pity alone, through the power of passion: ere long comes the loss of pity.

As it is said in the *Upāyakauśalya Sūtra:* "For example, young sir, suppose a man who has the science of charms to be bound in fivefold fetters by the king; whenever he should wish to come forth, at once by force of the knowledge of one charm he could burst all his bonds and come forth: just so, young sir, if a Bodhisatva who is fertile in resource takes pleasure in the five kinds of desire and abides filled with these; whenever he wishes, by a single thought of omniscience based on the strength of knowledge after having enjoyed all the kinds of desire he is born in Brahma's world."

And why is not the same said of hatred ? because of its most blameworthy nature, and because if pity is lacking resource is also absent.

Confident that to attain other's good is more important than one's own good, if he be moved by wrath even in admonishing another, he checks this for the future in consequence of repentance. What is the fault in not putting a check upon wrath ? The fault is the loss of pity from the fault of cherishing the wrath. We shall explain later that the cutting off of this is a fault of cutting that goes to the root. Even if this is good for that being, nevertheless by the loss of the Bodhisatva's pity would come the loss of a great chain of good to the world.

In the *Āryasatyaka Parivarta* also the type of the son is to be understood as chosen, because of tenderness. And the prohibition of excessive pity is due to the knowledge of the world's [1] good for the sake of winning the world. And being hindered if a benevolent [166] Bodhisatva [2] should receive an obstacle that Bodhisatva would be worthless to both.

The fault in passion is now also explained. " A man who follows lusts is a blind man : he will slay his parents. A man who follows lusts will kill the virtuous. Therefore let him always eschew them."

It is seen that one who is attached to his own welfare disregards the pain of others. That is true, it is seen. So also one who does not consider the suffering of others as his own ; but he who does, lacks both faults.

As it is said in the *Candrapradīpa Sūtra* : " As for instance, Ānanda, if any man should be burning from the sole of his foot right up to the crown of his head, all aflame, one great blazing : and if some one should go up to him and say, ' Come, my good man, when your body is not extinguished, dally, love, gratify yourself, fully pervaded with the five pleasures : what think you then, Ānanda ? Would he indeed, when his body was not extinguished, dally, love, gratify himself with

[1] So Tib. der ha caṅ sñiṅ rje : read तत्राति° in line 17.

[2] Reading °कामो बोधिसत्वो.

the five pleasures?' Ānanda said: 'No indeed, sir.' The Blessed One said: 'It is more likely that that man would dally, love, gratify himself (to put an imaginary case) and be fully pervaded with the five pleasures, when his body is not extinguished, than that the Tathāgata when formerly living as a Bodhisatva, and seeing people afflicted with the three kinds of calamity, in need, felt satisfaction, or peace of mind," and so on. And in the world when a son is impaled in view of mother and father, they do not think of attachment to their own welfare by reason of their natural pity. Secret relations with wives or maids who are protected by the family or religion or the royal standard,[1] would not be forbidden love. If there is here good for people, or no detriment to them, there is no sin when one understands the motive. But in the case of women devoted to chastity, as they realise their aim, one must avoid them and revere them as mother or sister, with no other kind of good living, from doing good to people. Then would that hold also for a Brother? Not so; [2] because he achieves the welfare of beings by means of continence.

[167] So it is said in the holy *Akshayamati Sūtra*: "But he has not to care whether it be in season and out of season." Then if he sees the greater advantage for beings let him transgress the rule.

In the *Upāyakauśalya Sūtra*, about the student Jyotis who has lived chaste for 42,000 years, it is shown that pity might arise in one who stands on the seventh step.[3] "'If I were to break this vow I should go to hell. Nevertheless I can endure the misery of hell, provided this woman be happy. Let her not die.' So, young sir, Jyotis turned and took the woman by the right hand and said, 'Rise, sister, do with me what you will.' . . . And so I myself, young sir, by an impulse of pity, though vile, and full of desire, was set back for ten thousand ages. See, young sir, the deed which in the case of others

[1] Page 166[11] read वा कुल° according to Tib. For the protectors see M. Vyut. 281.

[2] Read न तस्य, omitting with Tib. सपरेख.

[3] That is, at the height of attainment of charity.

would lead to hell, turns to birth in Brahma's world in the case of a Bodhisatva who is fertile in resource."

Again in the same place he says: "If the Bodhisatva should produce a root of good in one being, and should fall into such a sin as would cause him to fry in hell for a hundred thousand ages, he must endure to fall into that sin and bear that hellish pain rather than to omit the good of that one being."

Again in the same place he says: "Here, young sir, whenever the Bodhisatva fertile in resource falls into any sin by the power of the Bad Friend, from this he learns a fresh lesson. 'I must not enter Nirvāṇa with these elements; but I must make up my mind to this: a crore of deaths must be passed through for the sake of bringing people to maturity. I must not have heartburnings; however my course may be, I will bring people to maturity. But yet I will atone for this sin as is right. For the future I undertake to cease.' If, young sir, the Bodhisatva who has left the world, to put an imaginary case, should overcome all the four root sins, and by that fertility in resource should dispel them, I call that sinlessness in the Bodhisatva."

[168] In the holy *Ratnamegha* the slaying of a man who was intending to commit a deadly [1] sin, is allowed.

And in the *Śrāvaka-Vinaya*, in the passage about root sins, there is said to be no sin in the releasing of animals for pity's sake.

And in passion there is this quality, that when the Bodhisatva has allowed passion to arise a happy new birth is obtained; but not by wrath.

As it is said in the *Upāyakauśalya Sūtra*, concerning the love of the girl Srīdakshiṇottarā [2] for the Bodhisatva Priyaṁkara, "By the vow of Priyaṁkara the woman who should look on him with passionate mind would put off her womanhood and become a man, an exalted being. Behold, Ānanda, such

[1] There are five ānantarya sins, "that bring immediate retribution," see Childers, p. 327, *pañcānantariyakammam*.

[2] Tib. dpal yon can-gyi mchog. This Bodhisatva had made a vow that any girl who should be enamoured of himself should be sacred.

are his qualities: by whom some beings go to hell, by the same when he has brought them to birth amongst heroes, they fall into passion, they go to heaven, they become men. . . . Who would feel hatred towards Bodhisatvas great and glorious like Bhaishajyarāja, whose very sin gives happiness? How much more he that should honour them!"

Thus when there is this opportunity for the good of creatures, a sin arising from passion is declared to be no sin.

And in the *Upāyakauśalya Sūtra* it is fully explained how that like a courtezan the Bodhisatva who has succeeded in his good efforts leaves the creature with indifference.

But this is the reflection of one who has not attained a stage of meditation, but has walked in the six Transcendent Virtues,[1] not of any other, so we may dismiss the topic.

Therefore no place must be given to hate, for it is said in the *Upāli-paripṛcchā*: "For Bodhisatvas, Śāriputra, there are two most heinous sins. And what are these two? One connected with hate, one connected with delusion. Of these, Śāriputra, the first [169] sin is to be published directly in a Chapter of Ten Brethren. The sin of the hand is to be published as serious in a chapter of five, the touching of a woman with the hand and looking at her with the eye. The sin of evil thought, Śāriputra, he should publish as serious to one man or two. The five unpardonable sins,[2] sin as regards women, girls, the hand, the shrine, the order, and such-like sins, these the Bodhisatva must publish by day and night in the presence of the Thirty-five Blessed Buddhas."

In this case, here is the formula of confession. "I, N or M, take refuge with the Buddha, I take refuge with the Law, I take refuge with the Order. Glory to Śākyamuni the Tathāgata, the Saint, omniscient. Glory to Vajrapramardī. Glory to Ratnārśiṣ. Glory to Nāgeśvararāja. Glory to Vīrasena. Glory to Vīranandī. Glory to Ratnaśrī. Glory to Ratnacandraprabha. Glory to Amoghadarśī. Glory to Ratnacandra.

[1] Dh.S. xvii. Charity, morality, patience, energy, meditation, wisdom.

[2] Dh.S. lx. Matricide, parricide, slaying an arhat or a Buddha, causing divisions amongst the priesthood.

Glory to Nirmala. Glory to Vimala. Glory to Śūradatta. Glory to Brahma. Glory to Brahmadatta. Glory to Varuṇa. Glory to Varuṇadeva. Glory to Bhadraśrī. Glory to Candanaśrī. Glory to Anantaujas. Glory to Prabhāsaśrī. Glory to Aśokaśrī. Glory to Nārāyaṇa. Glory to Kusumaśrī. Glory to Brahmajyotirvikrīḍitābhijna the Tathāgata. Glory to Dhanaśrī. Glory to Smṛtiśrī. Glory to Suparikīrtitanāmagheyaśrī. Glory to Indraketudhvajarāja. Glory to Suvikrāntaśrī. Glory to Vicitrasaṁkrama. Glory to Vikrāntagāmī. Glory to Samantāvabhāsavyūhaśrī. Glory to Ratnapadmavikramī. Glory to Ratnapadmasupratiṣṭhita-Śailendrarāja, Tathāgata Saint Omniscient." So [170] they pray and supplicate all the chiefest Tathāgatas Saints Omniscient that are in all the universes. "Let them take heed of me, the Blessed Buddhas; all that in this birth or in other births in the succession of births without beginning or ending has been easily done or caused to be done or consented to by me; whether something that belonged to a shrine or to the Order has been taken or caused to be taken or was consented to being taken; if the five unpardonable sins have been done, or caused to be done, or consented to being done; if I have kept closely to the ten wicked courses of action [1] or taught others to do so, or consented to the doing, by which hindrance of merit I might go to hell or enter an animal or Yama's realm, or be born in bordering countries of foreigners, or come into being amongst long-lived deities, or become crippled in my organs, or embrace false doctrine, be indifferent to the arising of Buddha; all those hindrances in the presence of these blessed Buddhas full of knowledge and vision, witnesses and judges knowing and seeing, I publish, I reveal, I do not hide, in future I forgo. May these blessed Buddhas behold me, whatever in this birth or in others or in the course of the endless succession of births as it runs, I have given in alms, even so much as a morsel to an animal, what virtue I have kept, the root of good in chaste living, the root of good in bringing creatures to maturity, the root of good in the thought of en-

[1] Childers, 25*b*. Dh.S. lvi.

lightenment or in the transcendent wisdom, let all this be put together in one lump and weighed and compressed in the transcendent supreme wisdom with ever-increasing applications of merit; as it was applied by the former blessed Buddhas, as future blessed Buddhas shall apply it, as the blessed Buddhas who are now present in the ten regions are applying it, so also I do apply it. All merit I delight in, all the Buddhas I supplicate: May I have the supreme wisdom. All these who have passed away and also those to come and those who now are noblest of men, conquerors: with all these, beings of infinite praise, like oceans of virtue, I take refuge in an attitude of adoration. May the Bodhisatvas endowed with the powers of mercy that walk the earth for the good of all creatures, mighty, protect me, always a sinner.[1] I take refuge with the many Bodhisatvas.

[171] "Thus, Śāriputra, the Bodhisatva must purge his sins, putting first [2] those thirty-five Buddhas, with earnest attention paid to all the Tathāgatas: and to him thus purged of all his sins then and there the blessed Buddhas show then faces for the emancipation of all beings. They show manifold manifestations of themselves, that they may bring to maturity confused and foolish men still unconverted. . . . It is not possible for all the multitudes of ascetics and Pratyeka Buddhas to purify the state of sin and wickedness from which the Bodhisatva is freed by calling upon the names of those blessed Buddhas day and night by engaging in the recitation of the Triskandhadharma, and entering into meditation."

The practice of self-reproach has been described; and the practice of the opposite [3] is to be described. Here from acquaintance with the profound sacred books sin is annulled.

As it is said in the *Vajracchedikā*: "Whoever, Subhūti, young men or young women, shall learn doctrinal books such as these . . . shall study these, they shall be despised, utterly despised; and why so? All the deeds that in former births they have done leading up to harm, these by that state of

[1] The Tib. confirms the sense of "a sinner."

[2] So Tib.

[3] Page 159.

contempt as soon as the law is seen they shall cast aside and shall obtain a Buddha's wisdom."

By faith in the Void also there comes purging from sin according to what is said in the *Tathāgatakosha Sūtra* :[1] "He, Kāśyapa, that is a father and a Pratyeka Buddha, even he would be uprooted from life by that chiefest of murders, that chiefest of thefts, that is to say, the taking away of things belonging to the Three Jewels : that chiefest of lustful and deceitful deeds, that is, if it be a mother or a friend saint that he would violate[2] : that chiefest of lies, that is false accusing of the Tathāgata : that chiefest of calumny, that is [172] disparaging of the holy Order : that chiefest of harshnesses, that is, reviling of the holy ; that chiefest of idle talk, that is, distraction of those who love the right ; that chiefest evil intent, that is, meditating unpardonable sins : that chiefest covetousness, that is, the thought of taking the gains of those who walk aright : that chiefest of all false doctrine, that is, the heresy of clinging to the world. These ten paths of evil, Kāśyapa, are heinous. If, Kāśyapa, a being should be involved in these ten paths of evil so heinous, and if he should accept the Tathāgata's teaching about causation, if he recognizes that there is no such thing in the world as self or a being or life or a man who eats or enjoys the fruit of them, if he accepts that all is really and essentially illusion, also without impurity and naturally clear, and believes that all things are originally pure, for such a being I declare no coming to misery."

And it is said in the *Karmāvaraṇaśuddhi Sūtra* : "Again, moreover, Mañjuśrī, the Bodhisatva who sees what is sin and what is no sin, what is discipline and no discipline, what is impurity and purification, what is the region of mundane existence and what Nirvāṇa ; he receives purification that stops the effect of action."

And in the *Trisamayarāja* is described how to apply the antidote for sin. "Closing his eyes, meditating on Buddhas and

[1] =Tathāgatagarbha S. See Add. Note on text, p. 171.

[2] Insert l. 16 after *ca : tāṁ cādhyāpatyet*. The sense "violate" is required, but has no authority in Skrt. ; the Tibetan has it, however.

Bodhisatvas, [173] he should recite the Hundred Syllables 8000 times; as soon as he shuts his eyes he beholds the Buddhas and Bodhisatvas, and his sin passes away: or he should pass round a shrine from left to right, and recite this 8000 times, placing in front of the shrine-image one of the books of the Good Law. That is the process."

Or let him recite the *Cundādhāraṇī* until he sees in sleep the tokens of the destruction of sin: namely, when he dreams of uttering various cries,[1] or partaking of milk and whey and so forth, vomiting, staring at sun and moon, passing through the air, overcoming a black man, a bull, or blazing fire, beholding a congregation of Brethren and Sisters climbing upon milk-trees, elephants, bulls, mountains, thrones palaces, boats, by hearing the Law, the annulling of sin is to be indicated.

In the *Tathāgatabimba-parivarta* also is described how to apply the antidote for sin. "As a man smeared with urine would take a good wash and perfume himself, and that evil smell would be dispersed and gone; so disperses the sin of one who has done the five unpardonable sins. And he who is versed in the ten paths of evil, resting his faith on the Tathāgata, would present the image of the Tathāgata, and that sin also is not discerned, especially when he is possessed of the thought of enlightenment, especially if he has left the worldly life and lives in virtue."

In the *Pushpakūṭadhāraṇī* also it is said: "Now again, O Siṁhakrīḍita, whoso attends upon the Tathāgata for a year, or a thousand years, or a hundred thousand: and whoso at the shrine of the Tathāgata who has entered Nirvāṇa having achieved the thought of enlightenment should lay down one flower for the worship of the Tathāgata, and should offer water in the palms[2] of his hands, or sprinkle with water, or present a brush and remove yesterday's leavings, or should make the gift of ointment or flower or light with mind transported, and once repeat the formula, 'Glory to this Buddha, the Blessed Such-and-such,' then a doubt or uncertainty or mistake. O

[1] The text is obscure, and differs from Tib. [2] Reading प्रसृता°

Simhakrīḍita, lest the man should go into a state of misery for one age or a hundred or a thousand—that is impossible."

[174] And in the *Bhaishajyaguruvaidūryaprabharāja Sūtra* also it is said: "They who keep the Five Precepts of instruction, they who keep the Ten Precepts of instruction, and they who keep the Bodhisatva's ordinance the 400 Precepts of instruction, and the Brethren who have retired from the world and keep the 250 Precepts of instruction, and the Sisters who keep the 500 Precepts of instruction, and those who are fallen from the system of rules which they originally accepted, that is from some precept of instruction; if they are afraid of misery, they shall use the name of the Blessed Tathāgata Bhaishajyaguruvaidūryaprabharāja, and do worship according to their means. They need fear no more falling into misery.

"Then the Blessed One addressed the Elder Ānanda. 'Do you believe, Ānanda, do you credit, what I say in praise of the virtues of the blessed Tathāgata Bhaishajyaguruvaidūryaprabharāja? Have you doubt or uncertainty or misgiving in this profound range of the Buddha?' Then Elder Ānanda said to the Blessed One: 'I have not, blessed sir, doubt, uncertainty, or misgiving as to the doctrines set forth by the Tathāgata; and why so? The Tathāgatas are not wont to use speech or mind save when the body is cleansed. Yonder sun and moon, blessed One, so mighty and strong, might fall to earth; Sumeru king of mountains might move from his place; but the Word of the Buddhas could not fail. But, blessed sir, there are beings, their senses without the faculty of faith,[1] who hearing the range of a Buddha do not believe. This is what they think: "How can the name of Tathāgata, by just remembering it, give so many advantages?" They do not believe or credit; they reject it. It shall cause them long time evil, mischief, unhappiness, calamity.' The Blessed One said: 'If his name, Ānanda, shall fall on the ear of any out of place and out of season, they would go to a life of misery and misfortune. Hard it is, Ānanda, to believe a Buddha's range. That you, Ānanda, believe and credit, [175] that is to be

[1] See Childers, Dict. p. 139.

regarded as the Tathāgata's power. There is no scope here for disciples and Pratyeka Buddhas, except the great beings the Bodhisatvas, who are bound to one birth only.' "

In the same place it is said: " Whoever else of the faithful, young men or young women, that take upon them the eightfold vows of virtue, or keep the precepts of instruction for one year or for three years, who have this purpose and this intent: ' By this root of good we would arrive at the blessed paradise in the western region where is the Tathāgata Amitābha: ' who shall have heard the name of the Blessed Tathāgata Bhaishajyaguruvaiḍūryaprabharāja: [1] when they die the eight Bodhisatvas by their magical power show the way; they appear without birth in lotuses of various colours; [2] and some again arrive in the world of gods. When they have arrived there the former root of good does not dwindle. For them there will be no fear of a life of misery or calamity. When they are born thence they become kings in this world, lords inspired of the four continents. They establish many thousands of millions of beings in the eight good paths of action. Others again come into great kshatriya families, or great Brāhman families, great householders' families with much wealth and riches laid up in their storehouses and treasure chambers. They become handsome and have many dependents."

In the same place it is said: " Again, whatever woman shall have heard or understood the name of the Blessed Tathāgata Bhaishajyaguruvaidūryaprabharāja, that may be expected to be her last embodiment as a woman."

And it is said in the *Mañjuśrībuddhakshetraguṇavyūhālaṁkāra Sūtra:* " I reverence in order Jñānottaraprabhāketu, Praṇidhānamati, Śāntendriya, and Mañjughosha. [176] The woman who should bear in mind the name of these Bodhisatvas will not become a woman."

Now we have briefly discussed the use of the Antidote. Expiation now follows.

As it is said in the noble *Kshitigarbha Sūtra*: " By abstaining

[1] MS. °prabhavājasya. [2] See Childers, s.v. *opapātiko*.

from the taking of life one becomes a Bodhisatva, a Great Being, giving security to all beings: causing no fear, no agitation, no excitement, by reason of that root of good when its action is ripe. Whatever he has done or caused to be done or consented to, body, voice or mind, from his first entering the cycle of the five forms of existence or coming into the river of transmigration, hindrance in action, hindrance by sin, hindrance in conduct caused by taking life; by abstinence from taking life he annuls all that mischief." . . . And so on to "he makes all to have no effect. In the thronged assembly of gods and men he becomes beloved, free from disquietude, long-lived."

So on again, until: "Young sir, the Bodhisatva who all his life long abstains from taking what is not given, gives security to all beings; only he lives satisfied with his own gains, without contending with rivals, and without pride: [177] not desirous of unlawful takings by reason of that root of good." . . . And so on to "he annuls and stamps out the hindrance in action caused by taking what is not given . . . all this he makes of none effect. . . ."

Thus also the ten paths of good are thus described which destroy evil that is their enemy.

Moreover, in the *Candrapradīpa Sūtra* the destruction of all sin by abstinence from malice is set forth. As he says: "I shall endure the false speaking of fools, and their reviling, I will bear with their threatening, O my reader.[1] I shall atone for the sinful actions done by me formerly, malice done by me to other Bodhisatvas."

So much for the power of Expiation; we now come to the power of Taking Refuge.

Here the *Sūkarikāvadāna* must be cited.

"They who take refuge with the Buddha do not come to a life of misery. When they put off their human bodies they receive divine bodies."

Just so there is destruction of sin with reference to the Law and the Order.

[1] Tib. has vocative here.

But in the holy Maitreya-*vimoksha* is described the cleansing of sin by the thought of enlightenment. " This is like the fire at the final conflagration of a cycle of time, because thereby all bad deeds are burnt up; it is like a hell for the extinction of all wicked actions. . . . For instance, young sir, quicksilver is resplendent like gold: one measure of this gilds a thousand measures of copper; but this measure cannot be absorbed by those thousand measures of copper, nor made into copper. Just so one drop of the quicksilver of the production of the thought of omniscience, accompanied by the knowledge of the application of a root of good, working upon all the hindrances in acts and passions like the copper, [178] makes all things the colour of omniscience. And this quicksilver, the production of the thought of omniscience, cannot be soiled or absorbed by the copper of all sinful deeds. For instance, young sir, just as one lamp in whatever house or room it enters, as soon as it enters, dispels the blinding darkness even of a thousand years, and makes it light: even so one lamp coming from the thought of omniscience, in whatever creature's thoughts it enters the indwelling gloom and blind darkness of ignorance, as soon as it enters, it dispels the blinding darkness of the hindrances in sinful acts even when accumulated throughout countless ages of time, and makes a blaze of knowledge. Just as, young sir, great Nāga kings with the magic jewels in their royal tiaras fear no enemy's approach, so also the Bodhisatvas, with those magic jewels the thought of enlightenment and great compassion, fastened in their royal tiaras, have no fear of the hostile approach of misery and unhappiness."

In the holy *Upāli-paripṛcchā* also it is said: " Here, Upāli, if a Bodhisatva who has taken his stand in the Great Vehicle, fall into sin in the forenoon; at mid-day if he lose not the thought of omniscience the quantity of the Bodhisatva's virtue would remain infinite. If he should fall into sin at mid-day, at eventide if he lose not the thought of omniscience, the quantity of the Bodhisatva's virtue would be still infinite. Thus watch by watch the rule goes. So, Upāli, the instruction of the Bodhisatvas standing in the Great Vehicle is full of watchful care. And so the Bodhisatva should not repent excessively for wrong-doing, nor be excessively regretful. But if a man of the Pupils' Vehicle should fall again and again into sin, it must be understood that the mass of the pupil's virtue is destroyed."

CHAPTER IX

THE PERFECTION OF PATIENCE

[179] THUS guarding against the uninterrupted upgrowth of wickedness full of pain,[1] and shaking off the bond of hindrances in action, he should busy himself with the purification of passion.

Here at the very outset he should *Be Patient.*[2] For without patience at the beginning of the hearing strength is exhausted through not being able to bear the weariness; and one who hears not, knows not the way to tranquillity, or the way to cleansing from passion. Therefore without weariness *Seek to hear the Word.*[2] Tranquillity is difficult even for one who knows,[3] when he is living in company. *Then to the forest-cell repair.*[4] Even there if one be not able to calm his perplexity his mind is not tranquil; this is what is meant by *Centre thy mind on thought intense.* And of this condition of thought there is no fruit otherwise than by purification from passion; this is what is meant by *Fix it on the Impurities.*[4] Such is the meaning of these maxims of purification from passion.

Now comes the exposition. Here patience is said to be threefold in the *Dharmasaṅgīti Sūtra:* Patience in the acceptance of unhappiness; patience in reflecting upon the Law; Patience in supporting the injuries of others. Here the enemy of patience in accepting unhappiness is the dread of actual unhappiness in the approach of things undesirable. He that has lost what he desires, and he that is bent on happiness, both these have melancholy, and hence comes enmity and despondency

Hence he says in the *Candrapradīpa Sūtra:* "Not bent on happiness; not downcast in adversity."

[1] So Tib., but MS. "full of happiness."

[2] Kārikā 20.

[3] Reading jñānavato.

[4] Kārikā 20.

And it is said in the *Ratnamegha Sūtra:* "Those personal pains, lamentations, unhappiness, despondencies, and anguish of mind he endures and bears with."

[180] In the holy *Ugradattaparipṛcchā* also it is said: "Moreover, householder, the Bodhisatva who lives in a household must eschew partiality and hostility, unspotted by the eight worldly conditions.[1] If he has property, if he has wife and son, if he has wealth, riches, goods, he must not be puffed up, he must not be excited. In no adversity must he be cast down; he must not be despondent, and thus he must regard them: 'All that is composite is made of illusion, its mark is that it is in a state of flux.[2] These indeed come from the ripening of my deeds; to wit: mother, father, son, wife, maid-servant, manservant, attendant, hireling, friend, courtier, kith and kin, these are not my own, and I am not theirs.'"

Moreover: "If there is a remedy, what is the use of despondency? If there is no remedy, what is the use of despondency?[3] Even in the remedy one might fail if despondent and dazed by anger. From despair one's power goes, and one is caught in a worse trouble; by thinking of this in vain they pass a short life again and again. Therefore by practice one should renounce that useless thing like something worthless."

And how is the rejection of despondency practised? By casting away weakness and softness of mind. As it is said in the *Ugradattaparipṛcchā:* "In one whose mind is free from the likeness of cotton-wool."

And in the holy *Gaṇḍavyūha* it is said: "Girl, you must cultivate a mind unconquerable for the destruction of all passion; a mind invincible for the clearing away of all infatuation; a mind not to be shaken in the precipice and the whirlpools of the ocean of evil dispositions."

By practice nothing is difficult. For here even with the

[1] Gain, loss, fame, ill-fame, praise, blame, happiness, unhappiness.

[2] Tib. rnam-par bsgrabs-pas. The translation is a conjecture from the general sense of the two first elements.

[3] Restored from Bodhic. vi. 10; see note *ad loc.*

more ignorant classes, [181] just porters, fishermen, ploughmen and suchlike, by the habit of pain even in a thing of smaller fruit the mind becomes callous with healed scars and is not overcome by faintness; much more in a matter whose fruit is to attain the incomparable lot of all the world's joys and all the joys of the Bodhisatva. So the vulgar attack those who injure them, and who are struck by their own bad actions, and are to die by natural death; how much more should there not be effort and endurance of pain to attack the enemies, that injure for the longest time, pilferers of the good gotten by pain, killing the condemned in hell,[1] jailors of the prison of existence, destroying the region of the door of exit, who cause more deadly hurts even to those well-disposed towards them, unprovoked enemies, foes firmly fixed through endless ages, sins that are our enemies; especially of one whose loins are girt, fighting for the emancipation of the world caught prisoner by Māra's demons. There by practice of small[2] pains the practice becomes more and more severe. As the perception of happiness and unhappiness comes from the power of habit; so in all cases of unhappiness arising, the habit of associating the feeling of happiness causes that feeling to be present. This resulting fruit receives a spirit of contemplation that feels happiness in all things.

It is said indeed in the *Pitāputra-samāgama:* "There is, O Blessed One, a spirit of contemplation called that which finds happiness in all things; by the acquiring of which spirit the Bodhisatva feels in all things pain as pleasant, not painful,[3] nor indifferent. Even when he is undergoing hellish treatment the feeling of pleasure is present. Even when he is suffering a torment in human life, his hands being cut off, and feet, and ears, and nose, the feeling of pleasure is present. Even when he is being beaten with rods, or with split rods, or with whips, [182] there is the feeling of pleasure as he lies in prison. . . . When he is

[1] Tib. dmyal-ba ñid-gyi gsad-sar gsad-byahi, "in the place of slaughter which is hell," perhaps नरकस्थानवध्य°.

[2] In line 8, read *tatrālpa°* (with Tib.) and *Kashṭak°*. See Bodhic. vi. 14.

[3] Bt. with Tib. inserts *na duḥkhām.*

being fried in oil, pounded like sugar-cane, crushed like reeds, burnt with blazing oil or butter or ghee, the feeling of pleasure is present. When thrown into the mouth of fire, into the mouth of the lion, rolled and scorched,[1] . . . chopped up in penny-bits, roasted in a baking-pan, trampled by elephants, there is the feeling of pleasure. When his eye is being torn out, when he is being roasted alive on a spit, or haled off to the execution ground, and thrown down headlong, there is the feeling of pleasure, not the feeling of pain, nor of indifference.[2] And why is this? For as the Great Being the Bodhisatva long time behaved thus, this prayer formed itself: 'May those who entertain me, obtain the joy of calm and tranquillity; may those who protect me, who maintain me, respect me, honour me, revere me, all receive the bliss of tranquillity; and may they who curse me, who afflict me, who torment me, tear me with knives until they utterly uproot me from life, all partake of the joy of full enlightenment; may they awaken the incomparable and supreme enlightenment.' With these thoughts and actions and these aspirations he seeks and ensures, he cherishes and multiplies the feeling of joy in relation to all beings; and by the ripening of this course of action, he receives the spirit of contemplation that finds happiness in all things. At the time when the Bodhisatva has obtained the spirit that finds happiness in all things, at that time he becomes imperturbable, not to be caught by all the deeds of Māra." That is the sum of the matter.

Such practice fills with all self-sacrifice, accomplishes the hardest penance in all doings, makes steadfast in all patience, confirms in all strength, gathers all the elements of wisdom in ecstatic meditation; therefore let it always be preached.

[183] As he says in the *Candrapradīpa Sūtra:* "With dignity let him always be kindly; let him always be bent on gentle consideration." [3]

It is also said in the *Akshayamati Sūtra*. "Here what joy

[1] Tib. *skam rim bya-ba lta dril tam*, some obscure torture.

[2] Bṭ. with Tib. inserts *na duḥkhām*.

[3] Tib. zhi-bahi lta-ba-la, "peace."

is meant? From perpetual meditation on the Law, kindness, serenity, gladness, a mind not despondent, not crushed, not craving. Sweeping away of all desire for lusts, establishing of a desire for all righteousness. Gladness of heart, cheerfulness [1] of body, stimulation of intelligence, exaltation of mind, delight and pleasure in the body of a Tathāgata, proficiency in detecting beauties, that is, primary and secondary marks; no weariness in hearing good law, kindness, serenity, gladness in the attainment of confidence in the true law, the righteous exaltation of one content; a wisdom never hostile towards all beings; strength of will; no slackness in the search for the Buddha's doctrine and in the desire to hear it; confidence in the lofty teachings of the Buddha; emancipation and the fostering of thought that has left the Vehicle of partial knowledge; the cultivation of thought that is not cramped with jealousy; desire to give to him that asks; in and after giving, the decency of the Three Circles [2] and delight in giving; always pleasure in the virtuous; pleasure in helping those whose conduct is evil; with cleanliness of personal conduct giving confidence in passing beyond all dangers of a bad destiny; [3] application of Tathāgata's merit; firm impenetrability; no hostility of mind when others' ways of speech are unkindly and bad; tenderness and patience; humility; respect, reverence, and regard towards teachers; always a smiling face, no frowns; a habit of first greeting, no insincerity, no cheating, [4] pureness of conscience, no abusiveness, no guile; a habit of always praising, and looking to one's own stumbles; firmness in calamities, graciousness in things delightful; he must love the Bodhisatva as a teacher, the Law as himself, the Tathāgata as life, [184] preceptors as parents, all beings as sons, preceptors and instructors as the Buddha, good conduct

[1] See now M.V. i. 577. It is a synonym of *prīti*.

[2] Probably alludes to decent dress; see Childers, *timaṇḍala*. But it may be: "let the joy be pure in three respects," *i.e.* when the giver does not believe in the existence of giver, receiver, or gift.

[3] See Tib. 114 a. 4.

[4] See Childers, *nippesiko*, read °ष्पे°; Mahavyut. 127, 54.

as the head, that chiefest part of the body, the Perfections as his hands and feet, preachers as all precious things, directors as all delightful pleasaunce, contentment as health, inquiring into the Law as medicine, those who exhort and remind as physicians. This alertness in all the senses is what is called gladness."

And here when Bodhisatvas are taught, that saying adorns them which is said in the noble *Mahāmegha* :[1] " Their thoughts are always meditating on existence in hell, they take pleasure in this, they are traffickers to the town of hell, they long for hell, they are fond of its praises, they are familiar with its fire."

Here ends the patience concerned with enduring pain.

In the holy *Sāgaramati Sūtra*, moreover, patience is given as threefold : " Here, Sāgaramati, the Bodhisatva the Great Being, although by ignoble and wicked beings, by Māras or by deities mightier than Māra, by Māra's servants or messengers, he be hurt, impelled, disquieted, threatened, tormented, is not therefore broken in the Jewel[2] of the production of omniscience ; the intent of his mind is not broken away from its strong purpose of deliverance and great compassion towards all beings ; not broken away from the effort towards perpetuating the Three Jewels ; not broken away from the practice of good for the accomplishment of all righteousness ; not broken away from the collection of a heap of merit causing the perfection of primary and secondary marks ; nor from the zeal caused by aspiration for the purifying of Buddha's field ; nor from the producing of a body and a life that involve the renouncing of all things ; nor from the perseverance in not seeking one's own felicity so as to bring about the ripening of all beings. He thus resolved [185] endures scoffing, contempt, contumely in the face of all beings ; he endures the despiteful speech of all beings, and their ways of speaking abusive and wicked ; he endures the injury of all beings, he bears the burdens of all

[1] That is, they give themselves as substitutes to save others.

[2] Tib. sems bskyed-pa rin-po-che de-ltar bskyed-nas=cittotpādaratnam evam utpādya, " having produced the jewel of thought."

beings, or carries them, and is not broken down or despondent or despairing or crushed: he shows strength, he produces power, he uses strength, he makes the effort, he strives, he restrains the thought of infatuation. He being reviled revileth not again, tormented he torments not again, annoyed he annoys not again, he meets not anger with anger. Thus he makes up his mind. . . .[1]

"But if those beings, as many as in multiplying multiply over the ten regions, each with a pair of swords or spears or javelins or spikes, should chase me behind, saying: 'On whatsoever place in the earth that man, standing or sitting or walking up and down or lying, shall cause to arise the thought of enlightenment or of almsgiving . . . or of insight, or of the root of good in hearing the word, on that spot of the earth we shall tear his body asunder into a hundred pieces like a leaf of the jujube, annihilate and destroy it. If all those beings should revile me and blame me, upbraid me, dishonour me, address me with lying and harsh words, bent upon doing wickedness; if they should tear up and cut up and destroy and annihilate my body in a hundred pieces like a jujube leaf; even so I must not conceive an angry thought against any being. And why is this? There have been innumerable myriads of transmigrations, when I have been in hell or in an animal or in Yama's world, or as a man; when this self, all full of craving for love and food, without the hearing of the Law, getting a livelihood by evil means, living wickedly, has been chopped limb from limb in a hundred pieces, cut up, minced, tormented with all manner of torments, and yet from that cause I have done no good to myself or to others. But if, in the infinite future, all these beings should tear up my body,[2] cut me up, chop me in pieces, even then my omniscience is not renounced, nor are all beings, nor the good will of righteousness. And why is this? Because all this bodily annoyance is a transformation of the body; [187] it does not approach the hundredth part of the pains of

[1] See the text for the continuation, taken from the Tibetan version.

[2] Add काये.

hell, it is quite out of comparison. I can endure even to live in hell, but I must not give up the laws of Buddha nor the great compassion I have undertaken towards all creatures. . . . But the conduct which causes destruction, that conduct we renounce. And what is that? It is love of the body, dwelling in the body, clinging to the body; abandon the body and you abandon destruction. With this view of conduct, Sāgaramati, the Bodhisatva endures the ill-treatment of all beings. . . . This rejection and renouncing of the body, this indifference to the body, this for him is the Perfection of Giving. In that when the body is being torn to pieces he diffuses good-will amongst all beings and is not crushed with the pangs, this for him is the Perfection of Conduct. In that when the body is being torn he is patient, for the sake of the deliverance of those even who tear it, and is not injured in thought, and manifests the power of patience, this for him is the Perfection of Patience. The strength by which he refuses to give up the will of omniscience, and holds fast to it by force of thought, and just follows the course of transmigration, and holds to the root of good: this for him is the Perfection of Strength. In that when the body is being dissolved he is not bewildered in preserving that jewel of omniscience which he has gained, and has regard only to wisdom, and takes care only of peace and tranquillity, this for him is the Perfection of Meditation. In that while the body is being torn he regards the body as like a herb or a stick or a wall, and understands that the body is illusion, and considers that the body is naturally impermanent, unhappy, without personality, at rest, this for him is the Perfection of Wisdom." Such is the description.[1] . . .

Yet again he thinks after the following fashion: [2] "That being is lazy, without virtue; he reviles me and censures me. Come! we will take strength, we will be eager, seeking for the root of good. Now this very being must be first seated by me in the Buddha's circle; [3] afterwards I must awaken the incomparable supreme wisdom [188]. . . . We must gird up our

[1] See Mahāvyut. 54. [2] From 187^{16}–188^{5} wanting in Tib.

[3] The holy spot under the Bo-tree.

loins for the good of such beings, untamed, unprotected, not tranquil. . . . Come, let us take refuge in the nature of things. Who injures or is injured here? He though he seek finds not a thing that injures or is injured. He does not find the notion of self or other, and being freed from the wrong idea,[1] he is patient."

In the *Bhagavatī* also it is written: "This is the thought he cherishes. 'I whose duty it is to appease the quarrels of all beings, I myself quarrel. My gains are hard gained, if I answer as I am spoken to. I whose duty it is to be the means of progress for all beings, I myself say to another, The same to you, or return a harsh answer. This I ought not to say; I should be as without speech, I should be as a dumb sheep in quarrels and bickerings. When I hear others' ways of speech ugly, unkind, abusive, I ought not to make my thoughts angry. In the presence of others this is not meet or proper, that I recognize the faults in another's heart. This is not proper, that I think even the faults of another's heart worth listening to. Why is that? My purpose must not be weakened by me, whose duty it is to make all beings happy by providing all happiness, and completely to emancipate them, by awakening in them the incomparable supreme wisdom; in that case I perish; nor must I be angry for the great offences of others; in that case I go into delusion and agitation. This is my duty to do; with firm energy I must exert myself; I must not be agitated, even if my life is being taken: I must not show a frown on my face.'"[2]

And in the *Bodhisatva-prātimoksha* it is said: "Those who are angry he consoles and calms, he soothes and comforts them."

[1] Read उपलब्ध्यो°. [2] Reading मुखे.

CHAPTER X

THE PERFECTION OF STRENGTH

[189] WHEN thus established in patience, he should apply strength in hearing the word. Otherwise the very hearing makes for his destruction. As it is said in the *Candrapradīpa Sūtra*: "If he goes never so deep into the Law, and should not observe virtue, being intoxicated by his learning,[1] not even by his deep learning could he be saved from going into states of misery by his evil conduct."

But the praises of hearing the word are given in the *Nārāyaṇa-paripṛcchā*. "Thus, young sirs, wisdom comes to him that hears, cessation of passion to him that is wise; in whom passion has ceased, for him Māra does not appear."

Here he recites in full a Birth of the great sage Uttara and says: "O Vimalatejas, to the Bodhisatvas who love the Law, great Beings, reverend, respectful, even the blessed Buddhas dwelling in other worlds, show their faces and preach the Law to them. For the Bodhisatvas, O Vimalatejas, who love the Law, the Great Beings, in the midst of mountains and caves and trees the treasures of the Law are laid up. Countless pictures of the Law are in books and the palm of the hand. O Vimalatejas, for the Bodhisatvas who love the law, the deities that have seen the former Buddhas convey to them the teaching of the Buddhas. . . . When their life is exhausted the blessed Buddhas and the deities bring them the power of life. By protection of the Buddhas and the deities, if they wish they are established for a thousand years. . . . Unto an age or the remainder of an age or as long as they wish, the Blessed Buddhas

[1] Reading °यशो° and श्रुतेन मत्त with Tib. *thos-pas rgyags-nas* 117, l. 4.

take away even old age and disease from the Bodhisatvas who revere the Law, they bring them memory, [190] bring them a great existence and intelligence. . . . They dispel heretical views, and bring them true insight. By respect for the Law, O Vimalatejas, all fear of attack is taken away from the Bodhisatvas, the Great Beings. Therefore now, O Vimalatejas, the Bodhisatva must be devoted to skilfulness in the task of hearing the word."

What kind of learning is described in the *Bodhisatva-vinaya?* As it is said in the holy Akshayamati *Sūtra:* "There are eighty ways of entering on the hearing of the word; to wit: The way of will, of resolve, of intention, of endeavour, of infinitude, of the Good Friend, of reverence, of formal respect, of good speech, of attention, of applying the ear, of thought, of not being distracted, of being intent, of considering it as a jewel, of considering it as remedy, of calming all diseases, of conferring memory, of illuminating destinies, of brightness in mind, of the approach to knowledge, of eagerly hearing the Law of Buddha, of fostering renunciation, of noble self-control, of the pursuit of great learning, of cherishing respect and affection, of bodily cheerfulness, of a joyful heart, of unwearied study, of studying the law, of studying religious duty, of studying the preaching of others, of learning what he has not learnt, of learning transcendental knowledge, of not striving for other vehicles, of studying the Perfection of Knowledge, of studying the *Bodhisatva-piṭaka*, of studying the *Saṃgraha-vastu*, of studying the *Upāyakauśalya*, of studying pious conduct, of studying the full consciousness of memory, of reverence, of studying skill in production and skill in non-production, of impurities, of studying mercy, of studying dependent origination, of impermanence, of pain, of non-self, of calm, of void, sinlessness, absence of intention, the way of not accumulating Karma, of accumulation of good, of the protection of beings, of actions continuing through their fruits, of self-dependence, of preserving one's own thoughts, of not relaxing strength, of reflexion on the Law, of the ripening of sin, drawing to us what helps, and of assailing the sins that are our adversaries, of protecting the seven treasures, of taking away all poverty, of praising those who know all, of pleasing the wise, of agreeing with the noble, of conciliating the ignoble, of seeing truth, of avoiding the faults of the elements of being, [191] of weighing the faults of the composite, of guarding the good, of avoiding all sins, of what is useful to self and others, of not repenting good actions, of specific attainment,[1] of acquiring all the Buddha's ways."

Again in the same place he says: "He who is devoted to the accomplishment of righteousness, to him alone accomplishment of knowledge comes. Then what is this accomplishment of righteousness? It is that having little business, doing little, saying little, busying little, but pondering the meaning of the word in wakefulness during the earlier and later parts of the night; [2] seeking ever more and more; no turbidity of thought; obstructing the depravities of the mind; knowledge of defencelessness in sins; absence of wickedness; not excessive repentance; confidence in religious duties; profundity in the law, devotion to the law, intentness upon the law; fulness of energy, being like to a blazing headcloth in the search for wisdom; [3] being absorbed in that; no languidness in conduct; no laying down of one's yoke; specific attainment; avoiding society; keeping to one monastery; pleasure in the forest life; pleasure in holy customs, no fickleness in ascetic practices, delight in the precincts of religion; not remembering worldly speech; seeking transcendental things; not letting the memory be stolen away; following up the course of the meaning; orderly succession of thought; restraints drawn from constancy [4]; ensuring wisdom by the requisites thereof; [192] adorning oneself with shame and modesty; earnestness in following wisdom; extinguishing unwisdom; cleansing of the eye of wisdom of one who is covered with ignorance, delusion,

[1] See Ch. 584*b*. When in meditation a specific thought has been grasped and jhāna attained.

[2] *i.e.* giving only a small time to leep.

[3] Tib. ye-śes tshol-ba-la mgo daṅ gos-la me ḥbar-ba lta-ba daṅ de-la ma chags-par gnas-pa daṅ. I do not understand the simile.

[4] So Tib.

darkness and gloom; perfect purity of intelligence; amplitude of intelligence; constancy of intelligence; full-blown intelligence; directness of intelligence; independence of character; not thinking much of one's own qualities; proclaiming the qualities of others; doing good actions; no putting off the yoke of the ripening of actions; knowledge of the purification of actions."

What is to be heard? This is said by the Blessed One in the *Jñāna-vaipulya Sūtra:* "Profitable writings are to be learnt, those without profit are to be eschewed. That is to say, those concerned with casuistry and penal law, charms for procuring death, the science of controversy, with youthful sports, with demonology. . . . also any other writings that are opposed to deliverance and make for delusion, all these must be eschewed by him who is established in the Bodhisatva's Vehicle."

To cleanse the thought by thus hearing, he must resort to the forest. But how is the household life allowed in the *Ugradattaparipṛcchā* even to him who has the true disposition? Because even one who is strenuous may be unable. Then there would be no sin if he had to do with another's wife, and so forth? Not so,[1] because even if he is unable, it is wicked by nature; whereas the household life is culpable by convention.

[1] The Tib. shows that न is a separate sentence.

CHAPTER XI

PRAISE OF THE FOREST SECLUSION

THIS stands fast by the rule of the *Ugraparipṛcchā;* when the religious man has fallen into the faults of the householder's life, to purify his soul he must resort to the forest. So also it is said in the *Candrapradīpa Sūtra:* "Never indeed shall one obtain the supreme and highest wisdom if he follows his lusts, with attachment to sons and wife, and follows the household life which he ought to loathe. They who avoid lust like a fire of cow-dung, without [1] attachment to sons and wife, and terrified flee from the household life; not hard to get for them is that highest wisdom. There never was a Buddha aforetime, nor shall be in future, nor is there now, who could attain that highest wisdom whilst he remained in the household life. Renouncing kingship like a snot of phlegm, one should live in the woodland in love with solitude; renouncing passions, rejecting pride, they awaken wisdom unsoiled, incomposite. . . . With food and drink, with clothes, flowers, and ointments, the incomparable Conquerors are not so much honoured as by those who have renounced the world and practise the ways of the ascetic life. And he who, longing for wisdom for the sake of all beings, disgusted with all bad things, should make the seven steps towards the forest, from that he becomes excellent in merit."

But if one, from the courteous invitation of different beings, through love of social life or of gain and the like, hesitate on the threshold of seclusion, this case is also there described.

[194] "The wise do not quarrel with fools; they entertain fools and dismiss them: nor do they become intimate with

[1] The Tib. uses an expression which suggests the reading *ajanitva*.

fools, for they think that men of wicked minds are there present. The wise do not pay court to fools; for they know that fools are always themselves. If they pay court to fools for some time, again they become like no friends to them. The wise put no trust in fools in this world, aware that fools are always themselves. Fools are naturally alien to them in character: where could one get a friend amongst the worldly? When admonished by a fellow in the faith, those foolish persons show anger and hatred and distrust; knowing this the wise do not put trust in them. Fools flock to fools, as foul with foul; but the wise congregate with the wise, as butter mingles with cream."

Thus it is also said in the same place:

"Full happy are always they on earth for whom everything is indifferent; and they who dwell in caves [1] enjoy the ascetic's happiness; and they who own nothing, and those who have no belongings, they walk the world lonely as a rhinoceros, they go like the wind in the sky. [195] They would be full happy in the world whose mind does not cling to the world: their mind is always like the wind here, and attachment is indifferent to them. To live with the hated makes one unhappy, to separate from the dear is also a cause of suffering; but those who have abandoned both, they are happy, who have pleasure in the Law.

Again in the same place it is said: "He has always few duties, he has eschewed the faults of the worldly, he never quarrels, he is devoted to what is right; such are the qualities of him who lives in the forest. He is always weary of the world,[2] he has no delight in the world, for him there is no increase of afflictions; as he lives in the woodland great praises are his. No question arises for him to dispute; he is always delighted with peace, and walks in solitude. Restrained in voice, mind and body, many are his virtues as he dwells in the forest. Deliverance comes to him; easily he learns serenitude of purpose. As he follows the purpose of the forest life these qualities are all his, dwelling in the forest."

Again he says: "In the forest seek alway solitude, leaving

[1] Tib. *nags*, *i.e.* वन for घन

[2] So Tib.

the delight in village and town. Be always like the solitary rhinoceros: soon ye will obtain the boon of tranquillity."

And in the holy *Rāshtrapāla Sūtra* he says:

[196] "Who leave the household life, with its innumerable faults, be always free from anxiety; they have delight in the forest, virtuous, their passions calmed, compassionate. The society of women is not with them, nor have they ever intercourse with men; solitary they live like the rhinoceros, pure of inclination, innocent. They take no pleasure in getting, they are not depressed if they get not; of modest desires, content with anything they get, free from delusion and hypocrisy."

And in the *Ugradatta-paripṛcchā*: "I must not frequent the society of the world, for it is not mine to cultivate the roots of good in a single being." But if having heard the word and finding so splendid an opportunity, he should not cleanse his thought, being devoted to gain and the like, that same single being would go astray in this world and in the world of gods.

For in the holy *Ratnakūṭa* it is said: "As some man, Kāśyapa, who should perish of thirst although carried along by a flood of water, so in this world some ascetics and brahmans who have learnt and studied many scriptures, do not dispel the thirst of passion, the thirst of hatred, the thirst of infatuation; these, although carried along by the great flood of the Law, perish by the thirst that is sin, and fall into the pit of misery."

Therefore certainly one should resort to the forest.

"These are the places he should resort to. Where the distance is not over-great for his seeking alms, [197] and not too near; where is water, clear, pure, not turbid, easy to get with little trouble; places overshadowed with trees, with flowers, fruit, and leaves, with no danger from rabid dogs, where caves are and mountain slopes, easy to traverse, peaceful, incomparable; these are the places he should resort to. Once settled in these places, he recites what he has read before thrice in the night and thrice in the day in a tone not too high and not too low, not with senses agitated, not with wandering thought, in all tranquillity, reflecting on the Book, apprehending the causes, putting away indolence. And if the king should visit the Brother in that forest, or one of royal authority, or others, brahmans or kshatriyas, townsfolk or countryfolk, he must welcome them with respect; and thus he must say: 'Be seated, great king, in the seat prepared for you.' If he sits down, both should sit; if he does not sit down, both must remain standing. If the king is not to be depended upon, the Brother should admonish him. 'It is great gain to you, O King, if in your realms there are dwelling moral and virtuous men and learned ascetics and brahmans, not persecuted by robbers and miscreants.' If he is steadfast and of good conduct, with senses under control, a good man, capable of instruction, then the Brother should deliver a general [1] discourse. If the king does not take this kindly, he must address his discourse to influencing the king's feelings. If the king does not take this kindly, he must declare the loftiest dignities of the Tathāgata. Let him approach brahmans and kṣatriyas, townsfolk and countryfolk, behaving as befits each. He only who is learned is able to win the heart of those that hear the word; and those beings receive satisfaction in his presence and serenity and delight."

[198] And in the *Ugradatta-paripṛcchā* he says: "Moreover, householder, thus must the Bodhisatva examine himself who has left the world and dwells in the forest: 'To what end do I live in the forest? Not only by the forest life does one become an ascetic. Many live there who are untamed, uncontrolled, not devoted, not diligent. Thus beasts and monkeys in troops, flocks of birds, robbers and caṇḍālas live there, and they are not possessed of the ascetic's qualities. I must do more to fulfil that purpose for which I dwell in the forest, that is the ascetic's purpose.' . . . Again, householder, the Bodhisatva must thus examine himself who has left the world and dwells in the forest: 'To what end have I come into the forest?' Thus he must diligently ponder. 'It was fear that brought me to the forest. Fear of what? The fear of worldly society, the

[1] *Vicitra* is a technical term in Skrt. and Pali, but it is not clearly explained; but it is contrasted here with a direct appeal to the emotions, through the fear of death, etc.

fear of company; the fear of passion, hatred, delusion; the fear of pride, intoxication, hypocrisy, pain; the fear of praise, envy, and jealousy; the fear of form, sound, smell, taste, touch; I was afraid of the ideas of individuality and possession, afraid of arrogance and of doubt, afraid of the Māra of the elements of being, the Māra of sin, the Māra of death, the Māra of the gods;[1] I feared the mistake of thinking the impermanent to be permanent, the impersonal to be personal, the impure to be pure, unhappiness to be happiness; I feared thought, mind and consciousness; I feared the arising of obstacles and hindrances; and feared the false view of individuality; I feared the bad friend; I feared gain and honour unseasonable talk, the error that the unseen is seen, the unheard is heard, the unthought is thought, the unperceived perceived, the delusion that one who is not an ascetic is an ascetic; I feared mutual hatred; I feared the element of desire, the element of form, the element of no form; I feared to fall into the several ways of existence; I feared birth in hell, as an animal, as a preta: in a word, I was in fear of all evil ideas. It was the fear of all such terrible things that led me to go into the forest. . . .[2] Moreover, householder, when the Bodhisatva has left the world and settled in the forest, if he feel fear or terror, this is how he must school himself: 'Whatever fears may arise, they all arise from self-seeking. . . . But if when dwelling in the forest I should not renounce all clinging to self, nor belief in self, the notion of self, the feeling of a self, nor thirst for self, nor idea of self, nor the assertion of individuality, nor the heresy of self, [199] nor resting on a self, nor imagination of a self, nor protecting the self; useless would be my forest life. Moreover indeed, householder, life in the forest is not for him who has the idea of self or of others.[3] . . . Dwelling in the forest, householder, is a dwelling apart from all things, without the company of all things.[4] . . . As, householder, the herbs

[1] For the different Māras see Dh.S 80, Childers, p. 241*b*.

[2] See Childers 121*b*, and M. Vyut. 155.

[3] He believes neither in "self" nor in "others," but in void (śūnyatā).

[4] Mrs. Rhys Davids, *Buddhist Norm*, 205.

and bushes, the plants and trees growing in the forest fear not nor are afraid or terrified, and fall not into panic ; so, householder, the Bodhisatva dwelling in the forest must regard his body as like to the herbs and bushes, plants and trees, like wood, like plaster on a wall, like an apparition ;[1] he must realize that all is illusion. Who fears hell ? who is afraid ? If he fears or is afraid, he must thus thoroughly meditate on his body : ' In the body is no self, no being, no living one, no man, or person, or human being, or human creature, fear is an illusion of what is not. I must not yield to this illusion of what is not. Therefore as herbs and bushes, plants and trees grow in the forest without sense of self or possession, so I must dwell in the forest without a sense of self, without a sense of possession, recognizing and realizing that all things are like the forest.[2]

" And why so ? The forest life is without pleasure, without sense of self or possession.' . . . Moreover, householder, the Bodhisatva who has left the world must reflect that the forest life was ordained by the Buddha, and therefore he must live in the forest ; for thus there is the fulfilment of the pure Law. ' When the root of good is established, I will descend into village and town and market-town, kingdom and capital, and preach the Law.' . . . But if, householder, the Bodhisatva who has left the world goes amongst the multitude for the purpose of preaching or recitation, he must be respectful and courteous to teachers and preceptors, he must show respect to Brethren old and young and middle-aged, he must be diligent, self-helping, doing no hurt to others, and he must not be exacting in service ; and thus he must reflect : ' The Tathāgata also, the saintly and supreme Buddha, [200] was worshipped of the universe, including all the worlds of the gods, Māras and Brahma, of all creation with ascetics and brahmans, was to be revered of all beings ; yet even he did not claim observance from any one ; how much more we unlearned, but only eager

[1] A pseudo-self ? *ātmapratibhāsavat* is quite obscure.

[2] Mrs. Rhys Davids, *Buddhist Norm* (Williams & Norgate, 1913), p. 205, on Pali *aranna sanni*.

to learn ! nay, shall we not be the servants of all beings ? shall not we also be busy about the service of others, and not claim observance from any one ? ' And why so ? If, householder, a Brother is exacting in service, his acquisition of virtuous qualities is hindered ; and those whom he wins to himself think thus of him : ' This man wins us to get our service.' "

Again in the same work he says : " But, householder, if the Bodhisatva who dwells in the forest, desirous of hearing the Law, desirous of the preaching of teachers and preceptors, or to visit the sick, should go to a place of sitting or sleeping [1] near a village, he must make up his mind to return back again in the evening. If, again, the preaching or recitation depends on others, he must keep a cave-and-forest mind, as when he dwells in his hermitage. That is true forest life when in everything is the idea of the forest, meditation on the Law, ardour."

In the holy *Ratnarāśi Sūtra* it is written : " And if again, as he dwells in his place in the forest when yet a worldling that has not attained fruition, noisome beasts should appear, he should feel no fear, no terror, but this should be his thought : ' I have already renounced the life of the body and come into the forest ; I must not fear here, nor be terrified ; nay, I will have pity and put away hatred, and keep fear away. And if even so these noisome beasts should deprive me of life and devour me, I must reflect : It will be great gain to me if substance shall be taken from my unsubstantial body ; but these noisome beasts, since I cannot find meat to please them with, will eat my flesh and enjoy themselves. . . .' If again while he dwells in that forest place demons shall approach, of good colour or of bad colour, he is neither to conciliate them nor to attack them. If the deities who have seen the former Buddhas visit this forest Brother, [201] and ask him a question, then that forest Brother is to preach the Law to those deities according to his strength and ability so that they may understand it. If again they should put profound questions, which that forest Brother should not be able to solve, he must not be proud, but he must say, ' I am not learned ; I will meditate, I

[1] Tib. omits " to a place of sitting or sleeping."

will strive in the Buddha's salvation ; a time and a season shall come when I shall have heard and learnt all the Law, and shall solve every question.' They say : 'Well, may it become clear to you ; we are eager to hear the Law.' . . . Then as he dwells in his forest place he must take the image of the herbs and bushes, plants and great trees : 'How do these come to be ? As these, without being or sense of ownership, without sense of self, or possession, not moving, without business, spring up and decay, and there is none that makes them spring up, or destroys them ; so this body, that resembles a herb or wood or plaster, with no sense of ownership, no sense of self, or possession, not moving, without business, by a chain of causation springs up, by the defect of this chain of causation is destroyed ; and yet there is nothing that really arises or is decayed.' "

And again it is said : " Settled there in the forest thus he must reflect : 'Even if I have come into the forest, alone, without a fellow, if I have no companion to do well or ill by me, yet there are the gods, nāgas, rakshas, and the Blessed Buddhas, who know the intent of my heart. They are my witnesses : shall I dwelling here in this forest place pass into the power of evil thought ? If I who have come so far alone, with no fellow, without support, without sense of ownership or possession, should I think about lust, ruin, or mischief, or any other evil imagination, I should be indistinguishable from the beings who are involved in the world and in society ; then these gods, nāgas, and rakshas will be disappointed, and the Blessed Buddhas will be offended.' "

CHAPTER XII

PREPARATION OF THE THOUGHT

WHILE thus dwelling in the forest he *applies his mind to contemplation.*[1]

For it is said in the *Bhagavatī*: "He walking in the Perfection of Contemplation for the good of those beings avoids distraction of thought. And why so? Because this is his reflexion. 'Even worldly meditation is hard to accomplish with a distracted thought; how much more the incomparable supreme wisdom! Therefore I must not be distracted in thought until I shall attain the incomparable supreme wisdom.'"

Again it is said therein: "Moreover, Subhūti, the great Being, the Bodhisatva, when first he has begun to think, walking in the Perfection of Contemplation, falls into the ecstasy by thoughts connected with omniscience. Seeing forms with the eye, he is not affected by them; wherefore whatever covetousness and despondency or other sinful and evil conditions would take possession of his thoughts if he did not restrain the organ of sight, to restrain these he applies himself, and watches the organ of sight. So when he hears sounds with the ear, or perceives smells with the nose, or tastes savours with the tongue, or feels touch with the body, or recognizes conditions with the mind, he is not affected by them. Wherefore, whatever states would take possession of his thoughts if he does not keep his organ of thought in control, to restrain these he applies himself, and watches the organ of mind. Going or standing, sitting or lying or speaking, he does not leave his condition of tranquillity.[2] He does not fidget with hands or

[1] Kārikā 20. [2] Omit *asam°*.

feet or twitch his face, he is not incoherent of speech, his senses are not confused, he is not exalted or uplifted, not fickle or idle, not agitated in body or mind ; tranquil is his body, tranquil his voice, his mind is tranquil ; in secret and in public his demeanour is contented. . . . Frugal, easy to feed, easy to serve, of good life and habits ; even in a crowd dwelling apart ; his mind unchanged whether he get or not : [203] not uplifted, not cast down. Thus in good or in evil, in praise or blame, in good or evil report, in life or in death, he is the same unchanged, not uplifted and not cast down. Thus with foe or friend, with helper [or hurter], with noble and ignoble, with sounds confused and not confused, with shapes pleasant or unpleasant, his mind is unchanged, not uplifted and not cast down, without satisfaction or dissatisfaction. And why is this ? He regards all things as having the Void for their special characteristic, as not existing, as not created, as not produced" ; that is the matter in sum.

There by encouraging benignity in the despondent mind he should stimulate it ; but in an exalted mind he procures tranquillity by thoughts of impermanence.

He should remember the versicle given in the holy *Rāsh-ṭrapāla* for the purpose of counteracting both despondency and exaltation.

"In many millions of ages a Buddha sometimes arises, a friend of the world, a great sage. Now that chiefest opportunity is come, to-day he must reject sloth if he desires emancipation."

Thus, if I think, "All that is composite is unreal, like illusion, like a dream, soon there must be parting from all that is dear ; no one is here permanently ; strive and make effort always for the Perfections, the spiritual Stages, the Powers ; never let slip your strength until you awaken the most excellent wisdom."

And it is said in the holy *Lalita-Vistara* : "The three worlds are ablaze with old age, disease, and pain ; all is burning with the fire of death, helpless ; in fleeing from existence all the world wanders perplext, like a bumble-bee in a jug. [204] Unstable are the three worlds, like the autumn clouds ;

like the scene of a play is the course of birth ; like mountain torrents light and swift in speed, life in the world is gone as lightning in the cloud. In the earth, the gods' place, the path of the three states of unhappiness, people are under the power of ignorance and the thirst for existence, foolish, as the five modes of existence go round, like the turning of a potter's wheel. This world, with all its beloved shapes and delightful sounds, delicious tastes, agreeable sensations, is entangled in the net of sin as an ape in the net of a hunter. The pleasures of sense always involve fear and strife, they cause anger, they bring much pain and distress ; like a sword blade, like a poisonous plant, thrown away by holy souls like a pot of excrement, robbing the memory, causing darkness, producing the causes of fear, always rooted in pain, causing thirst for existence to grow like a creeper, ever full of fear and strife are the sensual pleasures. Dangerous like fire-pits ablaze these lusts are considered by the holy ; like deep bogs, like a sword-point, like a razor-edge smeared with honey ; as a serpent's head, as a pot of excrement, so are those lusts known to be by those who know them ; so like a spike, like a lump of bird's flesh, a little quarrel of dogs, like moon in the water, those lusts, like a mirrored image, like an echo in the hills, like an apparition, like a scene on the stage, like a dream, they are known by the holy. [205] Those sensual pleasures remain but for a moment, like illusion and mirage, like the empty bubbles and foam on water, false, imaginary, so are they known by the wise. In the first stage of life one has a beautiful shape, one is dear, desired, esteemed, walks the way of fools ; but when the beauty of form is lost by old age, disease, and pain, they leave it as the beasts leave a dry river. One that has wealth and riches, that is mighty with much treasure, is dear, desired, esteemed, and walks the way of fools ; but when wealth is wasted and poverty comes men leave him as an empty desert. Like trees covered with flowers and fruit is a man who takes pleasure in gifts, a giver of joy ; when wealth is wasted and old age appears, a suitor then is like an unlovely vulture. One strong in influence and wealth, with beauteous form, causes delight to senses in the company of friends ; but when oppressed by old age, disease and pain, his wealth wasted, then he is unlovely like death. Decayed by old age, his youth all past, he is like a tree struck by lightning ; like a house worn out with old age, full of fear ; quickly tell of the escape from old age, O sage ! Old age withers men and women as a creeper kills a grove of sāl trees : old age steals strength, energy and force ; in old age a man sinks as in a bog ; old age makes beautiful things ugly, old age steals brightness and takes away the power of strength ; it always steals happiness and brings contempt ; old age causes death and takes away the sap of life. Full of hundreds of diseases, ruinous evils, unhappiness, it is like the beasts in a conflagration of the jungle. Considering that the world is full of old age and disease, quickly tell of the escape from pain ! [206] As the quality of cold in the winter season steals the sap from herbs and bushes, trees and plants, so disease steals the sap of youth in the world, while feeling, form and force decay. Disease in the world always makes an end of wealth, riches and all blessings, and causes contempt ; it causes repulsion and resentment, and burns as the sun in the sky. Death, departure, new birth, dissolution, separation from things beloved, never to come again or to meet again, like the leaves and fruits of the forests, like the stream of a river. Death brings all under its power and dominion, death carries off all as a river carries a tree. Without companion or fellow a man wanders about, attended by the fruits of his own deeds, helpless ; death devours the hundreds of breathing beings, as the sea-monster swallows swarms of creatures, as the Garuḍa swallows the serpent, as the lion devours the elephant, as fire destroys the herbs and plants."

And in the *Rājāvavādaka Sūtra* he says : " If, great King, in the four regions four great mountains should move together, firm, strong, unbroken, uncleft, not hollow, compact, one solid whole, touching the sky and tearing up the earth, grinding under them all the herbs, trees, branches, leaves and foliage, with all the living and breathing creatures, it would not be easy to escape by speed or strength, or to turn them aside by drugs or charms or spells ; just so, great King, those four great terrors move together, which it is not easy to escape by speed or strength, [207] or to turn aside by drugs or charms or spells. What four ? Old age, disease, death, misery. Old age approaches, great King, grinding out youth, disease grinding out health, death grinding out life, misery grinding out all good fortune. And why so ? As, great King, the lion, king of beasts, full of beauty and swiftness, terrible with splendid claws and teeth, chases the herds of animals, and seizing one deals with it as he will, and that animal is helpless within the mighty ravening jaws ; even so, great King, a man wounded with death's arrow, life's fever over, without support, his vitals being torn, his joints being rent asunder, flesh and blood being dried up, with face burnt, parched, distracted, hands and feet shaking, helpless, incapable, smeared with spittle, nose-droppings, stinking urine and ordure, with only a breath of life left in him, taking a new existence from the actions of this, terrified by Yama's satellites, plunged in black night, choking in his last gasp, alone, without compassion or comrade, leaving this world, entering the next world, travelling by the great path, entering the great wilderness, plunging into the great abyss, coming into the great darkness, overwhelmed with the great flood, whirled away by the wind of past actions, going to a place where the marks of this world are not :[1] for him there is no other defence, no other refuge, nor other support except the Law. For the Law, great King, at that time is a defence and resting-place, a refuge and support. As for one who is starved with cold, the heat of fire ; for one without fire, warmth ; for one who is oppressed with heat, coolness ; for one who is on the road, a cool and shady grove ; for the thirsty, cool water ; for the hungry, good food ; for the sick, those versed in healing simples ; for the terrified, powerful companions ; all these are excellent protections : even so, great King, when one is pierced with death's arrow, life's fever gone, helpless, without refuge, without support, there is no other defence, no other support than the Law. Therefore now, great King, you

[1] That is, without the three nimittāni, *rāga dosha moha*.

must keep before your mind impermanency, change and decay, when in fear of death; righteously, great king, you must rule, not unrighteously; [208] and why so? Even if all goes well with your person, if it is well guarded, for a long time regaled and served with clean and pleasant food to eat, to drink, to relish, yet you will be encompassed by hunger and thirst when death shall come. Now clad in goodly garments of fine cloth and silk, cotton or linen, reclining on a splendid couch, when death shall come you shall be wrapped in clothes soiled with sweat. Thus, great King, if your person has perfumes for the bath, or for anointing, with flowers and fragrant scents and perfumes, ere long it will have a bad smell. Although now you are surrounded by troops of women in the women's apartments, with music of song and many instruments, happy and delighted, taking your pleasure all about, soon you will be very much afraid of death, and death will bring dejection and pain. Although now, great King, you dwell in houses anointed with ointments, well guarded with bolts, with windows carefully closed, many a sweet savour burning of scents and flowers, oils and cosmetics, hung with strings of ribbons and wreaths, covered with pearls and flowers, perfumed with vases of scent, you rest your feet on stools, and recline upon couches strewn with rugs and woollens, with quilts of down, covered with muslin and woven pillows on either side; but soon your vigour will be gone, and your body will be left on the earth in a loathsome charnel-ground, full of jackals, crows, and vultures, the flesh, bones and blood and grease of corpses. Although now, great King, you ride on elephants and horses and drive in chariots, with the noise of conchs and kettledrums, the sunshade spread above, fanned by chowries, attended by many elephants, horses, chariots and footmen, reverenced with myriads of salutations: yet when you perceive that your departure is at hand, your vigour gone, laid upon a bier, upheld by four men, carried out by the south gate of the city, with mother and father, brother and sister, wife, son and daughter, companions, menservants and maidservants, workmen and hirelings, their hearts grieving, hanging heads, hands uplifted, beating of breasts and loud lamentation, while 'O my son, O my lord, O my dearest, O my master,' the townsfolk and countryfolk continually do cry, you will be looked on with contempt, and brought to the charnel-ground, then devoured by crows and jackals and vultures, and those bones burnt in fire or left lying upon the ground, [209] or drenched with water, or mouldering in wind and heat and rain, scattered in all directions, and then they shall rot. Thus all conditions are impermanent, fleeting." That is the sum of the matter.

Thus sin is mainly passion, hate, and delusion; each of which ought to be nipped in the bud, and their causes eschewed.

In this connexion he speaks precisely in the holy *Ratnamegha:* "He uses the antidote for passion, and he shuns the causes whereby passion arises. What is this antidote for passion? what are these causes of its arising? Contemplation of impurity is the antidote to passion; a beauty of the district is a cause whereby passion arises. And what is contemplation of impurity? In this body there are hair, down, nails, teeth, dirt, filth, skin, flesh, bones, sinews, nerves, kidneys, heart, spleen, lungs, entrails, mesentery, upper and lower stomach, bladder, liver, excrement, tears, sweat, phlegm, snot, fat, humours, lard, marrow, bile, spittle, pus, blood, head, brain, piss. These things the Bodhisatva naturally considers, and as he considers them he thinks, 'Even he who should be foolish, deluded, incapable, bad, if he understood these things, [210] would not feel passion towards them; how much less would one who has wisdom!' Thus the Bodhisatva is full of the contemplation of impurity."

And in the *Bhagavatī* it is said: "Furthermore, Subhūti, the Bodhisatva, the great Being, walking in the Perfection of Wisdom, recognizes how this body is composed. As a butcher or a butcher's man kills a cow, and with sharp knife cuts it into four quarters, and examines it as he stands or sits; even so, Subhūti, the Bodhisatva walking in the Perfection of Wisdom, recognizes how this body is composed in its elements: 'In this body are the elements earth, water, fire, and air.' . . ."

Again he says, "If, Subhūti, a farmer has a sack full of all sorts of grain, rice, paddy, sesamum, and husked rice, vetch and beans, barley and wheat, lentils and mustard; a man of intelligence examining these would say, 'This is rice of such a sort, this is paddy, this is sesamum, this is husked rice, this is vetch, these are beans, this is barley, this is wheat, these are lentils, this is mustard.' Just so the Bodhisatva, the Great Being, walking in the Perfection of Wisdom, considers the body as it really is upwards from the soles of the feet, and downwards, the hair and head, nails, down, skin, how it is covered with down and full of all manner of impurities: 'In this body there are hairs, down, nails,' and so on to 'the head, brain, the oozings of eye and ear.' . . . Moreover, Subhūti, the Bodhisatva entering a charnel-place sees all sorts of dead bodies thrown down in the charnel-place, left in the place of corpses one day dead, or two days dead, or three, four, [211] five days dead, swollen, livid, putrid, eaten of worms; and thus he compares his body: 'This body also is of such a nature and of such composition; it not exempt from this condition.' Thus, Subhūti, the Bodhisatva, the Great Being, walking in the Perfection of Wisdom, continues contemplating the body from without. . . . Moreover, when he sees dead bodies cast out in the charnel-place six nights dead, being devoured by crows, eagles, or vultures, dogs or jackals, or worms of various kinds, he compares his own body: 'This body also is of the same kind and nature; it cannot escape this condition.' Moreover, when he sees dead bodies cast forth in the charnel-place, already being devoured, foul, stinking, he compares his own body as before. . . . Moreover, when he sees dead bodies lying in a charnel-house, a skeleton smeared with flesh and blood and the tendons attached, he compares his body, as before. Moreover, when he sees corpses in a charnel-house, all skeletons, flesh, blood and tendons all gone, he compares his own body as before. Moreover, when he sees in a charnel-house bones thrown about anyhow; here foot-bones, there shin-bones, there again the large flat bones, yonder hips and pelvis, [212] there the spinal column, here the neck or arm-bones, he compares his own body as before. . . . Moreover, when he sees in a charnel-house bones several years old, dried up in the winds like conch-shells, he compares his own body as before: 'This body also is of the same kind and character, and cannot escape this condition.' Moreover, Subhūti, the Bodhisatva, the Great Being, walking in the Perfection of Widsom, when he sees in the charnel-house bones several years old, crumbling away, black, gray, rotten, powdered into the likeness of dust, upon the ground, he compares his body: 'This body is of the same kind and character; it cannot escape this condition.'"

This is briefly the method of counteracting passion. For hatred, benevolence is the antidote, and not to see those that are disagreeable; or by encouraging the pleasure that comes from association in such matters as meals. There benevolence is a desire for another's welfare, prayer a desire for another's sake. Affection is unsullied by the two causes, the passion of lust or gratitude. That is the meaning.

Benevolence is threefold [1] in the holy *Akshayamati Sūtra:* "When Bodhisatvas first conceive the thought of becoming Buddhas, their benevolence is directed towards all creatures; when they have begun their religious practices, it is directed towards the suffering; it is without any object at all when they are patiently preparing for a future state."

Again, benevolence has the Buddhas as its object of thought, the Bodhisatvas, the disciples, all creatures as its objects of thought. Here when it has all beings as its object of thought, first it comes by accumulating benefit and blessing upon a beloved being with meditation. Upon such an one he should accumulate benevolence: then upon acquaintances; then upon strangers; then upon neighbours; then upon fellow-villagers; [213] and so with another village; and so on until he continues devoted to one region, spread over it, covering it. So with the ten regions. But this procedure does not apply to the benevolence towards the Buddhas and the rest.

This is described in the *Vajradhvaja-pariṇāmanā.* "As he walks in the practices of the Bodhisatva, whatever forms

[1] So Dh. S. cxxx.

are seen are either pleasant or the opposite. So with sounds, scents, tastes, touch, or mental objects, they are either pleasant or the opposite. The faultless and pure cause what is good, noble and bright, from which contentment results; and pleasure emerges, delight is produced, satisfaction comes, happiness is caused, rapture becomes manifest; dejection is repelled, vigour of thought is manifested and thought becomes active, the disposition becomes gentle, the senses are comforted; enjoying this happiness [1] he transfers it to others: 'With this transference of merit by all the Buddhas may those blessed Buddhas be endowed in greater measure with the inconceivable bliss of a Buddha's life, may they be possessed by the incomparable bliss of a Buddha's tranquillity, may they be established in greater measure with endless bliss, may they be endowed with the immeasurable bliss of a Buddha's emancipation, may they be possessed by the illimitable bliss of a Buddha's magic, may they be possessed by the inconceivable bliss of a Buddha's life in the Order, [214] may they be enveloped in the unequalled bliss of a Buddha's deeds of might, may they be exceedingly blessed with the bliss of a Buddha's strength, may they have unchanging [2] bliss by the pleasure of non-production in which all sensations are appeased, may they have undisturbed bliss in the incomparable course of a Tathāgata's bliss always united with the detached life. Thus the Bodhisatva, applying this root of good to the Tathāgatas, applies it to the Bodhisatvas; that is, he applies it for the fulfilling of unfulfilled prayers, for the purifying of those unpurified whose aspiration is perfect wisdom, for the consummation of all Perfections unconsummated, for establishing the thought of enlightenment like adamant, to prevent the loss of the unconquerable preparation for omniscience, for seeking the roots of good of the Bodhisatvas, for fulfilling the great resolution which is fixed in impartiality for all the world, for entering all the Bodhisatva s ways of life, for the clear knowledge of all the Bodhisatva's

[1] Tib. implies स तत्सुखं.

[2] Tib. implies °विचार°. For *anutp°* the Tib. is mi skye bahi bde.

powers, for acquiring omniscience in all the Bodhisatvas' roots of good. He then having applied this root of good for the welfare of the Bodhisatvas, thus applies the same root of good to those who abide in the Buddha's commands, disciples and Pratyeka Buddhas. Whatsoever beings hear the Buddha's voice even for the time of one finger-snap, or the sound of the Law, or who show respect to the holy Order, to them he applies the root of good for the incomparable and perfect wisdom, and for the fulfilling of the Buddha's remembrance, for the practice of remembering the Law, for respect to the holy Order, for the speedily seeing the welcome sight of the Buddha, for purification of thought, for penetrating the Law of Buddha, for acquiring illimitable virtues, for the purification of all supernatural faculties, for extinguishing all doubts in the Law. As he applies it to those who abide in the Buddha's commands, and to disciples and Pratyeka Buddhas, so this Bodhisatva [215] applies this root of good to all beings; that is, he applies it to turn them away from the road to hell, to keep them from birth as animals, for the happiness of avoiding Yama's world, to avoid all the ways of misery without exception, and to foster in all these beings the will to obtain the incomparable wisdom, that they may attain thought that aspires to omniscience, nor lose any of the Buddha's qualities, to induce that stage in which is the bliss of boundless omniscience, for the boundless purification of all beings, that all beings may attain boundless knowledge, . . . In him, whatever acts are concerned with robes, alms-bowl, lying or sitting, the needs of sickness, medicine, going to and fro, standing or sitting by the body and so forth, in the sphere of daily life, steadiness in deportment and inexcitability, acts of feeling, voice, and mind, good conduct, closure of the six senses, acts of clothing, rubbing, and bathing one's person, eating, drinking, and chewing, service of one's body in stretching out or drawing in, looking and watching, sleeping and waking,—in all this there is no act that is not applied to acquisition of omniscience for the Bodhisatva whose thought is busy with the good and profit of all beings, . . . whose mind is bent on the rescue of all the world, who strives ever after the root of good, avoiding infatuation and sloth, . . . his face turned away from all sin, his heart following all the instruction of the Bodhisatvas, with no obstruction in the road to omniscience, ensuring the stages of knowledge, loving the company of wise men . . . like a bee, gathering the root of good, his soul detached from the whole world,[1] not involved in the conditions of existence" . . . to the words " and even to dogs and other animals he throws a sop or a bite. He applies all this for the profit in happy births and deliverance of the same from this animal birth, from this flood of unhappiness, from this clinging to unhappiness, from these wretched elements of existence, from this wretched suffering, from this accumulation of unhappiness, from this wretched gathering of action, [216] from this source of unhappiness, from this root of unhappiness, from this abode of unhappiness; he applies it for the release of these beings, and by making them his object of thought he makes all beings the object of his thought and keeps them in mind. Then he makes the root of good subservient, that is, he applies it to omniscience, he enwraps it in the idea of wisdom. Then he guides the root of good, keeps it back from the thorny path of new birth, pushes it forwards by the Buddha's bliss without hindrance, draws it forth from the sea of existence, pervades it with benevolence that leads to the qualities of a Buddha."

And the following verses from the *Suvarṇabhâsa*, on the subject of benevolence and mercy, should be observed with respect, and rehearsed even with the voice.

" By the drum of the *Suvarṇabhāsottama Sūtra* let pains be assuaged in the three thousand worlds, pains of ruin, pains of Yama's world, and the pains of poverty here in the three worlds; and by this as it sounds the drum let vice in the world be ended, and let all beings be unhurt by fear, even as the great sages are without fear, their fears allayed; even as those are endowed with all holy virtues, oceans of omniscience as regards existence, so may people be seas of virtue endowed with all the constituents of tranquillity and wisdom. By this

[1] This sense is clear in Tib.

as it sounds the drum let all beings have the voice of Brahma, let them reach the highest summit of wisdom in Buddhahood, let them turn the wheel of the pure Law. [217] Let them stand for ages beyond imagination, let them preach the Law for the welfare of the world, let them destroy sin, let them conquer pain, let them extinguish passion with hatred and delusion. Let those beings who stand in a state of ruin, their bones and limbs burning in a blaze, hear the sound of the drum, and let them cry, Glory to the Buddha. Let all beings remember their births, a hundred births, millions of births, let them remember always the great sages, and let them hear their lofty words. By this when it sounds the drum let them always gain access to the Buddhas; let them verily eschew the deed of sin, let them do good and pure deeds. In all the regions of all things that have breath let all pains be done away in the world. Let all creatures that are maimed in their organs or docked of a limb be whole as they should be. Let those who are diseased, weak, without limbs, lying helpless in all places, all be set free from their disease quickly and be made whole in the organs of strength. They who are frightened by kings, robbers, and bravos, condemned to death, threatened with misery by hundreds of different fears, let all those in misery and pain be set free from those hundreds of fears great and awful. [218] Those who are tormented and oppressed by prison bonds, who are in all manner of misery, overwhelmed with many thousands of troubles full of pain and dread from many a danger, let them all be set free here from their bonds, the tortured be freed from their torments. Let the condemned have life, let those in misery all be made secure. Let the hungry, parched, or thirsty receive food and drink in plenty. Let the blind see beautiful shapes, let the deaf hear pleasant sounds, let the naked receive fine raiment, the poor a treasure. Let all beings be happy with plenty of wealth and riches and goodly jewels. May no one have pain or misery, may all beings be full of happiness, beautiful, pleasant, delightful; may all happiness be accumulated for them always. Let them by the mere thought be provided with food and drink to their mind, abounding in merit; let them have lute, drum, cymbal of sweet sound, running brooks, ponds full of lotus; just by a thought, let them have lakes of lotus golden and lilac, scents and garlands, ointment and perfume, aromatic powder, and flowers of all colours. Let them have rain for the trees thrice in the season, let them take them, let them be happy, let them do infinite worship in the ten regions to all the Tathāgatas, to Bodhisatvas and disciples, and the Law pure, spotless, and firm.[1] [219] Let all beings avoid the low course, and keep clear of the eight unlucky moments. Let them approach the supreme king conqueror, let them always have access to the Buddhas. Let all women always become men, and heroes, bold, intelligent and wise. Let them all walk towards wisdom, let them walk in the Six Perfections. Let them see the Buddhas in the ten regions, amidst the coral bowers, happily seated upon thrones set with jewels, and let them hear the Law revealed."

That is benevolence, in sum; the conduct that is antidote for hatred. For one that is subject to confusion, the manifestation of the Chain of Causation is antidote.

Now the Chain of Causation is described in the *Śālistamba Sūtra*. [220] Here what is the linking of cause to cause in the Chain of Causation internally? This: "The Potentialities are caused by ignorance," and so on to "old age and death are caused by birth. But for ignorance there would not be the potentialities," and so on to "but for birth neither would there be old age and death. Here if there be ignorance, the potentialities are the result," and so on to "if there is birth, old age and death are the result. Here ignorance never thinks: 'I cause the potentialities.' And the potentialities do not think: 'We are caused by ignorance.'" And so on to "Birth does not think: 'I cause old age and death,' nor do old age and death think: 'I am caused by birth.' Here it becomes clear that if there be ignorance, the potentialities are the result," and so on to "thus if there be birth, it becomes clear that old age and death result. Thus one must reflect

[1] Tib. read धर्मविरजनिर्मलसुस्थित (see note in text also).

upon the linking of cause to cause in the Chain of Causation internally. How is the linking of secondary causes to be regarded in the Chain of Causation internally? As from the union of the six elements. Of what six elements? They are earth, water, fire, air, space, intelligence; as from their union we must regard the linking of secondary causes in the Chain of Causation internally. Now in the links of this chain, what is the element earth? That element is called earth which causes the hardness that keeps the body together. That element is called water which achieves the task of aggregating the parts of the body. That element is called fire which assimilates the food and drink that are taken. [221] That element is called air which causes breathing in and out. That is called space which causes the porosity in the body. That element is called intelligence which causes name and form to keep together like a bundle of reeds, and the impure consciousness which is connected with the group of five organs of consciousness. If the secondary causes are not present, there is no body. When the internal earth element is unimpaired, then the other elements are unimpaired, water, fire, air, space, intelligence; then by the union of all, the body comes into being. Here the earth element does not think: 'I cause the hardness of the body.' Nor does the water element think: 'I do what is necessary for aggregating the parts of the body.' The fire element does not think: 'I digest the food and drink that the body takes.' The air element does not think: 'I cause the breathing in and breathing out.' The space element does not think: 'I cause the body to be porous.' The intelligence does not think: 'I am begotten by these causes.' Then where these secondary causes are, the body comes into being. Therein the earth element is not self, not a being, not a living thing, not a creature, not a human being, not a man, not a woman, not a male, not a neuter; and not I, not mine, nor any one else's. So with the elements water, fire, air, space, intelligence; none is a being, a living thing, a creature, a human being, a man, a woman, a male, a neuter, nor I, or mine, or any one's else. Here what is ignorance? The recognition in these six elements of the notion of one, of material, of permanence, of firmness, of perpetuity, of happiness, of self, of being, living, humanity, manhood, of individuality or possession; [222] these and the like examples of false knowledge are called ignorance. Thus when ignorance is present, passion, hatred, and delusion exist as regards objects of sense; and these, passion, hatred, and delusion as regards objects of sense, are called the mental conformations. The recognition of things is cognition. The four elements of being springing from attachment which are immaterial and produced with cognition, are Name; the four great elements and the form derived therefrom, is Form; putting these together we get Name and Form.[1] The senses connected with name and form are the six organs of sense. The union of the three things is touch; by touch comes sensation; close to sensation comes thirst; the development of thirst is the clinging to existence; from this clinging springs the action that leads to rebirth, existence; the manifestation of the elements caused by this is birth; the ripening of the elements is old age, decay, death; when one dies or becomes deluded or is deeply attached to himself the inner burning is pain, the crying out is lamentation; the arising of joylessness connected with the five kinds of consciousness is-misery; the mental unhappiness connected with memory is despondency; and all the other like unhappinesses are the kinds of despair. . . .

"Moreover, not perceiving reality is false perception, unintelligence ignorance. Thus where ignorance is, [223] three kinds of mental conformations are produced. These are called the mental conformations caused by ignorance leading to merit, leading to demerit, and leading to immobility.[2] The understanding of conformations leading to merit, also leads to merit; the understanding of conformations leading to demerit, leads also to demerit; the understanding of those

[1] See Dh.S. xlvii. 341.

[2] This is explained as what leads to the Fourth Dhyāna, and it is so called since the effects of the act cannot be cancelled. See Warren, *Buddhism in Translations*, p. 492, Index s.v. *Karma*, and *Points of Controversy*, Pali Text Soc. Transl., p. 359.

that lead to immobility, leads also to immobility. This is called the understanding caused by the mental conformations. So with name and form. By the growth of name and form, things happen [1] by the six doors of sense. That is what is called the six organs of sense depending on name and form. From these six organs of sense six classes of contact arise; this is called the contact depending on the six organs of sense. Whatever be the kind of contact, such is the sensation. This is called the sensation depending upon contact. When one feels this, especially enjoys it, is delighted, seeks it and practises it, this is called thirst depending on sensation; a clinging to delight and enjoyment, that cries, 'May I never be separated from dear forms and joyful forms!' The more one prays, the less one is ready to renounce. This is called the attachment depending on thirst. Thus praying he produces action that causes existence by body, by voice, by mind. That is called the existence depending upon attachment. The production of the elements that appear in existence is called birth depending upon existence. The decay that comes from the assembling and ripening of the elements resulting from birth, [224] is called old age and death depending on birth. . . . Thus this chain of causation with twelve links caused each by another comes from interdependence. It is not impermanent nor permanent, not composite or incomposite, not feeling, not subject to destruction or annihilation, not a matter of detachment, proceeding from a time without beginning,[2] uninterrupted; it runs along like a river. And of this twelve-linked chain of causation, four links make for concentration by their causality. What are these four? Why, ignorance, thirst, action, consciousness. Here consciousness is a cause by being like a seed, action because it is like the ground, ignorance and thirst because they are naturally sin. Action and passion produce the seed consciousness; then action cultivates the seed consciousness, and thirst lubricates it, ignorance waters it.

[1] This is obscure in both Sk. and Tib.

[2] See this text with slightly different readings in *Mūlamadhyamakakārikās*. p. 566 (St. Petersburg).

Without these causes the seed does not exist. Here action does not think: 'I cultivate the seed consciousness'; thirst does not think: 'I lubricate the seed consciousness'; ignorance does not think: 'I water the seed consciousness'; nor does the seed consciousness think: 'I am produced by these causes.' Moreover, when the seed consciousness lies in the field of action, lubricated by thirst, watered by ignorance, it grows up in the mother's womb in such and such a place of rebirth;[1] [225] a sprout of name and form appears; and this sprout is not self-made, not made by another, nor made by both, not fashioned by a lord, not matured by time, not dependent on one cause, yet not arisen without cause. And then by union of mother and father, in the woman's courses after the other contributory causes have acted, the seed consciousness being full of affection, produces in the mother's womb the sprout name and form, although things are without master or owner, without possessor, without claimant, like space, having the marks of illusion, the causes primary and secondary being not lacking. For instance, by five effective causes the sight-consciousness is produced. What are these? The sight-consciousness is produced as a consequence of eye, form, looking, space, and the idea that springs from these. Here the eye plays the part of the recipient of the visual knowledge, form plays the part of the object, light causes the manifestation, space provides that there is no obstacle, the resulting idea gives the impression. These causes absent, there is no sight-consciousness. When the organ belonging to the eye is unimpaired, so also are form, look, space and the resultant idea. Therefore by the union of all there is sight-consciousness. Here the eye does not think: 'I do for sight-consciousness that which depends on the eye'; form does not think: 'I play the part of the object'; look does not think: 'I cause the appearance'; space does not think: 'I provide that there is no obstacle to sight-consciousness'; the resultant idea does not think: 'I give the impression to sight-consciousness'; sight-consciousness does not think: 'I am produced by these causes.'

[1] Reading *pratisandhau* as in 226[1].

Here again it is manifest that when these causes are present, sight-consciousness arises. So one must do with the other senses, according to each. In these cases there is nothing that passes from our world to the next world; [226] but the fruit of action appears, because the primary and secondary causes fail not. As in the lack of fuel there is no fire, even so the seed-consciousness produced by the action and passion, arising in this place or that, produces the sprout of name and form in the mother's womb, although things are without master or owner, with no possessor, no claimant, like space, having the marks of illusion, the causes primary and secondary being not lacking. There [1] the internal chain of causation is due to five causes; but what are these five? Not permanence, not destruction, not transition, but small causes and large results, and a succession of similar events. How is it not due to permanence? Because some elements of being are ended by death, those that appear at the conception are others; but those elements which are the first are not also the second. Moreover, when the first class of elements are being held in check, the others appear. Therefore it springs not from permanence. And how not from destruction? When the second elements appear, it cannot be said that the first elements have been held in check nor that they have not been held in check; but while the elements that are ended by death are being checked the others appear, as when the pole of a balance rises or falls. Therefore it is not by destruction.

"How is it not by transition? Because the component elements arise within the one birth from a different class of being. Therefore not from transition. How is it from small causes and the consequent large results? A small act is done; [227] a great result follows. Therefore it is from small causes and their great results. How is it from appropriate succession of events? Whatever description of act is done, that description of result follows. That is why it is from appropriate succession of events. Whoever, reverend Śāriputra, regards this chain of causation even as it is, truly described by the

[1] Reading as before with Tib. तथा°.

Blessed One, in his true wisdom, always without a living principle, bereft of living principle, true, not erroneous, not born, not produced, not made, not composite, making neither resistance nor obstacle, propitious, without danger, indivisible, imperishable, without cessation, who considers it as not existing, void, . . . sapless, suffering, impermanent, miserable, empty, non-individual, he does not go back to the beginning: What was I long ago, prithee, or what was I not? Who was I in my past course? Nor does he go on to the future: What shall I be in my future course, prithee, or what shall I not be? or who shall I be? Nor does he refer to the present: What is this, or how is this? What are we, what shall we be?"

And it is said in the holy *Daśabhūmaka:* "Here ignorance, thirst, and clinging are the description of the way of passion; the conformations and existence are the description of the way of action; the rest is the description of the way of suffering. Moreover [228] what is said of the 'conformations depending on ignorance' refers to the past; from 'consciousness' to 'feeling,' refers to the present; from 'think' 'to action' refers to the future, and so it goes on again. . . . Thus he thinks: Combination makes composite, dissolution makes the contrary, agglomeration makes composite, dispersion makes the contrary. Very well, it is we who know the composite to be very evil and bad, that will get rid of this combination and agglomeration, yet for the ripening of all beings we will not enter the eternal peace." This in brief is the purification of delusion.

[1] See the *Wheel of Life* in Mrs. Rhys David's *Compendium*, p. 263.

CHAPTER XIII

SUBJECTS OF INTENT CONTEMPLATION

THUS the man diligent in thought would undertake the intent contemplations. Here the Intent Contemplation of the Body is concerned with impurity.

This is explained by minute analysis in the *Dharmasaṅgīti Sūtra*. "Moreover, young sir, the Bodhisatva thus contemplates the body: 'This body is just a collection of feet and toes, legs, chest, loins, belly, navel, backbone, heart, ribs and flanks, hands, forearms, upper-arms, shoulders, neck, jaw, forehead, head, skull, accumulated by the action that causes existence, [229] the abode of sundry passions, ideas and fancies, in hundreds of thousands. Many other ingredients are brought together therein, such as: hair of the head, down, nails, teeth, bones, skin, flesh, fatty secretion, sinews, fat, marrow, oil, liver, urine, excrement, mesentery, blood, phlegm, bile, pus, snot, membrane of the brain. Thus it is a collection of many things.' Then what is this body? As he regards it he thinks: 'This body is like space.' Thus he contemplates the body like space. 'That is all space,' he thinks. For the full understanding of the body his intellect does not direct itself to anything else, does not divert itself thither or fix itself there."

Again it is said: "This body has not come from earlier time, nor passes into another time, nor dwelleth in past and future, except as far as it is so suggested by inexact suppositions; not a doer nor one that feels; not rooted in beginning, end, or middle; without master or ownership or possession. It is called by extraneous names, body, or shape, or enjoyment, or abode, or frame, or corpse, or organ of sense. Unsubstantial is this body sprung from the parents' blood and seed, in nature impure, putrid, and ill-smelling, disturbed by passion, hatred, delusion, fear, despair, thieves, always liable to felling, falling, breaking, scattering, crumbling, full of a hundred thousand different diseases."

And in the holy *Ratnacūḍa* it is said: "Impermanent indeed is this body, abiding no long time, and death its end; he who knows this lives not untranquil for the body's sake. He even gains vigour. He gains threefold vigour, to wit: [230] vigour of body, of enjoyment, of life. Knowing that the body is impermanent, he enters a state of slavery and pupilage to all creatures, and busies himself for their service. Knowing that the body is impermanent, he avoids doing any of the body's faults, crooked or wicked or hypocritical acts. Knowing that the body is impermanent he takes comfort by his life, but does not commit sin for life's sake. Knowing that the body is impermanent, he does not cling to enjoyments with thirst; he becomes like one who sacrifices himself wholly. Moreover, young sir, the Bodhisatva meditating upon the body attaches the bodies of all to his own, and thus he thinks: 'The bodies of all creatures must be established by me in the establishment of the Buddha-body; and as the Tathāgata's body is incorruptible,[1] just so he regards the nature of his own body. He being acquainted with the nature of the incorruptible, regards the bodies of all as of the same character.'"

And as it is said in the *Vīradatta-paripṛcchā*: "To wit: this body grows by regular stages and decays by regular stages, an upheaping of infinitesimal atoms, hollow inside, flexible, distilling through the nine crevices and the hair-holes, as an anthill in which serpents dwell, like the ape of Ajātaśatru,[2] treacherous to his friends, like a bad friend naturally false, like a clot of foam naturally weak, like a bubble of water arising, bursting, melting, naturally deceitful like a mirage, like a plantain tree sapless when it is broken,[3] unreal by

[1] Reading, with the MS.: °कायो ऽना°.

[2] So Tib.; a legend not identified.

[3] Tib. bśig-na as if भज्य°.

nature like illusion, imperious like a king, seeking opportunities like an enemy, like a thief not to be trusted, like an executioner void of feeling, eager for mischief like a foe, like a murderer attacking the life of wisdom, [231] without personality like an empty village, like a potter's vessel lasting until it breaks, like a bag full of all sorts of dirt, running with impurity like a dish of malt, . . . like a wound not able to endure a touch, piercing like a thorn, like an old house to be propped up by repairs, like an old boat to be patched up, like a jar of unburnt clay that needs careful keeping, . . . ever unstable like a tree on a river-bank, like the stream of a great river ending in the ocean of death, like a great house full of all unhappiness, like a poor-house for the destitute not fenced about, open to bribes like a jailor, . . . like a young child always to be watched."

Again he says: "He who is proud of beauty, and thinks much of this body, this heap of impurities, he is seen to be foolish of wit: he goes carrying a pot of excrement all unknowing. His nose carries a sort of pus, he always wears a stinking garment, there is gum like worms in the eyes of a man; what passion can be felt for this, or what pride?

"As a child takes a live coal and thinks, Let it be rubbed and it will grow bright; but it goes out instead of growing bright, since the child's idea is wrong: so when a clean-minded man thinks he will cleanse this body, though well perfumed and sprinkled with a hundred sacred waters, it is destroyed, impure from the power of death.

"[232] Thus comes dissolution. The Bodhisatva must regard the body as just running from the nine apertures. He must regard the body as a dwelling-place for eighty thousand broods of worms. . . . The Bodhisatva must regard the body as the food of others, of wolves, jackals, horses, flesh-eating demons; as an excellent machine, a collection of tools fastened together by bones and sinews; as not independent, but composed of food and drink." That is the substance of the matter which is developed in that book.[1]

Feeling is a subject of intent contemplation, just as it is

[1] Reading क्षयः : and giving this phrase to line 5.

said in the holy *Ratnacūḍa Sūtra*: "Here, young sir, the Bodhisatva, using the intent contemplation which realises the nature of feeling, conceives great compassion for beings who are attached to the pleasures of feeling. Thus he schools himself: That is happiness where is no feeling; and so he develops the intent meditation upon feelings in order to annul the feelings of all creatures; and he girds up his loins for the restraint of their feelings. For himself he does not aim at the destruction of feelings. Whatever feeling he has, it is permeated with great compassion. When he feels a pleasant feeling, he conceives great pity for all beings who indulge passion, and rejects all inclination to passion in himself. When he has an unpleasant feeling he conceives great pity for all beings who indulge hatred, and rejects all inclination to hatred in himself. When his feeling is neither pleasant nor unpleasant, he conceives great pity for all beings who are subject to delusion, and rejects any inclination to delusion in himself. In pleasant feeling he is not gratified; he puts gratification away from him. In unpleasant feeling he is not displeased; [233] he puts displeasure away from him. In indifferent feeling he is not a prey to ignorance; he puts ignorance away from him. Whatever feeling he has, he understands that it is impermanent. If it be unpleasant feeling, he knows it is not himself. In pleasant feeling he knows it is impermanent; in unpleasant feeling he knows that it is a thorn; in feelings indifferent he is calm. Thus what is pleasant is impermanent, what is painful is as pleasant, what is indifferent is unsubstantial," and so forth.

And in the holy *Akshayamati Sūtra* it is said: "Touched by painful feeling, he conceives great pity for all beings who are in any of the misfortunes of sin. . . . Thus moreover feeling is infatuation, feeling is acquisition, feeling is attachment, feeling is obtaining, feeling is error, feeling is wrong imagination," and so forth.

In the *Dharmasaṅgīti Sūtra* also it is said: "Sensation has been defined as experience; but by whom is that sensation felt? There is no experience other than sensation. Thus the intelligence and memory must be applied to sensation. As wisdom, so this sensation is calm, pure, bright."

That briefly is the intent contemplation of feeling.

But the intent contemplation of thought is as set forth in the holy *Ratnacūḍa*. "Thus he inquires into his thought. But what thought? Thought is glad or sorry or deluded. What about past, present, or future? Now what is past [234] is exhausted; what is future is not yet come; the present cannot stand still. Thought, Kāśyapa, is to be found inside, not outside, not between the two. Thought, Kāśyapa, is formless, unseen, not solid, unknowable, unstable, homeless. Thought, Kāśyapa, was never seen by any of the Buddhas. They do not see it, they will not see it; and what has never been seen by the Buddhas, what they do not see and will never see, what kind of a process can that have, unless things exist by a false conception? Thought, Kāśyapa, is like illusion, and by forming what is not comprehends all sorts of events. . . . Thought, Kāśyapa, is like the stream of a river, unsettled, breaking and dissolving as soon as it is produced. Thought, Kāśyapa, is like the light of a lamp, and is due to causes and secondary causes. Thought, Kāśyapa, is like lightning, cut off in a moment and not abiding. Thought, Kāśyapa, is like space, disturbed by any chance passions. . . . Thought, Kāśyapa, is like the bad friend because it produces all miseries. . . . Thought, Kāśyapa, is like a fish-hook, having the look of pleasantness[1] in unpleasantness. So it is like a blue-bottle fly, because it has the look of purity in impurity. Thought, Kāśyapa, is like an enemy, because it causes many tortures. Thought, Kāśyapa, is like a strength-sucking goblin, because it always searches for a weak point. It is also like a thief, because it steals all the root of good. Thought, Kāśyapa, delights in form like a fly's eye. Thought, Kāśyapa, delights in sound like a battle-drum. Thought, Kāśyapa, delights in smell like a pig in the dirt. Thought, Kāśyapa, delights in taste like a maid that enjoys the leavings of food.[2]

[1] *i.e.* the bait looks pleasant to the fish.

[2] Reading °भक्त° in 234a; Tib. *zas-kyi lhag-ma*, 246, b. 6.

Thought, Kāśyapa, delights in touch, like a fly in a dish of oil. And thought, Kāśyapa, being sought all around is not found: what is not found is not gotten; what is not gotten, is not past, present, or future; what is not past, present, or future is beyond the three paths (heaven, earth, and the lower regions); what is beyond the three paths neither is nor is not," and so forth.

[235] Again, it is said in the holy *Ratnacūḍa Sūtra*. "Examining thought he does not see it as internal, he sees it not outside him, nor in the conformations, nor in the elements, nor in the organs of sense. Not seeing thought, he follows the course of thought, asking, 'Whence does thought arise?' He thinks, 'When there is an object thought arises. Then what else can be its object? Thus the object is the thought. Only if the object is different the thought is different; then there will be a double thought. So the object is the thought. Then how does thought see thought? Thought does not see thought. As the same sword-blade cannot cut the same sword-blade, as the same fingertip cannot touch the same fingertip, so that the same thought cannot see the same thought. . . . Moreover, young sir, thought moves to and fro, never abiding, like a monkey or like the wind . . . it goes far away, bodiless, lightly turning, sensual, moving amid the six objects of sense, linked to one thing after another; such is thought: its stability, its intentness, its immobility, its being fixed upon tranquillity, its concentration, this is what is called the stability of thought." [1]

[236] Again, it is said in the holy Akshayamati *Sūtra*: "I must make effort towards edification. The real nature of thought must not be lost sight of. What nature? and what edification? Thought is like illusion, such is the nature of thought; and by edification I mean renouncing all one's possessions and directing this renunciation towards the purification of the fields of all Buddhas."

Now the intent contemplation of the elements of Existence. [2]

As it is said in the same place: "The Bodhisatva who considers the elements as elements, dwelling upon them, does

[1] So Tib. gnas-pa. [2] Dharma.

not see any elements from which a Buddha's element cannot come, or wisdom, or the path, or escape. He knowing that all the elements are escape,[1] attains to the calm of great pity unhindered. As to all elements and all passions, he takes the notion that they are not genuine. These elements are without passion, passion' they have none. Why so? There is no heaping up of passions, they are not accumulated, there is no natural lust, hate, or delusion in them. From the perception of these very passions comes wisdom. What passions are naturally, that wisdom is naturally. Such is the intent contemplation of the elements."

It is also said in the holy *Ratnacūḍa*: "Now, young sir, when the Bodhisatva contemplates the elements and dwells upon them, thus he thinks: 'Nothing but the elements arises when they arise; when they are checked only the elements are checked. But in them there is no substance,[2] there is no being, or living thing, or creature, or human being, or man, or person, or member of mankind, who is born or grows old or comes to birth or arises. That is the condition of the elements. If they are brought about, they arise; but if they are not brought about, they do not arise. Whatever kind they are when brought about, [237] of that kind they arise, good or bad or indifferent. There is none that can bring the elements about, nor can the elements arise at all without cause."

In the same place he says: "Even when he considers the elements that have very little profundity [3] he never loses remembrance of the thought of omniscient wisdom."

Again, in the holy *Lalitavistara Sūtra*: "The aggregations are impermanent, unstable, naturally brittle like an unbaked pot, like a borrowed article, like a city built in the dust, lasting for a time only. By nature those conditions are subject to destruction, plaster washed away by the rainy season, like sand on a river's bank, dependent on secondary causes, naturally weak. They are like the flame of a lamp, their nature is to be destroyed as soon as they arise, unstable as the wind, sapless and weak like a clot of foam. [238] The aggregations are

[1] So Tib. [2] Read °भावो वा with Tib. in line 15. [3] So Tib.

without energy and void, like the stem of a plaintain tree, when one considers, like illusion, confusing the thought, like an empty fist used to coax a child. Everything that belongs to the aggregations is concerned with primary and secondary causes; the generation of fools knows not that it is due to the interlinked chain of causation. As the grass rope arises from muñja-grass by twisting, or the well-buckets are turned by a wheel, but there is no turning in them one by one; so the turning of all the components of existence is dependent upon the combination with each other, the turning is not in each of them from before, behind, or within. As the sprout springs from the seed and yet the sprout is not the same as the seed, not other than that and not that: so their nature is not to be destroyed and not eternal. [239] The aggregations are caused by ignorance, and they do not really exist. They are the same as ignorance, they are naturally empty and without energy. From the seal one sees the impression, and no transference of the impression is perceived, the impression is not in the seal and yet the impression comes from nowhere else: so the aggregations are not permanent nor are they destroyed. Visual knowledge is produced from form by reason of the eye, but not in the eye is that which comes from form, nor is the image of the form in the eye. These conditions are unsubstantial, impure; yet they are imagined as being substantial and pure: but the visual knowledge which is false and mistaken is born from that. The wise man sees the arising and decay of cognition, its arising and going away; the ascetic sees that it is gone nowhere, not present, void, like illusion. [240] Like the lower and upper kindling, the combination of these with the hands forming a triad, thus from this cause fire is produced; being produced and having done its task it is quickly destroyed. Then a wise man inquires whence it is come or whither it goes, he looks in every part or direction, but neither the going nor the coming is perceived. The causes of action are the conformations, the organs and objects of sense, the elements, thirst, ignorance; because of the conglomeration arises the being, and this is not perceived as really existing. Dependent on throat, lip, palate, tongue, the syllables are changed and uttered; but they are not in the throat or made by the palate, but they are not perceived in every one of these. This arises by the power of voice, mind, and intelligence in combination; mind and voice are invisible, are not perceived without or within. Wise men perceive the arising and the dying away of voice, sound, noise, or echo, so transient and empty; all voice is like an echo. [241] As string and wood and hand form a triad, and the sound that arises therefrom comes by the flute or lute or other instrument: then a wise man inquires whence that has come and whither it goes; he looks in every direction, but the coming and going of the sound is not perceived. So all the aggregations come about by primary and secondary causes; but the ascetic by perceiving their nature sees that the aggregations are void and without energy. The elements of the aggregations and the objects of sense are void within and void without, creatures separate and homeless, things whose nature is like air."

It is said in the *Lokanāthavyākaraṇa*: "Void are the conditions and nameless: why do you ask about name? Emptiness: nowhere are gods or nāgas or rākshasas. Men or no men, all are known as that. By name is namehood, empty; in name there is no name. Nameless are all the conditions, but illuminated by name; but what is the nature of name has been neither seen nor heard, is neither arisen nor disappeared. Of what do you ask the name? Name is a matter of habit, declarations are made by name. This one is Ratnacitra by name; that other man is Ratnottama."

CHAPTER XIV

SELF-PURIFICATION

[242] THE subjects of intent meditation have been described. Thus he whose thought is fit for religious meditation,[1] able with perfect wisdom to do away the ocean of pain for the rest of the world in the ten districts, should realize the emptiness of all elements of being so as to treat the power of all the conditions past, present, and future under the sky. Thus the emptiness of all individuality is made clear; and by cutting them off by the root, passions do not arise.

As it is said in the holy *Tathāgata-guhya Sūtra*: " Just as when a tree is cut at the root, Śāntamati, all the twigs and leaves wither away; so, Śāntamati, all passions are extinguished by destroying the heresy of individual existence."

The praises of realizing the Void are infinite.

As in the *Candrapradīpa Sūtra*: " He that does not reject the teaching of the Sugatas, verily that hero does not fall into the power of women. [243] He gets delight in the salvation of the Sugatas who knows that the very nature of the conditions is peace.[2] He will ere long be here a lord of men, he will be a healing physician, giver of happiness, he utterly draws out the arrow from those in pain, who knows in tranquillity the very nature of the conditions. He by the power of tranquillity is a man towering among men. He buffeted with sticks and clods is not angry, torn limb from limb he is not disturbed, who knows that the very nature of the conditions is peace. He will not fall into the ways of woe, he will always bear the marks and tokens of beauty.[3] His higher knowledge will be

[1] The rest of the sentence is very obscure, and it is not in the Tib.

[2] So Tib. quite clearly.

[3] Perhaps the marks of a future Buddha.

conspicuous always; he shall stand in the presence of the Sugatas, he is a hero."

And in the *Bhagavatī* it is said: "Moreover, Sāriputra, the Bodhisatva, the Great Being, who wishes to develop the Buddha-body, [244] and to acquire the 32 marks of the great man and the 80 subsidiary marks, and the remembrance of former births in every birth, and the continuance of the thought of enlightenment, and the persistence in the conduct of a Bodhisatva, who wishes to avoid all bad friends and companions, to give pleasure to all Buddhas and Bodhisatvas and good friends, to subdue all Māras and deities that belong to Māra's troop, to clear away all mental blindness, to get rid of the obstacle caused by phenomena,[1] must learn the perfection of wisdom. Moreover, Śāriputra, the Bodhisatva, the Great Being, must learn this perfection by the wish, 'May those ten regions praise me in which the Blessed Buddhas appear.' Moreover, Śāriputra, the Bodhisatva, the Great Being, absorbed in one thought, who in the eastern region desires to pass beyond the elements of the world, which are like the sands of the river Ganges for multitude, . . . and so with all ten regions, he must learn the perfection of wisdom." That is the substance of it.

On this topic, it is described in the *Pitṛputrasamāgama* how all phenomena are without substance, but it is not denied that they are connected with the fruit of action; that they have no properties of their own, but it is not denied that they are connected with the world of appearance.

"This man, great King, is composed of six elements, has six contacts with the world of sense,[2] eighteen processes of mind. When I say, 'The man is composed of six elements,' what is the meaning of that?[3] There are six elements: Earth, water, fire, air, space, intelligence; these, great King, are the six elements." And so on to "These six contacts with

[1] Compare Dh.S. cxv., where this class is called *jñeya*.

[2] Dh.S. 33.

[3] This seems to be the general sense, according to Tib., which omits *na khalu punar ekad yuktam* altogether. The text is corrupt.

the world of sense. What six? The eye is a contact with objects for the showing of forms. The ear, for hearing of sounds. The nose, for the perceiving of smells. The tongue, for distinguishing tastes. The body, for feeling sensations. The mind, for distinguishing things. These, great King, are the six contacts with the world of sense. . . . And the eighteen processes of the mind: what are these? Here when the man has seen forms with the eye, he proceeds to consider all connected with the question of pleasure or displeasure. So with hearing and voice, etc. Thus with each of the six senses, [245] by distinction of three cases, pleasure, displeasure, and indifference, we get eighteen processes of the mind. . . . And what, great King, is the internal element of earth? Whatever in the body is perceived as hard or solid. But what is that? Hair and down, nails, teeth, and so forth. That is called the internal element of earth. And what, great King, is the element of earth outside? Whatever outside is perceived as hard or solid, that is the element of earth outside. Now, great King, when the element of earth is found within, it does not come from anywhere, when it is checked it is not stored up anywhere. There comes a time when a woman thinks, concerning herself, 'I am a woman'; having thought this concerning herself, she sees a man outside her, and thinks, 'This is a man'; having thus thought she falls in love with the man, and desires union with the man outside herself. The man also thinks, concerning himself, 'I am a man,' and so as before. By their desire for union the union takes place: because of the union, an embryo is conceived. Here, great King, neither the thought nor the thinker exists. In the woman is no woman, in the man is no man; thus the thought is produced without being or truly existing, and the thought does not exist in itself.[1] As the thought, so the union, and so the embryo, does not exist by any independent being. And if anything does not exist from independent being how shall it produce hardness? So thus, great King, having understood the thought one must regard the hardness. Now that hard-

[1] Tib. read °पः for °पा.

ness when it arises does not come from anywhere, and being checked is not stored up anywhere. There comes a time, great King, when this body finds the end of its course in the cemetery. Then that hardness putrifying and being checked does not go to the east, nor to the south, nor the west, nor the north, nor up, nor down, nor to an intermediate point. So, great King, must be understood the internal element of earth. [246] There comes a time, great King, when in a part of the world in space stands Brahma's palace made of precious stones. Its hardness, great King, does not come from anywhere. The spheres and the great spheres [1] stand firm, strong, solid, adamant; even their hardness when it arises does not come from anywhere. Mountains like Meru king of mountains, Yugandhara, Nimindhara, Īśādhāra, stand as long as the hills may last: all the universe of Trisāhasramahāsāhasra stands fast, in height 84 thousand leagues, and in the midst stands the great earth, 68 hundred thousand leagues; even that hardness, great King, when it comes does not come from anywhere.[2] There is a time, great King, when this world comes together. Then this mighty earth is burnt by fire or is deluged with water or scattered by wind. As it is burnt by fire not even soot is produced, just as when ghee or oil is burnt by fire no soot nor ashes is produced; so from this universe of Trisāhasramahāsāhasra burning with fire not even a residue of soot or ashes is produced; and as when salt is dissolved in water, or when birds are scattered by a hurricane, not a bit of the earth remains. So we are told. Here, great King, the arising of the element of earth is void, and its destruction is void, and when the element arises its nature is void. So, sir, the element of earth is not recognized as being this element except by convention; and this conventional expression is not woman and is not man. Even so, sir, this must be regarded as it really is by exact knowledge. Now what is this element of water? The water that is in the body of each separate person; that which consists in water, the watery nature, is

[1] See Childers, s.v. *cakkavālaṃ*.

[2] The MS. has āgacchan, and *na* must obviously have dropped out of the text.

grease; that which consists in grease, the greasy nature, is the liquidity accepted and received. But what is this? tears, sweat, snot, [247] oil, serum, marrow, fat, bile, spittle, pus, blood, milk, piss, and so forth, all this is the internal element of water. . . . A time comes, great King, when on seeking a thing beloved the tears flow; or when one is smitten with pain, or by the action of heat, the tears flow; or the eyes water in the wind; . . . this watery element does not come from anywhere. A time comes, great King, when the internal watery element is dried up; when it dries up and ceases it does not go anywhere. . . . Verily when the world comes into being two and thirty palls of cloud come up all round containing everything; they overshadow the universe of Trisāhasramahāsāhasra. From these the god Īśādhāra rains for a space of five intermediate ages, so for five ages rains the god Gajaprameha, for five ages Acchinnadhāra, for five ages Sthūlabinduka. After this the great earth extends up to Brahmaloka covered with water. But this element of water, sir, so vast, arising, does not come from anywhere. There comes a time, sir, when this world arises; and as the world arises there is the appearance of a second sun, and from the appearance of this second sun lakes, ponds, and rivulets are dried up. So with a third sun the great lakes and rivers dry up. When a fourth sun appears, the great lake Anavatapta is utterly dried up. By the appearance of the fourth sun the water of the ocean is dried up and exhausted to the depth of a league; so two leagues, three, four, five, ten, twenty, thirty, forty, fifty leagues, until 40,000 leagues are left . . . until a depth of two palm trees is left, till it is neck-deep, till the water is of the depth of a cow's hoofprint. There comes a time, sir, when there are only scattered spots of water left in the great ocean. . . . There comes a time, sir, when not a drop of water is left in the ocean enough to wet the first joint of the finger. But all this watery element, sir, disappearing, does not go anywhere. . . . Verily, sir, the arising of this watery element is void, and its disappearing is void, and even when it is there, this watery element [248] is by nature void. So, sir, this watery element is not [1] perceived as such by nature except by way of convention: and this conventional expression is neither woman nor man, as before. . . . What is the internal element of fire? Whatever in this body is felt and received as fire, fiery, hot. But what is that? Whatever makes that body warm or hot; whatever causes it properly to digest what is eaten, drunk, chewed; excess of which causes feverishness. . . . What is fire outside the person? All without that is felt and received as fire, fiery, hot. But what is that? Whatever men seek for from things connected with fire-sticks or grass by means of powdered cowdung or cotton or similar fluff, which arising burns even a village or even a district . . . or even a continent, or a thicket of grass or a forest or firewood until it burns out, and so forth. In this case, sir, the internal fire arises, but it does not come from anywhere, and when it ceases it does not go anywhere into store. Thus without being it is, and having been it goes deprived of its nature. . . . So whatever in this body is air, airy, lightness, buoyancy. But what is that? These: rising and falling airs, wind in the side, back, or belly, knife-like, razor-like, piercing, needle-like, wind-swellings, spleen, breathings in and out, rheumatism, and so forth. Without the body there are winds in front, to the right, behind, to the left, with dust and without dust small and big. There comes a time, sir, when a great hurricane arises, [249] which blows down the highest trees, even walls and mountains; this done, unnoticed it is gone. And that which men excite with a corner of the robe, or the bellows, or a fan . . . This is called the outside air. And its arising is as before. . . . What is the internal element of space? Whatever within this body and in each several body entering and pervading of the nature of space that can be described as within it, not occupied or penetrated by skin, flesh, or blood. But what is this? What in the body is the aperture of the eye . . . the mouth, the door of the mouth, throat or gullet, by which one eats, into which it descends, through which what is eaten or drunk or consumed or swallowed oozes downwards; all that

[1] Reading °त्वेन नो° as p. 246[14].

is called the internal element of space. So without also: what is not occupied or penetrated by form, not surrounded, hollow and empty; that is meant by the element of space without the body. Comes a time, sir, when because of action the organs of sense appear and occupy the element of space; then the term 'internal element of space' is used. But it does not come from anywhere. There comes a time when all that bears form becomes space. And why is that? Because the element of space is indestructible, firm, immovable. Just as the region of Nirvāṇa is incomposite, so, sir, the element of space must be regarded as present everywhere. For in time a man, sir, might cause to be dug in some dry spot a well or a pond or a pit or pool, what think you, sir? Has the space come from anywhere? He said: 'No, Blessed One.' The Blessed One said: 'For instance, the man, sir, might fill up again that well or pool or what not, what think you, sir? has that space gone any whither?' He said: 'No, Blessed One. And why so?' [250] 'Because the element of space has nothing to do with going or coming, nor with manhood or womanhood.' The Blessed One said: 'So, sir, the space without is immovable, unchanging; and why so? The element of space is void by its nature, negative by its nature, it has nothing to do with manhood or womanhood. Thus it must be truly regarded by perfect wisdom. Now what is the element of Intelligence? Recognition of objective form dependent upon the organ of sight . . . So, sir, the recognition of any colour or shape is called the element of intelligence acted upon by the sense of eye. . . . So, sir, the perception of the six objects of sense through the six senses is called the element of intelligence. But verily, sir, that element of intelligence is not dependent upon the senses, not drawn from the objects, not placed between them, not within, not without, not between both. Verily, sir, that element of intelligence, having recognized a thing, ceases; when it rises it does not come from anywhere when it ceases it does not go anywhere. Its very arising is void, its disappearance is void; when arisen also, by its nature it is void. So, sir, the element of intelligence is void by its very nature ; it is not recognised except by convention. And this convention is neither man nor woman. Thus this must be truly regarded by perfect wisdom. Now, sir, what is the organ of sight ? The sensitive parts[1] of the four great elements ; that is to say, of the elements of earth, air, fire, and water. Thus the sensitive part of the earthy element is not[2] the organ of sight, the sensitive parts of the elements air, fire, water, are not the organ of sight. And why so ? Because the sensitive part of the earthy element is not the organ of any sense, nor has it arisen by any sense-perception. . . . The sensitive part of the airy element is not the organ of any sense or arisen by any sense-perception. And why so ? [251] These things are incapable of motion, perfect, like Nirvāṇa. Thus, sir, investigating each of these things one does not recognize the organ of sight except by convention. And why so ? Void is the sphere of the earthy element by its nature, . . . void is the sphere of the airy element by its nature. And when things are void by their own nature, what tranquillity[3] or agitation of them can there be ? And when there is neither tranquillity nor agitation of things, how will they see form ? Thus the organ of sight is utterly void by its very nature and that from the beginning is not perceived, and in the future is not perceived ; because it neither comes nor goes, its very position is not perceived since it is essentially negative. And what by its nature does not exist, that is neither male nor female. What self-consciousness can this bring ? And self-consciousness, sir, is the province of Māra, lack of self-consciousness is the province of Buddha. And why so ? Because things are all void of self-consciousness. . . . And what, sir, is the sense of hearing ? The sentient organ derived from the four great phenomena. . . . So, sir, all things are directed towards release, involved in the nature of things,[4] ending in

[1] See *Dh-Sṇi.*, pp. 173–4 (*Buddhist Psychology*, Mrs. Rhys Davids).

[2] Insert न as in the rest of the passage.

[3] Here *prasāda* (sphere) is used in another sense.

[4] The meaning is that they are all void ; but the exact sense of these compounds escapes me.

the airy element, powerless, incompetent, inexpressible, not to be expressed. When the senses are arrested, sir, these are called "matter." The sight is arrested in form, therefore the forms are called the matter of sight. So hearing is arrested in sounds, and so forth. When we say that the sight is arrested in form, we mean that there is a falling upon it or an arresting upon it. So the sight falls on forms in three ways: upon agreeable forms with the idea of agreeableness, upon repellent forms with the idea of repulsion, upon forms indifferent with observation. So the mind upon things, and so forth. These matters are called the province of the mind, for here the mind moves and ranges; therefore they are called the mind's province. When the mind, sir, moves pleasantly on forms not disagreeable, by that passion arises in it. When it moves with repulsion upon disagreeable forms, [252] by that hatred arises in it. Upon forms indifferent it moves bewildered; by that arises bewilderment in it. So with sounds and the rest a threefold idea arises as before. Here, sir, the senses are like illusion, material objects are such stuff as dreams are made of. Take an example, sir. A man asleep might in his sleep have to do with some young woman; awakened from sleep he might remember that young woman. What think you, sir; does that woman exist in the dream?' He said: 'No, Blessed One.' The Blessed One said: 'What think you, sir? Would that man be wise who would remember the young woman in his sleep or believe in the dalliance?' He said: 'No, Blessed One. And why so? Because the young woman in the dream does not exist at all nor is to be found; then how could there be any dealings with her, except in so far that he who believes in her existence really feels failure or fatigue?' The Blessed One said: 'Even so, sir, a foolish, untaught worldling when he sees agreeable forms believes in them, and believing in them is pleased, and being pleased feels passion, and feeling passion develops the action that springs from passion, threefold by body, fourfold by voice, threefold by mind; and that action, developed, from the very beginning is injured, hindered, distracted, changed, not going towards the east, not south nor west nor north, not up nor down, nor to the intermediate points, not here nor across, nor betwixt both. But when at life's end the time of death comes, when the vitality is checked by the exhaustion of one's allotted span, by the dwindling of the action that is his share, [253] the action becomes the object of the mind in its last consciousness as it disappears. As for instance when a man is awakened from sleep the idea occurs to his mind, This is a girl. So, sir, by the object a first consciousness belonging to rebirth arises from two causes, the last consciousness as its governing principle, and the action as its support: he is born either in hells or in the womb of beasts or in Yama's realm or in a demonic body, or amongst men or gods. And if this first conception belonging to the birth immediately after it has been destroyed, a new series of thoughts arises; where the experience of the ripening of the act is to be felt. There the arresting of the last consciousness is known as "rebirth," the manifesting of first consciousness is known as "arising." So, sir, nothing goes from our world to another, but rebirth and arising take place. So, sir, the last consciousness when it arises does not come from anywhere, when it ceases it does not go anywhere; action arising does not come from anywhere, ceasing it does not go anywhere; first consciousness too arising does not come from anywhere, ceasing does not go anywhere. And why so? Because it is naturally negative. The last consciousness is of itself void, action is of itself void, the first consciousness is of itself void, rebirth is of itself void, arising is of itself void. And the irresistibleness of action comes into play and the experience of ripening, and then is there no doer, no feeler, except by conventional name. [254] For example, sir, a sleeping man in a dream might fight with an enemy; the same awakening might remember him. Now what think you, sir? Does the enemy exist in the dream? or is there any fight with an enemy?' He said: 'No, Blessed One.' The Blessed One said: 'Then what think you, sir; would that be a wise man who should believe in the enemy in that dream? or in the fight with the enemy?' He said:

'No, Blessed One. And why so? In dreams an enemy does not exist at all, then how could there be a battle with him? unless in so far that he who should believe in it really would feel failure or fatigue.'. The Blessed One said: 'Just so, sir, a foolish, ignorant worldling when he sees with his eyes forms that are disagreeable [1] believes in them, and believing is repelled, and being repelled he is angry; angry he forms action born of sin, as before.[2] Another example, sir. Suppose a sleeping man, attacked in his dream by a demon and terrified falls into stupefaction; awakened he remembers this demon and this stupefaction, what think you, sir, does this demon exist in the dream, or this stupefaction? . . . Even so, sir, a foolish, ignorant worldling when he sees with his eye forms that ought to be despised believes in them, and believing is deluded, and deluded forms action born of delusion, as before. Another example, sir. Suppose a sleeping man should hear in a dream a young woman singing with a sweet voice and a sweet lute, and she should court him with that sweet song; and he on awakening should remember that song: what think you, sir, a wise man should not believe in the song of the girl singing in his dream?' He said: 'He should not, Blessed One.' The Blessed One said: 'And why so?' 'Because, Blessed One, that girl in the dream neither exists at all nor is perceived; then how could her song exist? except in so far that he [255] who believes in its reality would feel failure and fatigue.' The Blessed One said: 'Just so, sir, a foolish, ignorant worldling hearing with his ear sounds that are pleasing believes in them;'" and so on as before. So with smells, dividing always into three classes.[3] "'. . . Here, sir, the following must be my thought: Should I not thus be the eye of men and gods; a torch, a brilliant lamp; a bank, a ship, a quay; a prince, a chieftain, a guide, a merchant; I should run in front; delivered I should deliver, comforted I should comfort, emancipated I should emancipate. Sir, there has been in the past no limit to the sovereignty and

[1] °स्यास्यो° a misprint for °स्यस्यो°. [2] Reading °दु° for °गु°.

[3] Pleasant, unpleasant, indifferent.

dominion that I had. So, sir, the senses are all illusion, unsatisfied and unsatisfying, things are such stuff as dreams are made of, unsatisfying, causing dissatisfaction.'

"Here is a story of the emperor Anantayaśas, and it is told when he fell from heaven surrounded by all his royal attendants. As ghee, sir, or cream, or fresh butter, dropped upon hot sand, sinks in and does not stand firm; so, sir, King Anantayaśas sank and did not stand firm. Then King Priyaṃkara came up to King Anantayaśas as he sank, and thus he said: 'What declaration, sir, are we to give to the world? What is the last good word of King Anantayaśas?' He replied: 'You must say, King Anantayaśas, having been lord over the four continents, all his wishes fulfilled, possessed of the fruit of all trees out of season, having rid himself of all misfortunes, his desires fulfilled in all beings, amidst showers of perfume and gold, of fine gold and of all blessings, inhabiting the four great continents, sharing the seat of Śakra, but not freed from his excessive desire, always unsatisfied by his lusts, has perished. This is the declaration, sir, that you must give.' Having thus said, King Anantayaśas died. . . .

"[256] Therefore now, sir, I tell you, the nature of water in a mirage neither was nor is now nor shall be. So, sir, the nature of form, of feeling, of ideas, of the conformations, and of knowledge,[1] neither was nor is now nor shall be," and so forth.

Again it is said: "Thus much must be understood: to wit, the covering and the essence, the kernel and the husk. And that by the Blessed One has been fully seen, fully spoken, made clear, as being void. Therefore he is called all-knowing. As concerns the covering, the Tathāgata has seen this as being human experience; but the essence is inexpressible, not to be perceived or discerned, unexplained, unrevealed, . . . not active, . . . not gain and not no gain, not pleasure and not pain, not glory or its lack, not form and not no form," and so forth.

"There by the Conqueror for the sake of the world the covering was explained for people's good, that the world

[1] Reading °ज्ञानं.

might produce faith towards Sugata for happiness. Covering is dependent upon knowledge.[1] The man-lion told the crowds of men about the six states of existence; hell, animals, also pretas, asuras, men, maruts, low families and high families, rich families and also poor families," and so forth.

[257] And again it is said: "What is that thing which was prophesied by the Blessed One for the supreme wisdom? Is it form or feeling or idea or conformations or consciousness that the Blessed One declared in his supreme wisdom?

"This thought came to them: It is not form, . . . not consciousness that the Blessed One prophesied in his supreme wisdom. And why so? Neither form nor wisdom comes into being. Thus how can that which does not come into being know that which does not come into being?" (And so on to "consciousness"). ". . . Then since nothing can be perceived, who is Buddha, what is wisdom, who is Bodhisatva, what is prophecy? Void is form by its nature" (and so on to "consciousness"). ". . . All this is just convention, just names, just compact, just covering, just agreement. Thus wise men should not believe in it," and so forth.

In the same book again gods of the Fifth Heaven[2] said: "As we, O Blessed One, understand the meaning of what the Blessed One says, all things are the end of being, the infinite and the unveiled end, the independent end, and so forth.[3] All things are wisdom, Blessed One; they must be recognised as without essential nature, even the five mortal sins[4] are wisdom. And why so? Wisdom has no essential character, nor have the five mortal sins; that is why it is said, the five mortal sins are wisdom. Therefore those are laughed at who desire to be annihilated. And why so? If any one should fall into the circuit of existence, he is seeking for nirvāṇa."

Again it is said: "The culminating point of being, Blessed

[1] I do not understand this line, which is lacking in Tib.

[2] See Childers, 285a. They are dependent on themselves for happiness. I have altered the punctuation.

[3] That is, the Void.

[4] See Childers, 327.

One, is that which is said by the self-sufficing gods. Here we do not perceive even being, much less do we perceive an end. And why so? Whoever, Blessed One, perceives being, he also perceives an end of being, and he moves in duality." [1]

And in the same place the Master is praised by Sahāmpati Brahma. "As a man sleeps overcome with hunger, and dreams that he is satisfied with partaking of a hundred choice viands; yet there is no hunger, no viand, no being to dream, and all things are like a dream. [258] A man utters an agreeable voice in reading; he is pleasing to his hearers, and there is no passage of the voice, there is no voice, you do not apprehend it with pleasure, there is no doubt of it. As one hears the lovely sound of a lute, like honey, and there is really no sound: so a wise and understanding person, regarding the conformations, does not perceive any being there in fact. . . . As a man in this world hearing the sound of a conch reflects, and knowing whence it comes, does not regard the emptiness as having a nature of its own; so you, King of men, regard all things. As a man in this world analyses food which is agreeable, good, but without nature of its own, and as is the flavour so are those parts, so its nature; so you, great seer, regard all things. As in this world a man seeing a rainbow examines it bit by bit, as void, without qualities, and regards those parts as void like the rainbow; so you, great sage, regard all things. As one analyses a great city, and perceives a city according to its nature not its name, as he sees that all its parts are void, so you, great King, regard all things. As a man is pleased and delighted with a drum, and knows that the sounds are void, as he regards the nature of them one by one, so you, great sage, regard all things. [259] If one should strike that drum, it does not feel either repulsion or affection, as if the drum should reflect upon the constituent parts of the process, so you, great King, regard all things. If one should strike his drum, the sound does not think, 'I give pleasure to the people,' as if the sound should reflect upon the elements of that sound; so you,

[1] That is, he is perplexed by believing in being and in annihilation; we believe in neither, and so we are calm.

great King, regard all things. If one should strike the drum, that sound is not made up of parts, nor is it self-dependent, as if the sound should regard the elements of that sound; so you, great sage, regard all things."

And again it is said: "The excellent meditation[1] on Mercy has been preached by our Leader as having all creatures for its object; and when he has examined beings he clearly sees the world to be void of beings. In this the Best of Men is without blemish, his mind is without doubt; therefore let us worship thee the worshipful Sugata, thy mind perfect. Although you do not see pain and unhappiness, Sugata, scattered to the ten quarters, [260] yet you preach mercy amongst all beings, you the god above all gods. Thus, O conquering Bull, understanding the doctrine of the Conqueror in truth, therefore let us worship thee the worshipful chief and best of men. Śakyamuni gives no pain to beings, who takes their pain away.[2] All creatures are delighted and pleased, and their distresses are taken from them. So understanding the Buddha's doctrine, his ineffable doctrine, and having honoured thee, best of men, let us enjoy the fruit attained. A body is not obtained by the sage free from the body when he seeks it;[3] yet you have preached memory, and your memory has not been stolen away. It is said by the Sugata, Cultivate[4] those meditations which refer to the body. Having thus understood the Buddha's doctrine, excellent worship is done to the Protector. You should cultivate calm, the path of spiritual insight, for the suppression of pains. [261] O Blessed One, those impurities connected with desire are appeased, by which the earth is tormented, nevertheless that calm also, that spiritual insight and those impurities, all are void, O sage. Therefore let the gods in every place worship thee, the King, beyond all doubt," and so forth.

[1] See Childers, s.v. bhāvanā.

[2] Tib. seems to mean: "O Ś., you do not see the existence of beings or of pain, but you are able to take away their distress."

[3] Reading मार्गितः.

[4] Reading भावयथिमाः

Again it is said: "Void is the eye by its nature: and the thing whose nature does not exist, that is not material; what is not material that has no real existence; that which has no real existence, that does not arise nor cease. . . . That which in three ways is not perceived, that is not eye, not sense: how should its use be understood? as an empty fist it is delusive; . . . only in name not in fact it is perceived as empty, not a fist. So eye and sense are empty, like the fist it is delusive, not existing, inane; deceitful tricky things, fool's prattle, stupid infatuation; . . . only a name."

Again in the same place: "You, great hero, have shown that the great flood of depravities is like a shower of rain in a dream; and the destruction of depravities has been shown to all the intelligent to be like a head cleft in a dream; therefore honour be to thee, the all knowing."

In the same place, the Blessed One, questioned by Druma, King of the fairies, said to him: "When you say I do not understand void and prophecy, if there were anything not void the Conqueror could not give any prophecy of that. Why? Thus: It would be fixed in its own nature; it would be firm and unchangeable. It has no growth, no dwindling, no act, no cause. As the image that is seen in a bright mirror, in essence void: [262] so, Druma, understand these things; if reality is without change, you are perplexed about worship; you analyse, and having looked at the worship analytically, you ask what parts of it are unchangeable.

"And in that you do not understand inactivity and activity as I explained them. But consider how the waggon is put together part by part, and yet there is activity in it. And I have described action, yet no doer is to be found in the ten regions. As by the friction of the wind the blazing of a tree blazes up,[1] and neither maruts nor tree thinks, 'I produce the fire,' nevertheless there is the fire,[2] so are the doers of action. And when you say there is no heaping up of merit, and assemblage of good doings; be instructed in that also and hear the truth of the matter. As you say the measure of man's life is a

[1] Reading निर्वे°.

[2] So Tib.

hundred years in living, and there is no heaping up of years, this heaping up is like that."

And in the *Bhagavatī* it is said: " 'But, reverend Subhūti, when a thing arises is it existent or not existent?' Subhūti replied: 'Reverend Śāriputra, I would not wish to speak of a thing arisen as either existent or not existent.' "

[263] And in the *Dharmasaṅgīti* also it is said: " 'The true nature of things is a way of describing the void. And that void condition neither arises nor ceases.' He said: 'If things are thus said to be void by the Blessed One, then all things will neither arise nor cease. The Bodhisatva Nirārambha said: 'Even so, young sir, as you fully perceive, all things neither arise nor cease.' He said: 'When it was said by the Blessed One: Composite things arise and cease, what is the meaning of this utterance of the Tathāgata?' He said: 'The belief of the whole world, young sir, is convinced of arising and ceasing. Then the Tathāgata in his great compassion to keep men free from fear, taking his stand upon experience, said that things arise and cease; but in this he did not mean the existence or destruction of anything.' "

Again in the same place it is said: "Thus, Blessed One, the eye does not make contact with the forms of sight, nor the ear with sounds, because the mind does not make contact with mental objects. That is the fact. Then why does the eye not make contact with forms? Because there is no link between them; for the eye is not connected with a form, . . . the mind is not connected with mental objects, and where there is no connexion there is no contact. When there is only one isolated thing there can be no contact; and all things, Blessed One, are isolated, they do not know or discern one another, they do not form or fashion one another, they do not spring up or influence each other, they do not dwindle or grow, they are not affected or altered, do not pass into each other or vanish away; they do not belong to any one nor is any one theirs; these things, Blessed One, do not feel agitation or passion nor are purified. Thus, Blessed One, I know, thus I understand. And when I say, Blessed One, that I know and I understand, that means only a modification of the organs of sense;[1] but they do not think, This is a modification of us. He that knows this is not in contradiction with any one; and no-contradiction is characteristic of an ascetic. Thus from the seeing of things comes the vision of the Buddha, [264] from the Buddha's vision comes the vision of all things, from the vision of all things comes the vision of the primary and secondary causes, from this comes the vision of the void, and to see the void is not to see; not to see all things, Blessed One, is to see all things, which is the true seeing."[2]

Experience[3] has no foundation. How is it supported, how not supported? Like taking for a man a position that does not exist. And for one who believes in the void, how could there really be a position by reason of which that illusion which is a man could come into existence? Thus all things are without root, because really no root exists.

Thus it is said in the holy *Vimalakīrtinirdeśa:* "'What root is there of a non-existent assumption?' He said: 'The root is a false idea.' He said: 'What is the root of the false idea?' 'The root is not relying upon anything.' He said: 'What is the root of this?' He said: 'This not-relying, Mañjuśrī, has no root at all. So all things are supported on roots that have no support.'"

In short, this perfection of wisdom must be cultivated by him who desires purity of thought; this done, he must be clever at fighting passion, the enemy; he must not play the hero in a dwelling-house.

As it is said in the holy *Dharmasaṅgīti Sūtra:* "One who believes in the void is not attracted by worldly things, because they are unsupported. He is not delighted by gain, he is not cast down by not gaining. Glory does not dazzle him, lack of glory does not make him ashamed. Scorn does not make him hide, praise does not win him; pleasure delights him not, pain does not trouble him. He that so is not attracted by the

[1] āyatana.

[2] So Tib. *dharmadarśanād Buddhadarśanaṃ, Buddhadarśanāt,* etc.

[3] *saṃvṛti,* "the covering," p. 236 above.

things of the world, he is said to know the void. So one who believes in the void has no likes or dislikes; he knows that to be only void which he might like, and regards it as only void. He that likes or dislikes anything does not know the void, and he who makes quarrel or dispute or debate with any one does not know this to be only void nor so regards it," and so forth.

That in brief is the Cleansing of Thought.

[265] "In this way there is the highest purification when there is the vision of things. Here when one is stained with the five depravities,[1] or when the good friend is disheartened, how, in short, must one make effort so as to purify the thought quickly? By putting away self-esteem and contempt for others; the root of both those two is the view that there is really a self, that there are beings, and this view is easily abandoned by this exercise." Thus respect for others and contempt for self are cultivated.

"If there is a being, if there are the conformations, the uniformity is certain; for how could there be for a given being the quality of being self or other, which involves a contradiction? Again, grant that this conception be without foundation: living creatures cherish this from immemorial habit of imagination, and habit accomplishes the most difficult things. Since in these two cases all depends on habit, why should one abandon the respect of others which produces happiness, and desire something else for one's happiness? The causes of honour have been declared to be a jewel,[2] but there is no pleasure to me from honour connected with other people's misfortune in this world. Therefore in life let the Bodhisatva do the opposite to the conduct of one cruel and envious-minded, full of self-love. In such a man the high esteem of self, fostered by praise and blame and the like, grows by the power of hell as hell-fire grows fostered by the demons.

[266] "One does not think of the sound, It praises me, because it is without thought; that which troubles my spirit is to think, Another is pleased with me. If I am happy in his satisfaction,[3]

[1] Kleśa°, drshṭi°, sattva°, āyuh°, kalpa°: Dh. Sgr. 91.

[2] Tib. read °त्सिकय°.

[3] Join सामान्येन.

that happiness ought to be always and generally existent; if his happiness is indifferent to me, what matters it to me that he is pleased? What care I for another's pleasure, whether it be pleasure in me or in some one else? I have not the smallest bodily pleasure when another is pleased with me. Knowing that things are so, we must renounce the unfounded illusion; we must recognise that praise, blame, and honour have no effect. No virtue, no long life, no health, no strength comes from homage and salutations, just as the gesticulations of others do not affect him that they mock. Gaining or not gaining are not affected according as one is pleased or despondent. Therefore let me reject these fruitless agitations and have a mind like a rock.

"By rejecting social relations, purity of mind is quickly produced." On this point we have also the following thoughts.

"We recognize a person because an image has been frequently formed in the mind; from this comes affection, from this comes also repulsion. He that feels affection and repulsion has not eschewed sin; then all sorts of calumnies, and jealousy with envy, [267] love of gain and so forth, pride, such things find a place. Therefore with all diligence the sage should put away from him all social relations. Because of the resemblance, 'that' although different is regarded as 'the same,' for example the water of a river, but it is a mistake; consequently I must take my stand on the truth. That likeness is insubstantial and it will produce suffering; I and that and all else will ere long be no more."

CHAPTER XV

PURITY IN ENJOYMENT AND RELIGIOUS ACTION

NEXT after self-purification comes Purity in use and enjoyment due to the absence of hoarding; here it is explained apart. "How purely to enjoy discern, till all thy life is fully pure." [1]

As it is said in the holy *Ugraparipṛcchā*: "In this world, householder, the house-owning Bodhisatva seeks his enjoyments rightly and not wrongly, fairly not unfairly; he is right-living not wrong-living."

And it is said in the holy *Ratnamegha*: "When the Bodhisatva sees a generous giver, he does not pose. How does he not pose? He does not lift and set down his feet smoothly and daintily, but looks a yoke's length before him, [268] with a confident air, without swerving his regard. It is thus he avoids playing pretence in action. How does he avoid pretence in speech? The Bodhisatva does not for gain's sake and because of gain speak delicately and softly and pleasantly, does not utter compliant speeches. . . . How does he avoid pretence in thought? If a Bodhisatva, when pressed by a giver or a benefactor to take a gift, manifests moderation in his speech while cherishing in his heart covetousness, this is a fire within, young sir: moderation in speech and covetousness in the heart. Thus, young sir, the Bodhisatva does not get anything by hypocritical speech. . . . The Bodhisatva does not hint when he sees a giver or a generous man,[2] as 'I am worried about my robe, or my bowl, or medicine'; nor does he ask anything of that giver or generous man, or utter a word. Thus

[1] Kārika 21a.

[2] Correct text to दायकं दानपतिं वा. Probably वा should be added also in 267^{14}, 268^{9}.

the Bodhisatva does not get anything by hints. . . . When the Bodhisatva sees a generous giver, he does not say, 'Such and such a generous man gave me such a thing and I have done him such a service;' or 'he gave me this and that, thinking me to be pious, and out of compassion I accepted it, thinking him to be learned and without covetousness.' . . . This is a bodily wrong, I mean running to and fro for the sake of gain and because of gain, and it is evil conduct: a mental wrong is asking, [269] and a desire to injure in the presence of virtuous receivers of gifts. Thus the Bodhisatva gets nothing by improper requests. . . . In this world the Bodhisatva does not procure gain by false balance or false pretensions or broken trust or knavery. Thus the Bodhisatva gets nothing by wrong-doing. . . . The gains that belong to a shrine or the Law or the Order or those not given or not allowed, he seeks not nor makes his own. Thus the Bodhisatva gets nothing that is not pure. . . . What he receives he does not call 'mine,' does not treasure up nor hoard. From time to time he gives to ascetics and brahmins, from time to time he himself shares with parents, friends, courtiers, kinsmen, relatives, and as he partakes he is not inflamed by desire . not clinging to it, if he receives nothing he is not depressed, he is not annoyed, he does not allow his calm to cease in the presence of generous givers."

Then also this the Bodhisatva's Purity in respect of gain, like personal purity, would be for the good of others.

As it is said in the holy *Vimalakīrti-nirdeśa:* "Again, reverend Śāriputra, whoever enter this house, as soon as they have entered, no passions trouble them: this is the second miracle."

Again in the same place it is said: "Then from that food that whole company was satisfied, yet the food did not decrease; and all those Bodhisatvas and disciples, guardian deities of Śakra and Brahma, and others who ate that food [270] felt such a pleasure in the body as is the pleasure of the Bodhisatvas in the world named 'full of all pleasures'; from all their hair-holes such perfume was wafted, as is the perfume of the trees in the world that is scented with all perfumes."

And it is said again: "The Brethren, reverend Ānanda, who ate this food, if they have not attained the fixed determination,[1] they shall find it digested when they have attained it. With those creatures who had not yet developed the thought of enlightenment, when they shall find the thought of enlightenment developed it will be digested. They who have developed the thought of enlightenment, until they shall find themselves not without holy peace it shall not be digested." That is the substance of it.

Purification of religious action comes from behaviour pervaded by the Void [2] and by Pity.

For it is said in the holy *Gaganagañja Sūtra*: "He gives that gift, pure of the notion of I, pure of the notion of mine, pure of the notion of motive, of heresy, of reason, of kind,[3] of expecting profit, a gift pure in thought like the sky, . . . as the sky is infinite, so is the thought with which he gives; as the sky is outspread over all, so that gift is applied unto wisdom; as the sky is immaterial, so that gift is dependent upon no matter; as the sky is without feeling, so that gift is detached from all feeling; so it is without consciousness, not composite, with the characteristic of manifesting nothing; as the sky pervades all the Buddha's field, so that gift is pervaded with compassion for all creatures; . . as the sky is always transparent, so his gift is clear of the nature of thought; as the sky illuminates all creatures, so his gift gives life to all creatures; . . . as one created by supernatural power gives to another, so he is without imagination and without reflexion; without thought, mind, consciousness, not desiring anything; thus by the absence of duality, [271] his gift is clear of the natural marks of illusion. When he has this renunciation in giving, renunciation of the passions of all creatures by knowledge of wisdom, non-abandonment of all creatures by knowledge of expedients, so, young sir, the Bodhisatva becomes self-sacrificing in heart, and his gifts are like the sky."

[1] *niyāma*: when a bhikshu has attained a state of will from which there is no backsliding: certitude of nirvāṇa (or for a bodhisattva, of bodhi).

[2] That is, emptiness of lust, hate, and delusion.

[3] That is, it does not matter what the gift is.

And it is said in the holy *Akshayamati Sūtra :* "That is no gift that does harm to creatures, . . . that is no gift which is lacking in what has been said, . . . that is no gift where is contempt for those who deserve offerings amongst all creatures, . . . there is no gift with boasting, . . . that is no gift which distresses those who crave, that is no gift where is scoffing and wheedling, or hostility, there is no gift in what is thrown away, no gift without one's own hand, . . . that is no gift that is improper, or unseasonable, there is no gift in a pernicious charm, or in what does harm to creatures."

When it is said in the *Ugraparipṛcchā :* "Even strong drink he gives, thinking, 'This is the time for the Perfection of Giving, the time to give to each one whatever he craves. But thus will I do: those to whom I shall give strong drink I will cause to receive remembrance and full consciousness," the meaning is that one who is disappointed in the hope of obtaining strong drink will bear a heavy grudge against the Bodhisatva; hence comes a loss of sympathy; wherefore in default of other means to conciliate their good-will, strong drink should be given. As regards the gift of such things as a sword, if the gift be made after full consideration of advantage and disadvantage, there is no sin, as it appears from the same text; but in the scriptures such a gift is prohibited by a general rule. Thus the principle of Purity in gifts has been explained.

Purity of Conduct is thus described in the holy *Gaganagañja Sūtra :* "Do not abandon the thought of enlightenment, with a view to the purification of thought; be free from the mind of disciples or Pratyeka Buddha, with a view to the purity of standard." [1]

[272] Again, another view of purification of conduct. "The sky is pure, pure is his conduct; clear is the sky, clear is his conduct; calm is the sky, calm is his conduct; not exalted [2] is the sky, not exalted his conduct; peaceful is the sky, peaceful his conduct ; . . . indivisible is the sky, indivisible his conduct; and so forth. The sky is without obstruction; he whose thought has no dislike for any creatures has the purity of peace.

[1] *prāmāṇika :* quite unknown. [2] This seems to mean proud.

The sky is uniform ; he whose thought is one for all beings has the purity of peace ; and so forth. Suppose there be a great forest of sāl trees ; some one might come and cut down a sāl tree ; those that are left do not think, 'That tree is cut down and we are not ;' they feel neither pleasure nor dislike ; no thought, no fancy, no illusion. This peace of the thought of enlightenment is the supreme peace like the sky."

In the holy *Ratnacūḍa Sūtra* the subject is given at length. "This is what is meant by strength. What is that purity ? It is the knowledge of the body as [1] being an image of reflexion, the knowledge of voice as being something inexpressible, the knowledge of the mind as being altogether at rest. Then, armed with the resolution of compassion he is established in the resolve of great pitifulness. He enters on meditation which takes the mould of the void in all the best aspects. What is the void in all its best aspects ? That which is not without generosity, . . . not without expedients, not without pleasure and delight in deep compassion, not without the presence of the knowledge of truth, not without the regard for all creatures and the thought of enlightenment, not without wish, intention, resolve ; intentional generosity, fair speech, doing good for others,[2] done not without that same intention ; not without full consciousness and memory ; not without the earnest meditations, the right exertions, the constituents of magic power, the moral qualities, the forces, the requisites of supreme knowledge, the eightfold path, quietude, far-sightedness . . . peaceful by its nature, [273] not content amid sinful acts, regardful of all things, observant of the Buddha's righteousness, dull [3] by its own character, bold with respect to blessing, not busied with its own tastes, always busied with the Buddha's business, tranquil by peace always kindled by the ripening of beings ; this is what is meant by the void in all its best forms. . . . This, young sir, is the perfect meditation and the purification of conduct.

[1] Tib. *du* makes this clear. [2] See Childers, s.v. *saṅgaho*, s.f.

[3] Tib. *bem-po*=जडा.

"By this is to be understood the purification of knowledge; so also in all acts of merit."

So also it is said in the holy *Vimalakīrti-nirdeśa:* "The field wherein the wheel of the good law is rolled, wherein the great Nirvāṇa is manifested, the field where the virtue of the Bodhisatva is not abandoned, this is also the field of the Bodhisatva."

CHAPTER XVI

THE INCREASE OF GOOD CONDUCT

Now we have to describe three kinds of Increase. Hence the verse:

> "Many there are to take from thee:
> Little thou hast; what boots it thee?
> It gendereth not supreme content;
> Therefore increase it all thou mayst." [1]

Supreme content is Buddhahood: the meaning is, that this is not produced by just that purity which belongs to the disciple.

> "How to increase my body's weal?
> Increase thy vigour, scorning sloth." [2]

[274] The Vigour of this verse is described in the holy *Ratnamegha:* "In the multitude of beings, that being is not to be found who should destroy the Bodhisatva's strength by strength."

How comes the increase of this? As it is said in the holy *Tathāgataguhya Sūtra:* "When Ajātaśatra was amazed as reverend Vajrapāṇi showed his strength, and asked the Blessed One, he said: 'There are ten ways, sir, by which a Bodhisatva obtains strength like this. And what are they? In this world, sir, the Bodhisatva renounces body and life, but he does not renounce the Good Law. He bows before all creatures, and does not let his pride grow. He is compassionate to weak creatures, and does not dislike them. When any are hungry he gives them the best food. When any are frightened he gives them

[1] Kār. 22. [2] Kār. 23a.

protection. When any are ill he exerts himself for their complete cure. The poor he rejoices with plenty. At a shrine of the Tathāgata he does repairs with a lump of plaster. He lets people hear pleasant speech. He goes share for share with those afflicted with poverty. He carries the burdens of the weary and exhausted. These are the ten ways, sir.' "

[275] What is the increase of activity? The same as increase of energy: as it is described in the *Sāgaramati Sūtra:* " The Bodhisatva, Sāgaramati, must always practise energy by sustained effort. Keen of will must he be, and he must not drop the yoke. When the Bodhisatvas practise energy, Sāgaramati, it is not hard for them to get perfect and supreme enlightenment. Why is this? Where energy is, Sāgaramati, there is enlightenment. But when men are lazy, enlightenment is far far away. The lazy cannot be generous, . . . the lazy has no understanding, and no benefit for others."

And in the *Candrapradīpa Sūtra* it is said: " As a lily in the midst of the water he grows and grows."

This in brief is the increase of the body's weal.

" Enjoyment's increase comes from gifts,
Offspring of mercy and the Void." [1]

As it is said in the *Vajracchedikā:* " When a Bodhisatva gives a gift without believing in anything,[2] it is not easy to set a limit to the mass of his merit."

And in the *Mahatī Prajñāpāramitā* it is said: " Moreover, Śāriputra, when the Bodhisatva, the Great Being, gives even a small gift to all creatures, and he desires to make it immeasurable, ineffable, by applying his fertility in resource to wisdom in all its forms, he must practise himself in the Perfection of wisdom. So one who wishes to fulfil the desires of all beings, . . . and by providing them with gold and silver, parks and kingdoms, must practise himself in the Perfection of wisdom."

[276] And without mercy, nothing is accomplished by the

[1] Kār. 23b.

[2] *apratishṭhito,* lit. not abiding: he does not believe in the existence of giver or gift.

Bodhisatvas: so we shall say. This in brief is the increase of enjoyment.

Increase of merit is the root of all increase: this thought is called the binding on of the girdle.

> " With effort first, before all place
> Settled resolve and purpose firm;
> Set mercy too before thy face
> And so for merit's increase strive." [1]

The verse which begins " With effort," etc., as before, has for its aim to produce firmness, at the beginning of practice, by bringing again and again to mind the resolutions, etc., which were made when one was purifying the thought. He employs the words " at first " in order to prevent slackness: one must say, " As with skill and care in the use of weapons when time of battle is come, so at the time of practice I will make strong my resolution." Then how does he make strong his resolution?

As the holy Sudhana approaching the holy Maitreya made firm his bodily strength by considering how he had wasted [2] a world of bodies in the past because they were unable to practise virtue, controlling his thought and intention as he considered the many different ways in which his thought attached him to outside objects, ineffective towards purity of body and mind in the past, [277] he ponders the great importance of present intentions by considering the useless stream of his actions leading to worldly conduct and evil deeds; he develops this force to build the true conception of the conduct of all the Bodhisatvas, by considering that in the past his judgment had been affected by untrue ideas springing from illusion; he strengthens the force of resolution in a way superior to the conduct of all others by considering that his exertion for his own ends in the past was bad, by considering that all his past bodily action was insipid; he increases the power of the faculties which produce great comfort when used to acquire the qualities of a

[1] Kār. 24.

[2] Reading प्रयास as suggested by Tib.

Buddha, by considering that in the past his inclinations have been warped by wrong ideas; he cleanses the course of his feelings by undertaking the aspiration of all Buddhas which owing to right views is not involved in error in the present; by considering that his past strenuous effort was unsuccessful and ineffective even when there was such an effort;[1] he produces exaltation of body and thought by exerting great efforts to realise that the qualities of the present Buddhas are at hand, by considering that in the past he has been possessed of bodies, cast into the different evil states of existence, bodies of no use to himself or to others, which could not contribute to their life; he increases the impulses of joy and delight by assuming a personality capable of producing the qualities of all Buddhas, of serving all the world, of pleasing all good friends; he realises that this body, although it is produced in the womb, full of old age, disease and death, and union and separation, is capable of being the cause of a body of wisdom consisting in the resolution of a Buddha, a body which will be devoted to the practice of the rule of a Bodhisatva during ages to come, devoted to the ripening of all beings and to obtain the qualities of a Buddha, devoted to seeing the Tathāgata, [278] to traversing of the field of all Buddhas, to service of all who preach the law, to learning the doctrine of all Tathāgatas, a companion of the search for all righteousness, devoted to the accomplishment of the advice of all good friends and all the Buddhas' righteousness; so he increases the inconceivable power of merit and spiritual faculties.

In the holy *Akṣayamati-nirdeśa*, a Mahāyāna Sūtra, it is also said: "Lonely is the Bodhisatva, with no second and no companion, and he girds up his loins in the perfect and incomparable wisdom. He by a will that has been grasped by the strength of resolution gives no opportunity to another, but acts by himself. He is imbued with strength of his own strength. It is he who firmly resolves: 'Whatever ought to be gained by all beings, that I will cause them to obtain. Whatever all the holy Bodhisatvas, whatever those newly

[1] So Tib. but query *ayoga*

entered upon the Vehicle shall not obtain, that will I cause them to obtain. Generosity is not my helper, but I am helper of generosity. Morality, patience, resolution, meditation are not my helpers, but I am theirs. I am not supported by the Perfections, but they are so by me. So I would proceed with all those things by which we get our neighbour's good-will [1] and all the roots of good, . . . so I, alone, without second or comrade, standing upon the earth's circle hard as adamant, attacking Māra with his armies and his chariots, with knowledge produced by instantaneous insight, must develop the incomparable and perfect enlightenment.' "

In the holy *Vajradhvaja Sūtra* he says: " Just as the sun, offspring of the gods, rising is not stopped [279] by the default of those who are born blind, nor by the fault of castles in the air,[2] nor by the fault of the earth-dust of the four continents of the earth-spheres, nor by the fault of Rāha, King of the Asuras, nor by fault of quantities of smoke, nor by fault of the passions of Jambudvīpa, nor by fault of all sorts of shadows, nor by fault of interposition of mountains; so the Bodhisatva the Great Being, with wide and deep thought, by remembrance and intelligence, with unimpaired goodness, until he comes to the goal of his virtuous and wise action, is not kept by faults of malice in other creatures from the developing of the root of good, is not diverted by faults of foulness or heresy in other beings, he is not repelled by others' agitations, does not ungird the armour of enlightenment because of the mass of corruption in others, does not relax through the foul quarrels of others his resolve to save all the world, . . . [280] nor by association with foolish people, is not despondent through the faults of others. And why not? There is no hindrance in that multitude of things,[3] that is, to thwart the purification of all the world. . . . And that mass, the pain of all creatures, and the manifold action connected with hindrance, which causes that they by that hindering action do not see the Buddhas, do not hear the Law, do not know the Order; all that threefold

[1] Dh. S. xix.
[2] *i.e.* Fata Morgana, a vision of cities in the sky.
[3] This is acc. in Tib.

hindering action in them, accumulated by their own body through the mass of pain, do I take away in each several rebirth in hell and place of misery and society: may all those creatures be born out of those places, all that burden of pain I take upon myself, I assume, I endure. I do not avoid or run away, I fear not nor am afraid, I tremble not, I turn not back, I despair not. And why not? Certainly the burden of all creatures must be borne by me; that is not my own pleasure; it is my resolution to save all creatures, I must set all free, I must save all the world, from the wilderness of birth, of old age, of disease, of being born again, of all sins, of all misfortunes, of all transmigrations, of all depths of heretical doctrine, of destruction of the good Law, of ignorance arisen, therefore by me all creatures must be set free from all the wildernesses, caught as they are in the net of thirst, wrapt in the toils of ignorance, held fast in the desire for existence, whose end is destruction, enclosed in the cage of pain, attached to their prison; without knowledge, uncertain in promises, full of hesitation, ever in discord, finding unhappiness, without means of refuge, in the flood of existence, worldlings in the foaming gulf. . . . I walk so as to establish the kingdom of incomparable wisdom for all: I am not one tittle concerned with my own deliverance. All creatures I must draw out from the perils of transmigration with the lifeboat of all-wisdom, I must pull them back from the great precipice, I must set them free from all calamities, I must ferry them over the stream of transmigration. By my own self all the mass of others' pain has been assumed: . . . I have the courage in all misfortunes belonging to all worlds, to experience every abode of pain. I must not defraud the world of the roots of good. [281] I resolve to abide in each single state of misfortune through numberless future ages: and as in one abode of misfortune, so in all such abodes belonging to the worlds, for the salvation of all creatures. And why so? Because it is better indeed that I alone be in pain, than that all those creatures fall into the place of misfortune. There I must give myself in bondage, and all the world must be redeemed from the wilderness of hell, beast-birth, and Yama's world, and I for the good of all creatures would experience all the mass of pain and unhappiness in this my own body: and on account of all creatures I give surety for all creatures, speaking truth, trustworthy, not breaking my word. I must not forsake others. And why so? With all creatures for its object the mind of all wisdom has been developed in me, that is, for the deliverance of all the world. I am established in the incomparable all-wisdom not by desire of pleasure, not to indulge in the five senses, not to follow the concerns of lust; nor is it to accomplish the multitude of pleasures that are included in the sphere of mutual passion that I walk the Bodhisatva's path. And why so? Because all these worldly pleasures are no pleasures; that is the sphere of Māra, I mean, to follow lust. That road is beset by foolishness; dispraised of all Buddhas is that principle, I mean, to follow lust. Just so to follow lust means the uprising of all this mass of pain, and from this alone comes hell, animal-birth, Yama's world; all quarrelling and strife, all bickering and anger, are manifested just from this; and these creatures, following their lusts, are far from the presence of the Blessed Buddhas. And these lusts are an obstacle even to rebirth in heaven, how much more to the safe possession by all creatures of that most royal[1] and incomparable wisdom! And I beholding thus the immeasurable faults of lust, brief and blazing, therefore on that account I will not walk after them. . . . So must I apply my root of good that all creatures may gain exceeding great happiness, unheard-of happiness . . . the happiness of all-knowledge: I must be charioteer, I must be guide, I must be torch-bearer, guide to safety, [282] one who has obtained lucky times, master of resource, knower of good, I must take the place of the boat of all-knowledge amid the ocean of transmigration, I must be able to apply merit, I must be the guide to the other shore. . . . Now in this world with its four continents there are not so many suns rising to give light to the world as there are living creatures; but here is only one

[1] Tib. read rgyal-srid, °राज्यस्य, the realm of wisdom.

sun that rises to enlighten the whole world for them; and these creatures that come into the world have not each light by his own body, that they may know when it is day, or do their business, be it to cook the grain, or day by day in garden or town to take pleasure and enjoyment, or look at the heavens, or go to and fro in village and town and city or King's capital, each on his own business intent. . . . Here now, when the divine sun arises, one sun's disc without a second gives light to all creatures upon the whole earth. Just so, when the Bodhisatva the Great Being produces the roots of good and applies the root of good, this is his thought: 'These beings have not the root of good by which they might save themselves. How much the less can they save another? But I on account of all creatures produce roots of good and apply the root of good, that is, for the deliverance of all, to enlighten them and give them wisdom, to convert them and conciliate them, to perfect them, for their peace and delight, to take away their doubts, and so I must use these ways of the round sun. I must not wait for another; I must give no opening to another by casting away my resolution; my effort to save all must not cease amongst them; [283] I must not desist from my application of merit towards the destruction of all pain; small roots of good I must not try to get;[1] I am not to think of being satisfied with a mean application of merit."

And in the holy *Akshayamati Sūtra* he says: "He does not court ages in seeking for enlightenment: 'So many or so many ages I will hold to my resolution.' No; his resolution is eternal. 'If one day and night should be equal to all the total of time gone by, then with such-like days in one fortnight, in a month of thirty days, in a year of twelve months, and so on counting years up to an hundred thousand, may I create one thought of enlightenment, may I behold one perfect Tathāgata. In this manner and by this counting, with such thoughts and such manifestations of the Tathāgata as many as the sands on Ganges banks, may I learn the thoughts of each creature. In the same manner and by the same counting, by so many

[1] That is, I must not be satisfied with small ideals.

thoughts and so many manifestations of the Tathāgata may I produce my own line of thought for all creatures:' so he must resolve without desponding. This resolve of the Bodhisatva is an indestructible resolve. Such is the system to be followed in such things as giving, and in producing the things that belong to the supreme enlightenment,[1] and the marks of the Great Man."

Again, in the holy *Ratnamegha* it is said: "If the Bodhisatva learns of people's grasping greed and violence, he must not say, 'Away with these people so grasping and so violent!' and on that account be depressed and turn his back on the others. He makes a vow to have a very pure field in which the very name of such persons shall be not heard. And if the Bodhisatva turn his face away from the good of all creatures, his field is not pure and his work is not accomplished. Then the wise Bodhisatva thinks, [284] 'Therefore whatever beings of animal nature may be insignificant, timid,[2] stupid, deaf, dumb by nature, may I meet in my Buddha-field all who in animal form are not behaving so as to attain Nirvāṇa, not cured, rejected by all Buddhas and Bodhisatvas; these all I would seat in the bo-tree circle, and bring to the knowledge of supreme enlightenment.' As thus the Bodhisatva thinks, as his thoughts arise one by one, all the realms of Māra do quake, and all the Buddhas utter his praises."

Just so by desire of increasing merit his resolve should be firmly fixed; and now is to be declared why this resolution should be made firm.

Again, it has been explained in the *Dharmasaṅgīti Sūtra* to answer the question why this should be made firm. "In resolution truly, O Blessed One, is the root of the Buddha's qualities. He who has no resolution, from him all the Buddha's qualities are far away. But, Blessed One, when he has made his resolve, if there are no Buddhas, the voice of the Law comes forth from the firmament and the flowering trees. When a Bodhisatva has a pure resolve, from his own imagination come forth teaching and instruction. Therefore indeed, Blessed One, a Bodhisatva ought to make his resolve. As he can

[1] For these 37 dharmas see Dh. S. 43. [2] See note in text 284[1].

go that has feet, so, Blessed One, he has the Buddha's qualities who has resolution. As he lives that has a head, so, Blessed One, he that has resolution has the Buddha's enlightenment. As he can gain that has life, so, Blessed One, he gains Buddha-good that has resolution. As, Blessed One, when there is fuel,[1] the fire burns, when there is none, it does not burn: [285] so if there be resolution all the Buddha's qualities are kindled for the Bodhisatva, but if not, they are not kindled. Even as, Blessed One, if there be clouds the rain falls, without them it falls not; so, Blessed One, if there be resolution the Buddha's qualities appear. As a tree, Blessed One, whose root is decayed, is not wont to put forth flowers and fruit, so, Blessed One, he whose resolution is decayed is not wont to put forth any good qualities. Therefore, Blessed One, the Bodhisatva who desires a Buddha's enlightenment must make a good resolve, fully kept and protected, purified and established."

Now what is this resolve? It is declared in the holy *Akshayamati Sūtra*: "Now this resolve is genuine because it is not artificially made; not artificially made because it cannot be contrived; not contrived because well known; well known because without guile; without guile because pure; pure because sincere; sincere because not crooked; not crooked because straight; straight because not uneven; not uneven because strong; strong because unbreakable; unbreakable because firm; firm because not wavering; not wavering because not dependent, and so forth. And this is called resolution just because it arises from the repeated acquisition of one virtue after another." [2]

As it is said in the same place: "The resolve to escape comes by specific attainment," and so forth.[3]

By resolution is also meant benevolence to all creatures, compassion for all creatures; friendliness to the holy, pity for the unholy; respect for teachers, protection for the

[1] Tib. zhugs śiṇ mchis na zhugs ḥbar gyi=sati 'ndhane 'gnir, *etc.*

[2] An etymological explanation, referring to *adhika*, *adhigama*, and *adhyāśaya*.

[3] The Pali *visesādhigamo*, attainment of jhāna by meditating on a specific object.

unprotected, help for the helpless, refuge for those that have no refuge, a resort for those that have none, comradeship for those without comrade, straightness for the crooked, uprightness for the rapacious, [286] honesty for the false, genuineness for the overreaching, gratitude for the ungrateful, regret for the malicious, help for the unhelpful, truth for those who walk in error, humility for the proud,[1] absence of fault-finding for the fault-finding, silence for others' faults, protection for the sinful, no betrayal of faults for all the deeds of artifice, readiness to hear for all those worthy of honour, readiness to take all in good part for those who admonish," etc.

Thus I make firm resolve and determination, and putting compassion in the forefront I strive for brilliant success.

As it is said in the holy *Dharmasaṅgīti Sūtra*: "Then indeed the Bodhisatva Analokiteśvara, the Great Being, said to the Blessed One: The Bodhisatva, Blessed One, should not be taught too many things. One virtue should be fully mastered and learnt by him, in which are included all the virtues of the Buddha. And what is that? It is great compassion. In great compassion, Blessed One, all the virtues of the Bodhisatvas are included. Just so, Blessed One, when the precious wheel of a universal monarch runs, all the army goes with it; so Blessed One, when the great compassion of a Bodhisatva goes on, all the Buddha's virtues go with it. Just so, Blessed One, when the sun is risen all are busy about their various businesses, so, Blessed One, when great compassion has arisen then all the other virtues that produce wisdom are busy in action. [287] Just as, Blessed One, when all the senses are ruled by the mind they are abundantly active each in its own sphere, so, Blessed One, when great compassion is established, all the other virtues that produce wisdom are active abundantly each in its own action. Even as, Blessed One, when sensibility is alive all the other senses act, just so, Blessed One, when there is great compassion, the other virtues act that produce wisdom," etc.

Again, it is said in the holy *Akshayamati Sūtra*: "Reverend

[1] Reading *stabdheshu*.

Sāradvatīputra, even as the breathing in and out is the chief thing in a man's sensibility, so, reverend sir, in a Bodhisatva who has entered the Great Vehicle great compassion is the chief thing. . . . As there might be in a merchant or householder heartfelt love for an only and virtuous son, so there is heartfelt love for all beings in a Bodhisatva who has acquired great compassion."

How is this to be produced? When he has realised in himself that his own manifold pain or danger experienced before or now is extremely unwelcome, one possessed of mercy must conceive mercy for those he loves, and for those who suffer from present pain and disease, or those who are being dragged through the infinite course of transmigration, the infinite ocean of great pain.

As it is said in the holy *Daśabhūmaka Sūtra:* "He is astonished at this, like as those foolish worldlings deluded by ignorance, of whom innumerable existences have ceased to be, are ceasing, or will cease, thus perishing do not conceive disgust for the body, nay, they strengthen the trap of pain, nor do they cease from the fear of the stream of transmigration, [288] nor throw aside attachment for the conformations, nor are disgusted with the phantom of the elements, nor are aware of those blinded by the phantom of delight, nor discern the empty village of the six senses, nor cast from them the clinging and attachment for the notions of I and mine, nor uproot the thorn of pride and heresy, nor destroy the net of lust, hate, and delusion, nor dispel the darkness of ignorance and delusion, nor dry up the flood of thirst, nor seek the Daśabala for their leader; who having gone to the gloom of Māra's abode swim in the ocean of migration infested with the monsters of many evil imaginations, and without refuge there fall into agitation, and experience many pains, that is who come into birth, old age, disease, death, grief, sorrow, pain, despair; in truth I alone with no second bear such an accumulation of knowledge and of good works for those that are tormented with pain, without protection, undefended, unguarded, without resting-place, without refuge, blind, overgrown with the membrane of the egg of ignorance, plunged in darkness. By such an accumulation of knowledge and of good works collected, all these beings would obtain complete purification."

In the same place it is said: "Those beings indeed are fallen into the way of the wilderness and forest of transmigration, their faces set towards the precipice of hell, animal-birth, and Yama's world, [289] caught in the dangerous net of heresy, clouded with the darkness of delusion, walking in falsehood and lies, blinded, without a guide, . . . carried along the stream of transmigration, sunk in the river of thirst, caught by the great current, unable to see, walking along the precipice of desire, destruction, doubt, injury, imagination, caught by the water-demon of the heresy of individuality, plunged in the whirlpool of the darkness of desire, caught in the midst of lust for delight, lost in the desert of self-conceit, without resort, not uplifted above the habitation of sense-impressions, without the accumulation of good; these we must uplift by the great power of the root of good, and place on the precious land of the perfect knowledge of good, without misfortune and without darkness. These beings are tied in the bonds of great pain, despair, destruction, compliance, repulsion, affection and dislike, attended by grief and woe, in the iron chain of desire, hidden in the gloom of delusion, guile and ignorance, the fetters of the three worlds. These we must establish in the full and true knowledge of the three worlds, in the fortress of confidence, the assuaging of all pain, Nirvāṇa unbroken."

Thus by these praiseworthy resolutions and efforts strengthening each other, he should cause merit to grow. Then indeed

> "Good Conduct's ordinance of praise
> And all besides devoutly keep." [1]

[290] In the holy *Ugradattaparipṛcchā* indeed the reading of the *Triskhandhaka* is ordained for one who is pure and wears pure garments to be read thrice in a night and thrice in a day. "There are three Accumulations, called Confession of

[1] Kārikā 25a.

Sin, Delight in Merit, Solicitation of Buddha, so called because of the accumulation of merit. Here the praise is implied in the declaration of sin. This is according to the authority of the *Upālipariprcchā*, where it is said that confession follows after the homage to the Buddha. Prayer is included in Solicitation, because they have the same sense. But worship is not taken into account because it is impermanent by lack of power; mental or vocal worship is not mentioned because they are well known in other Sūtras. By mentioning the three all that is important is understood. Then the praise is, 'I reverence all Buddhas.'"

In the holy *Akshamati Sūtra* is described the Confession of one's own and others' sins in the heaping-up of merit; and in four versicles and in hymns of praise as sung; and in the versicles of the holy *Bhadracarya* and others.

And the Veneration is explained in the holy *Ratnamegha*: "Here whatever of the nature of flowers or fruit he has, without thinking them his own or his possession the Bodhisatva thrice each night and thrice each day offers to Buddhas and Bodhisatvas . . .; those [1] scented or perfumed trees and jewel-trees or wishing-trees are not held to be his own or his possession, these also he offers thrice each night and thrice each day to Buddhas and Bodhisatvas."

And in the holy *Trisamayarāja*, "the mountains of jewels which are on dry land, or in the water, the jewels of land or water in the ten regions, without sense of ownership or possession are to be given," it is said. "And in this way all drugs, [291] all flavours, all circles of water and fair lakes, all the circles of gold, all medicinal herbs in the cream of earth, most precious in taste or touch, which appears when the worlds are created, nectar-plant or wild rice, all that are in the northern continents and the more delightful articles of diet that are in the purified worlds." [2]

[1] The Bower MS. has *parpaṭaka* for Oldenlandia Corymbosa, whose bark and powder are used in drugs. See Index.

[2] Read स य इत्ये as in p. 291[5].

As it is said also in the holy *Ratnamegha:* "And all the most excellent things serving the Tathāgata's worship that he hears of in the Sūtrāntas, these he applies to Buddhas and Bodhisatvas of intent with intense effort of will."

So: "he meditates on the various things that belong to worship."

The Confession has already been described. But in the holy Akshayamati. *Sūtra* the Confession of one's own and others' sin is explained in the accumulation of merit; the Delight, in the *Bhadracaryā Gāthā*, or in the section of the *Candrapradīpa* on Delight; Solicitation in the same Bhadra*caryā*. The complete application of merit is to be found in the same holy *Bhadracaryā*, or see the *Vajradhvaja-pariṇāmanā*.

Or the Solemn Aspirations described in the *Dasabhūmaka*. As he says: "That is, to provide for the worship of the Buddhas all and every one without exception, he directs the First Solemn Aspiration, endowed with all the best qualities, purified by lofty aspiration, wide and comprehensive, extending to the extremity of space, dwelling on infinite futurity, uninterrupted [1] for all the multitude of ages and all the Buddhas who shall appear to provide great worship. [292] The Second Solemn Aspiration he directs for maintaining the method of the law that has been taught by all the Tathāgatas, to keep the enlightenment of all Buddhas, for keeping the preaching of all Supreme Buddhas, wide and comprehensive, extending to the extremity of space, dwelling on infinite futurity, uninterrupted throughout all the multitude of ages and Buddhas that shall appear for the reverence of the good law. The Third Solemn Aspiration he directs in the extent of all worlds without exception to see [2] all the life of the Buddha from the dying in Tushita Heaven, through conception, the movements of the embryo in the womb, birth, boyhood's play, wedded life, going forth from the world, austerities, approaching the bo-tree throne, victory over Māra, the seeking for supreme wisdom, turning the great wheel of the Law, until he attains complete Nirvaṇa, beginning with the practice of conciliation

[1] Tib. rgyun mi ḥchad pahi. [2] So Tib. See note [8], p. 295 of text.

and all the precepts of worship, in this always simultaneously striving, an aspiration wide and comprehensive, extending to the extremity of space, dwelling on infinite futurity, uninterrupted throughout all ages and Buddhas that shall appear, until he attains complete Nirvāṇa.[1] The Fourth Solemn Aspiration he directs, wide and comprehensive, extending to the extremity of space, dwelling on infinite futurity, uninterrupted throughout all ages and the Buddhas that shall appear, being wrapped in all the perfections, strong, large, without measure, without interruption, in order to purify every place, to cleanse every limb and sub-limb, for the earnest desire of cherishing thought to encourage the giving of teaching and instruction for the preparation of the Perfections by showing the paths of the world of the Bodhisatvas specific and general, in periods of destruction or of change. [293] The Fifth Solemn Aspiration he directs to ripen all the animal world without exception, all the whole animal world I say, with form or without, with consciousness or without consciousness or neither, with or without all that are egg-born, caul-born, sweat-born,[2] self-produced,[3] included in the three worlds, all who have come into the six modes of existence, all who have come into birth, included under name and form, for the appearance of all the Buddha's law, for the intelligent discrimination of all the modes of birth, to establish supreme wisdom, a prayer wide and comprehensive, extending to the extremity of space, dwelling on infinite futurity, trusting in the understanding of all æons and of the animal world. The Sixth Solemn Aspiration he directs for the various mistakes in the world, a prayer for the inner perception of the whole world without exception, wide and compressed, great and immeasurable, small and lofty, confused, topsy-turvy, level, discriminating the deceptions that relate to entering and descent, the approach to knowledge of the discrimination of the various entries in the ten regions; a prayer wide and comprehensive, extending to the extremity of space, dwelling on infinite

[1] until , . Nirvāṇa, not in Tib.

[2] As vermin.

[3] As superhuman beings

futurity, trusting in the understanding of all æons and of the universe. The Seventh Solemn Aspiration he directs for the cleansing of all the Buddhas' fields; the cleansing of the descent into all the fields and each, one and all, his prayer is full of the ornaments, the buildings and the splendour of an immeasurable Buddha's field, possessed of the path of purification in the removing of all sinful passions, full of beings who are mines of immeasurable wisdom, aiming at the lofty field of a Buddha, in order to teach and to satisfy all creatures according to their dispositions; [294] a prayer wide and comprehensive, infinitely extended in space, dwelling on infinite futurity, trusting in the understanding of all æons and of the Buddha's field. The Eighth Solemn Aspiration he directs for entry into the Great Vehicle: for the formation of a single fixed purpose in all Bodhisatvas, for accumulating unrivalled roots of good, for equality of all Bodhisatvas in one single object, for the meeting of Buddhas and Bodhisatvas in regular and uninterrupted assemblies, for causing a Buddha to arise as desired, for approaching the knowledge of a Buddha's majesty in the fostering of one's own thought, for attaining transcendent faculty in one who follows the imperishable, for research in all worlds, for obtaining a greeting in all circles of society, for approaching all rebirth in one's own body, for reaching the Great Vehicle transcending thought, for not interrrupting the walking in the ways of a Bodhisatva: a prayer wide and comprehensive, extending to the extremity of space, dwelling on infinite futurity, trusting in the understanding of all æons and of virtue. The Ninth Solemn Aspiration he directs for avoiding useless speech, in order to follow a Bodhisatva's conduct mounted upon the unchangeable wheel, to make body, voice and mind efficacious, to understand all the law of the Buddha as soon as spoken, to attain knowledge as soon as the sounds are uttered, [295] to annihilate passion on the instant by becoming tranquil, to gain the precious refuge of the Great Physician, to gain a body like a gem, to walk in all the conduct of a Bodhisatva, a prayer wide and comprehensive, extending to the extremity of space. dwelling on infinite futurity, trusting in the understanding of all æons and of virtue. The Tenth Solemn Aspiration he directs for the earnest desire of the Great Vehicle, in order to attain the supreme and perfect enlightenment in all worlds, to exhibit without departing one hair's breadth from the path all the birth and life of foolish and worldly persons, retirement from the world, supernatural transformations, the Bo-tree seat, turning the wheel of the law, and the Great Renunciation; to attain knowledge of majesty in all the Buddha's field; to cause a Buddha to arise as desired in all the worlds of beings, producing knowledge moment by moment, leading to tranquillity; to penetrate all ideas without pride by perfect enlightenment alone; to content the cravings of all creatures' thoughts by the mere utterance of speech; to continue uninterrupted the power of virtue by exhibiting the Great Renunciation; to show the sphere of the great knowledge by causing all the law to arise; to penetrate all worlds by knowledge of the law and perception of magic and delusion: a prayer wide and comprehensive, extending to the extremity of space, dwelling on infinite futurity, trusting in the understanding of all æons and of supreme enlightenment."

[296] And this phrase, "I apply," Blessed One, is to be used everywhere.

And in the holy *Avalokiteśvara-vimoksha* the same course is to be taken. "This root of good I apply to dispel the fear of falling for all creatures; to calm the characteristic fears of all creatures; to put away the danger of illusion for all creatures; to cut away the danger of fettering for all creatures, to hinder the danger of the approach of obstacles to the life of all creatures, to take away the danger of despondency in helping all creatures, to make cease the danger of lack of livelihood for all beings. I apply it to do away with the danger of ill repute for all beings, to annul the danger connected with mundane existence for all beings, to dispel the danger of company-fright for all beings, to dispel the fear of death for all beings, to prevent the fear of a state of misery for all beings; I apply it to cause illumination so as to make all people turn back from the rugged path of blindness, to dispel the fear as to association with the uncongenial, to hinder for all the fear of separation from what is dear, to dispel the fear of living with what is not dear, to set all creatures free from the fear of bodily torment, to liberate all creatures from fear of mental torment, that all creatures may get away from pain, hopelessness and despair."

[297] Again, this incomparable application is briefly put in the holy *Bhadracaryā Gāthā*.[1] "As Mañjuśrī the hero knows, and as the Buddha Samantatabhadra knows, following them, I apply all that good by that application of merit which was praised as chiefest by the Jinas who are in the past, present or future, I am applying all this good in this holy *Bhadracaryā*."

[1] Edited and translated by a Japanese scholar in a Strassburg doctor's Dissertation about 1913.

CHAPTER XVII

THE PRAISE OF WORSHIP

THE Ordinance of Praise and so forth has been described: whence is it known that merit increases thereby? From the holy *Avalokana Sūtra*. Thus it is there said:

[298] "He renounces the eight unfavourable moments which I have indicated, and he chooses that one moment when the Buddha arises in his purity. Fair, beautiful, provided with the marks, possessed of strength and power, he does not fall into sloth. Pre-eminent and wealthy is he, invincible and full of merit; reverencing the light of the world he does obeisance again and again. He arises in merchants' families rich and pre-eminent; he would be liberal, a hero, of free generosity, not envious; he would be a righteous king, monarch and lord of the four continents, he would rule all the earth with its circuit of ocean and mountains, of great prosperity, an emperor, possessed of the seven jewels, established in rule, he does obeisance to the Buddhas again and again. When he leaves this world he goes to heaven, rejoicing in the Jina's salvation, and becomes Śakra King of the gods, lord on the peak of Meru. He cannot tell all the praise of Buddha in countless ages who should venerate the shrine of the lord of the world.

[299] "Verily he is not blind or lame even in countless ages, who cultivating the heart of wisdom venerates the shrine of the Teacher. Firm in resolution, firm in strength, a chieftain firm in might, he speedily comes to good fortune by venerating the shrine. If one should honour thousands of millions of Buddhas for a like number of ages, he who in this last age, in this horrible time, should worship a shrine has greater merit.

Pre-eminent is Buddha, unequalled, to be venerated ; one who has walked in the pre-eminent way and attained excellence ; he who does worship to this chief of men becomes in consequence best and incomparably beautiful.

" Departing hence from mankind he goes to the Thirty-three, gets a palace there, magnificent, made of jewels. Who himself gives an upper chamber, is surrounded by his troop of fairies, and he who puts a garland on the shrine is born among the Thirty-three. He would get a divine lake full of the eight qualities of water, with golden sand bestrewn with jewels and crystals. After enjoying that bliss and fulfilling his time the wise man descends from the world of gods and becomes a prosperous man. [300] Thousands and millions of births he would be honoured, after giving a garland to the shrine. He becomes an imperial monarch and Śakra the lord, and Brahma in Brahma's world, for giving a garland to the shrine. If one gives a gift of leaves to the sainted lord of the world, for him all blessings increase both divine and human. He would sacrifice things small and poor and he does not come into being here the next time. If he makes a booth of festoons for the lord of the world's relics, he would become a powerful king with uninterrupted pomp. He is dear and cherished, honoured and praised of gods and nāgas and all the wise men in this world. Where that hero is born, illumined by the light of merit, those families are respected, those countries and those towns.

[301] " He who takes a speck smaller than a grain of mustard seed and burns incense on the Blessed One's shrines, hear me sing his praises and be your hearts serene, leaving obstinacy and sins. He virtuous walks over all regions, altogether full of health, firm in mind, vigilant ; he subdues pain, and walks in virtue, dear and beloved of the people. If he has a kingdom he reverences the Jina, the supreme, great in power, a wise emperor, golden coloured, with the various marks, and receives precious perfumes in all the world. As soon as born he receives the best clothes, silken garments divine, pre-eminent, well made. He is blessed with a beautiful body when he has clothed

the shrine of the lord with robes. He who does worship at shrines of the incomparable chieftains with robes, his nature in this world becomes unequalled, covered with the thirty-two marks.

[302] " On the palms of the hands resplendent pearl necklaces appear for many an endless age, lion-garlands with strings bright in colour, if one have enwrapt the Blessed One's shrine with robes. By placing a banner on the Blessed One's shrine and making the prayer ' May I become a Buddha in the world,' he becomes worthy of honour by the people, walking noble in the Jina's course. His person becomes golden coloured, he receives brilliant robes, well-made cotton coverlets, and fine silk fabrics. If he gives a flag to the mighty one without stain, he gets great wealth very soon, plentiful treasure is his, he is endowed with endless wisdom, his conversation is magnanimous. He does not plant a thorn in the thoughts of another, he is serene in mind, vigilant; fire has no power upon him, not poison or knife, he is looked up to by the people. [303] From now to the destruction of the world the Buddha's field is golden; it is not possible to weaken such a life and glory, if one fix but one light on the Buddha's shrine. His body is faultless in its proportions, he is healthy, iron-armed, undismayed, he walks in splendour through all the world, who sets up a light upon the shrine. Like as if Buddha fields a hundred thousand million were full of mustard seeds piled into mountains, so one cannot count or weigh or tell what is one light given to the Tathāgatas. He who gives one sunshade, adorned and brilliant to see, to the Blessed One's shrines, his person is incomparable in this wotld and covered with the 32 marks, by which the person of the Jina is resplendent, like the shining form of gold, or fine gold brilliant to see, all flowered over with lucky marks. He is endowed with supernatural knowledge and mighty glory, walks in best and noblest virtue, his enjoyment never diminishes, he is honoured and worshipped by gods.

[304] " He never delights in sensuality, he is heroic, pure in morals, good in virtuous conduct; he takes the vow and

dwells in the air of the forest, devotes himself to meditation and attains excellence. No diminution of knowledge is there ever for him, he loses not anyhow the thought of enlightenment; he lives in benevolence happy at heart, who has given a sunshade to the Blessed One's shrines. He who does worship to the mighty one with a musical instrument, he verily does not come into the power of sorrow's pangs; pleasant-voiced he becomes in the world of men, his tones [1] are calm and pure. Clear-eyed is he, with full consciousness, clear of hearing and lofty in thought, his sense of smell is extremely keen, who has played upon an instrument of music at the Blessed One's shrines. His tongue is very fine and excellent, full subtle and delicate, in sound fine and pleasant, red and crimson as that of the gods, uttering an infinite number of fine distinctions in sound. He surely becomes not a serpent or a creature without tongue,[2] nor lame and crook-backed, nor again one with bent limbs; his person is excellent and resplendent who has played upon an instrument of music at the Blessed One's shrines. No one surely feels displeasure [3] at him, god or nāga or serpent-demon: full of courage he walks the earth, who has played upon an instrument of music at the Blessed One's shrines. Thousands of millions of ages he is excellent of body and perfect in every limb, amiable and covered with lucky marks, for cleansing a shrine of the Blessed One who has attained Nirvāṇa. [305] A noble palace he obtains, of delightful scent, divine, excellent, of bright sandal wood; he has no craving at any time, after cleansing a shrine of the Blessed One in Nirvāṇa. At the time of destruction of the noble Conqueror's rule, he is never then to be found in Jambudvīpa; he is in heaven established at that time, if he has anointed with perfume a shrine of the Conqueror. All the lusts, disgusting, unclean, contemptible, he escapes, established in his mass of virtue; he walks along in that walk of holiness, who has anointed with prefume a shrine of the Conqueror. When he leaves this earth he is lord of the Maruts in heaven, he counts

[1] "Divisions of sound," Tib. [2] Said, for example, of a frog.
[3] *aprasādam*, as is clear by context; see also M.V. ii. 383[18].

his wealth in thousands without delay; he works the good of many deities, if he has anointed with perfume a shrine of the Conqueror. Excellent in speech he is, delightful in voice, dear and beloved, and revered by much people, his happiness is always peaceful, if he has anointed with perfume a shrine of the Conqueror. He avoids all spheres of ruin, he is near to the Tathāgatas, he always receives favour, happy and lovable, if he has anointed with perfume a shrine of the Conqueror.

"[306] He avoids all unlucky times, for him are the eight lucky moments in especial, he does unequalled worship to the Buddhas, who has given a covering of net to the Blessed One's shrines. He becomes a hero, firm of spirit, vigilant, takes no delight in the enjoyment of pleasure, attains renunciation, is not cast down, who gives a covering net to the Blessed One's shrines. He does not lose the thought of enlightenment, he is of virtue unbroken, well protected, gets righteousness without passion, all cleansed, who brings a net for the Blessed One's shrines. He avoids harsh speech at all times, always eschews foolishness, wide in wisdom he abides in virtue, who has brought a net for the Blessed One's shrines. He receives pure food, gets garments excellent and well-coloured, soft, fine to look at, who brings a net for the Conqueror's shrines. He that throws away from the Conqueror's shrines useless and withered garlands with joyful feeling, will avoid lusts, painful, hateful, terrible, and will please the caravan-leaders of the Daśabala.[1]

[307] "He becomes agreeable, pure of body, to be looked up to and revered by many, not even a king is angry with him, who takes away from a shrine the withered flowers. All bad roads are avoided, and the region of misfortune; that Bodhisatva is established in a mass of virtue, who takes down from the Conqueror's shrines a flower formerly placed there by other men. Griefs and faults he avoids undeluded, all the many diseases he avoids, consolation he has for endless ages, who takes away withered flowers from a shrine. He becomes Buddha, notable beyond all others, with no like, to be worshipped by men and gods, he becomes adorned and pure in body, who takes away

[1] The Bodhisatvas.

withered flowers from a shrine. And he that should give a beautiful celestial flower, mystic flowers,[1] or a trumpet-flower, or who should take away from the shrine one that is defiled, for him there would be a reward choice and unequalled. He that reverently does obeisance to the Lord's shrine, fixing his will on the whole Buddha's world, he becomes in this world respected and honoured, agreeable and reverend. All people flock to his kingdom in this world, gods and titans, nāgas and men; he rules all the thousands of worlds, in full flower, he rules the kings in his power also and the lords; all the beings that are in his kingdom, he will establish in the Buddha's pure wisdom. The spheres of misfortune are avoided, and he works for them the best and choicest good. [308] His conversation[2] is of pleasing report; full of virtues, to be revered for memory and mind, full of confidence he walks in the world, he has always as his purpose affection for the best. His conversation is with a voice beautiful and clear, he would be recognized by his voice so sweet and gentle; no one has lordship over him; he is one for the people to gaze at. He produces in the multitude joy in giving, pleasantness, beneficence, equality[3]; being reviled he would not be angry, who reverently does obeisance at the Buddha's shrine. He becomes the king of the gods when he enters heaven, or as a man he is king, there is never any decay in him who does obeisance at a shrine in this world. He would never fall into misfortune and he would avoid all low desires in the world, he is rich above all, with great treasure, who does obeisance at the Buddha's shrine. He never uses magical charms, he never is angry out of due season in the world of men, people are pleased and delighted with him, who utters one word to the Man of Virtue.[4] [309] Who takes a handful of flowers, and glad with jubilant heart sprinkles them over the lord of the world, he becomes meritorious in the world of men, and abiding in safety reveres

[1] *māndārava:* Erythrina fulgens.

[2] Correct text to परिचारो ॥. So 302[3].

[3] See Childers, *saṃgaho* s.f., for the four saṃgahavatthus. Dh. S. xix.

[4] Buddha.

the Conqueror. Griefs and faults and the stain of obduracy are not his; with unequalled austerities, his limbs well composed, revered by the multitude, he will avoid desires terrifying, hateful, horrible."

Again, it is said in the holy *Mahākaruṇa-puṇḍarīka Sūtra*: "Let alone the man, Ānanda, who should reverence me face to face; let alone worship of my body with things no bigger than a leaf of mustard; let alone the dedication to me of builded shrines; whosoever, Ānanda, thinking of the Buddha, shall cast but into the air only one flower—the ripening of their mass of merit is that these people,[1] as long as the transmigration which has no beginning, the former end of which is not known, who pass through so many ages, gain the place of Indra, of Brahma, of universal empire—the limit of this merit cannot be reached. Let alone thought of the Buddha, even the throwing of just one single flower into the air, if even persons only in sleep throw into the air but one flower thinking of the Buddha, that I declare to be a root of good, which issues in Nirvāṇa."

And it is said in the holy *Bṛhat-sāgara-nāgarāja-paripṛcchā*: "Bodhisatvas endowed with eight qualities always Bhujagādhipati, attain without interruption association with the Buddhas. And what are these eight? By instigating people to look on the image of Buddha; by doing service to the Tathāgata; by constantly speaking the Tathāgata's praises; by making a likeness of the Tathāgata; by instigating all to look on the Tathāgata; and in whatever Buddha's field they hear word of the Tathāgata, there they set their longings; they are never depressed; always in exaltation they crave the Buddha's wisdom."

How much more does he who asks increase of merit have his aim accomplished by association with the Buddha! the goal of which virtue none could attain but he who is all-knowing.

[310] As it is said in the holy *Gaṇḍavyūha*:

"Hard it is to hear of a Buddha even in hundreds of ages; how much more the sight of him, resolving all doubts, supreme!

[1] Omitting *saced*.

This illuminator of the world, having arrived at the understanding of all things,[1] when well seen, is a gate of merit for the three worlds, cleansing all creatures; a field full of great merit, a gladsome circle of wisdom, illuminating the infinite[2] world, increasing the mass of merit, breaking the net of pain, cleansing the mass of knowledge; they have no fear of unhappiness by whom the Conqueror is pleased. Wide is the thought of those who behold the chief of men; a force of wisdom arises incalculable and bright."

Again, in the same place he says: "For the good of all beings arise the Tathāgatas, great in compassion, mighty, turning the wheel of the Law. How can the Buddhas, devoted as they are to the good of all, be requited by all flesh even in countless ages? Better to roast in three states of suffering, most cruel, for a million ages, than not to see the Teacher, who put an end to all existence.[3] As many as the various states of unhappiness in all the world, better to abide long in them than not to hear the Buddhas. Why is dwelling even a long time in hell recommended? Because the sight of the royal Conqueror increases knowledge. [311] All pains are annulled when one sees the Conqueror, monarch of the world, and there is an entrance into wisdom, the field of the Supreme Buddha. One destroys all hindrances by seeing the Buddha, noblest of men; he increases infinite merit by whom enlightenment is attained."

So this is the opportunity for increasing merit by associating with the Buddha. Now even to see the likeness of the Tathāgatas has infinite fruit; how much more, by his very self?

For it is said in the holy *Sraddhābalādhānāvatāramudrā Sūtra*: "If any young man or woman, Mañjuśrī, should give day by day food of a hundred flavours to the Pratyeka Buddhas, as many as the dust of all the universe, and bright vestments, and thus giving should give for as many ages as the sands of Ganges; and if another young man or woman, Mañjuśrī,

[1] So Tib. quite clearly.

[2] Reading अमिते.

[3] Obscure: perhaps refers to *samsāra*.

should see the Buddha, whether in a painting or in a manuscript [1]; this produces merit infinitely greater than that; how much more then, if any hold out reverent hands, or give a flower, or give incense, perfume, lamp? This produces merit infinitely greater than that."

Again, in the holy *Bodhisatva-piṭaka* is described a way to increase merit. "He that cleans a shrine of the Tathāgata, he attains four purities of aspiration in perfection. And what are these? Perfect purity of aspiration in form,[2] in steadfast undertaking, in seeing the Tathāgata, in the multitude of lucky marks."

Again, in the same place it is said: "One who lays a flower on the Shrines of the Tathāgatas, or anoints them, attains eight things without deficiency: and what are these? No deficiency in form, no deficiency in enjoyment, [312] no deficiency in his surroundings, no deficiency in virtue, no deficiency in tranquillity, no deficiency in knowledge, in wisdom, in aspiration."

It is said also in the holy *Ratnarāśi Sūtra*: "Those beings that belong to the three states of existence,[3] let them all make shrines for each of the Tathāgatas, of such an height, as is Sumeru King of Mountains, and let them pay worship to each of these through as many ages as the sands of the Ganges are: and let a Bodhisatva, with a mind of untrammelled omniscience, put but one flower there, he would produce greater merit than all that merit aforesaid."

In the same place it is said: "Be all those who are in the infinite multitude of worlds established in the Great Vehicle; be they all possessed of imperial rule, and let each imperial ruler make a lamp as large as the great ocean, and kindle a light as tall as Sumeru, and offer such a light at each of the shrines of the Tathāgatas: yet if a Bodhisatva who has left the householder's life put a wick in some oil and light it and set it on a Tathāgata's shrine, that former offering of lights is not

[1] Tib. has "idol" for this.

[2] I do not understand this. No help in Tib.

[3] See Childers, *s.v.* bhavo.

worth one-hundredth part of this oil-wick . . . there's no comparison between them. . . . If again those who are imperial rulers should honour the order of Brethren, Buddha at their head, with soft cushions, and if a Bodhisatva who has left the household life and goes on alms-pilgrimage should share with the rest what is in his bowl, giving them to eat of it; this is greater and more precious than that. And if those imperial rulers should pile up a heap of robes as high as Sumeru and give to the Order of Brethren, of whom Buddha is the head, and if a Bodhisatva who has left the household life should give everything except his three robes to the Order of Brethren, whose head is the Buddha, established in the Great Vehicle, or to a Tathāgata's shrine: this Brother's gift of robes surpasses that aforesaid heap of robes. And if those kings singly should bestrew all Jambudvīpa with flowers, giving them to a Tathāgata's shrine, and if a Bodhisatva who has left the household life should place even one flower on a Tathāgata's shrine; that aforesaid gift is not one-hundredth part of this, . . . there's no comparison between them."

[313] It is declared also in the holy *Anupūrvasamudgata-parivarta:* " Looking at these four excellent advantages, the Bodhisatva is zealous in the worship of the Tathāgata. Which four? I shall have worshipped the best recipient, and others seeing me will learn to do so; by worshipping the Tathāgata, the thought of enlightenment will become firm; by seeing the two and thirty marks of the Great Man, a root of good will be accumulated: these are the four."

Thus to provide worship for the Tathāgata is a thing without superior; as it is explained in the holy *Sāgaramati-paripṛcchā Sūtra:* " These three ways of worshipping the Tathāgata are unrivalled, Sāgaramati. What three? When one develops the thought of enlightenment, when one comprehends the Law, when one develops the thought of great compassion towards all."

It is shown also in the holy *Ratnamegha:* " Bodhisatvas, young sir, are born untouched with the impurity of the womb, who have ten things: and what are these ten? These:

Making a Tathāgata's likeness; building up an old shrine; giving perfume and ointment to Tathāgata-shrines; washing the Tathāgata's likeness with scented water; sweeping and anointing the Tathāgata-shrines; body-attendance on parents and teachers, and on readers; body-attendance on holy men; and that too with heart not greedy but free from greed; and this good they thus apply, saying, 'By that root of good let all beings be born untouched with the impurity of the womb.' And they think with keen aspiration.[1] These are the ten things, young sir."

The advantages of rejoicing are described in the holy *Prajñāpāramitā:* "He that rejoices over the production of these thoughts [2] in the great Beings, the Bodhisatvas, who are just established in the Great Vehicle; he that rejoices in the production of these thoughts in those Bodhisatvas who are practising that way of life; he who rejoices in success of those Great Beings, the Bodhisatvas, who return no more to life; [314] how much greater a heap of merit, Blessed One, does that young man or woman produce?' This said, the Blessed One replied to Śakra, King of the gods. . . . 'Let it be possible, Kauśika, to conceive measure of the infinite multitude of worlds as compared with a tip of straw; yet it is not possible to conceive the measure of merit in these thoughts, full of rejoicing, in the Bodhisatva, the Great Being.' This said, Śakra King of the gods said to the Blessed One: 'Delivered over to Māra those beings must be judged, who hear not and know not, and do not feel this joy, that infinite is the merit of this rejoicing in the Bodhisatvas, the Great Beings, from the first resolution to become Buddha down to the moment when they have attained supreme wisdom. On Māra's side they will be, Blessed One.' The Blessed One said: . . . 'Those men or women, Kauśika, who rejoice at these thoughts, whether they be in the Bodhisatvas' Vehicle, or the Pratyeka Buddhas' Vehicle, or the Disciples' Vehicle, they will quickly please the holy Tathāgatas, the perfectly wise.' The Blessed One said:

[1] = the resolve to become a Buddha.

[2] Correct text 313[20] to *avinivartanīyānām api.*

Thus by those roots of good in thought, full of rejoicing, wherever these shall arise they shall be honoured, revered, respected, worshipped, praised, and reverenced; they shall not see disagreeable shapes or hear disagreeable sounds, nor shall they have disagreeable smells, tastes, or touchings; for them there need be no fear of birth in states of misfortune, but they may look for birth in heaven. And why so? Because they have rejoiced in all the bringing of happiness to all beings and roots of good for infinite beings, . . . and they having attained supreme enlightenment shall wholly emancipate countless and infinite beings.' "

Again in the same place he says: " All beings, Subhūti, in all the infinite worlds, as the sands of Ganges for multitude, could attain the supreme and incomparable wisdom, and having attained it [315] could enjoy the Four Esctasies through ages as many as the sands of the Ganges are: yet if a Great Being, a Bodhisatva possessed by this transcendental wisdom and skilfulness in using the means of salvation, shall rejoice over the mass of virtue, tranquillity, wisdom, emancipation, knowledge of emancipation, of the Buddhas past, present and future; putting together all the mass of virtue, tranquillity, wisdom, emancipation, and knowledge of emancipation of the student Pratyeka Buddhas also, in a lump, and weighing it, should rejoice over it all, with a jubilation perfect, best and most good, choice, fine, pleasant, excellent, unrivalled, supreme, unequalled, incomparable, with no like, if then having thus rejoiced, one should apply to supreme enlightenment the merit, that results from the rejoicing, then, Subhūti, that former mass of merit, containing the Four Ecstasies, belonging to the Bodhisatvas who have consciousness of their religious acts, is not worth a hundredth [1] part of the merit that results from rejoicing, . . . there is no comparison between them."

This same method is described as concerning the application of the merit. Or from the fact that this merit has been applied to a supreme end towards the quality of Buddha, there would be Buddhahood due to good actions and aspirations. Then

[1] For the rest of the enumeration, see Vajracch. p. 35.

how could there be a better growth of merit ? For this merit which is realised through the freeing of all creatures, is impregnated with knowledge, and admits of no doubt.

The praise of asking for instruction is given in the holy *Ugra-paripṛcchā*, in order to comprehend the Law for guarding one's life in numberless and infinite fields of the Buddha.

CHAPTER XVIII

RECOLLECTION OF THE THREE JEWELS

[316] In the Sixteenth Chapter was discussed the growth of merit; in this the chief subject is, What is the continual practice of faith and the other virtues.

As it is said in the holy *Tathāgata-guhya Sūtra:* "These, O King, are the four qualities of those established in the Great Vehicle, useful for specific attainment [1] without falling away. What four? Faith, O King, leads to specific attainment and hinders loss; and what faith? The faith by which one approaches the saints, and does not what one ought not to do. Reverence, O King, leads to specific attainment; by which reverence one hears a thing well said, and desires to hear it, and hears the law without closing the ears. Humility, O King, leads to specific attainment, by which one shows respect and honour to the saints, and so will do. Courage, O King, leads to specific attainment, and hinders loss; by which courage one gets readiness of body and mind, and safely performs all that has to be done. These, O King, are the four."

These, faith and the rest, must always be practised; so of others, which he speaks of in the holy Akshayamat *Sūtra,* these five powers. "What five? The power of faith, fortitude, of remembrance, of concentration, of wisdom. Here what is faith? That faith by which one believes in four things. And what four? He believes in right worldly insight in the matter of transmigration in the world: he becomes confident in the ripening of action, and knows, that whatever deed he shall do he shall have the fruit of it; not even for life's sake does he sin.

[1] See Childers, 584 *b*: ecstasy induced by dwelling on a specific thought.

He believes in the virtue of a Bodhisatva, and having entered on this life [317] he does not wish for any other Vehicle. Hearing all the doctrines consisting in the chain of causation, real, clear and profound, consisting in behaviour according to selflessness, not-being, not-living, not-personality, consisting in void, absence of attribute, sinlessness,[1] he has faith in them. He follows none of the heretical sects, he has faith in all the Buddha's qualities, confidence [2] in his strength and the rest; and having believed, his doubts gone, he attains those qualities of a Buddha. This is what is meant by the power of faith. And what is the power of fortitude? The qualities which he believes in by faith, he attains by the power of fortitude: this is what is meant by the power of fortitude. And what is the power of remembrance? The qualities which he attains by his fortitude he keeps from destruction by remembrance: this is what is meant by the power of remembrance. And what is meant by the power of concentration? The qualities that he keeps from destruction by remembrance, on these he fixes his thought by concentration: this is what is meant by the power of concentration. And what is meant by the power of wisdom? The qualities which he fixes his mind on by concentration, these by the power of wisdom he investigates and learns to understand, and this individual wisdom not dependent on another is called the power of wisdom. Thus these five powers, conjoined and developed, complete all the Buddha's qualities, and confirm that stage where he receives the prophecy that he will become a Buddha." [3]

The powers of faith and the rest must always be practised; as it is said in the holy *Ratnacūḍa Sūtra:* "In this place what, young sir, is the purification of the Bodhisatva's exercise of his powers? that by these same powers he becomes supported and not to be crushed by all the Māras: not to be captivated

[1] Dh. S. 73; Cp. Mrs. Rhys Davids, "Compendium of Philosophy," Aniruddha, p. 67.

[2] There are four vaisāradyāni: abhisambodhi°, sarvasatvaksayajñana°, antarāyikadharmānanyathātvaniscitavyākaraṇa°, nairvāṇikamārgāvataraṇa°.

[3] See Mahavyutpatti 8, Dh. S. 77, Childers, s.v. *vēsarajja*.

by the Vehicles of Disciple and Pratyekabuddha: not to be diverted from the Great Vehicle: unconquerable by all passions: firm in his promises once made: content in heart: strong in body: guarded by his powers: unconquerable by the leaders of sects," and so forth.

So much for the constant practice of faith and the other virtues with a view to increase of merit.

What is compassion? As he says in the *Candrapradīpa Sūtra:* [318] "All the worship of many kinds, immeasurable, which is found in countless millions of fields, if one perform all that worship always towards the noblest man, yet he of compassionate heart is out of all comparison by counting." [1]

What is it to remember the Buddhas and so forth?

It is described in the *Rāshṭrapāla Sūtra:* "I praise thee, like the colour of gold, with choice marks, with face like the bright moon; I praise thee full of unequalled wisdom; there is none like thee in the world stainless. Thy hair and nails are gentle, pleasant, friendly, bright, thy head-excrescence [2] is like the King of mountains. It is not possible to look on thy head-excrescence; the circle of hair shines between thine eyebrows, O Sage. Like the drops on a jasmine, a shell, the bright snow, like the blue lotus thy dear and beautiful eyes. With the same tenderness with which thou lookest upon this earth, I praise thee, clear-eyed Conqueror. A tongue long and thin and red, and thy mouth with which thou concealest it, and speaking the Law dost teach the world: I praise thee and thy sweet and lovely speech. Teeth clean, firm like the thunderbolt, thirty and ten moreover, set close together; smiling thou teachest the world; I praise thee with thy sweet and truthful speech. In form thou art unequalled, a Conqueror, with thy glory thou dost illuminate a hundred fields. Brahma, Indra, the lords of the earth are obscured, O Blessed One, by thy glory. [319] O Blessed One, legged finer than a deer, with the gait of elephant, peacock, or lion, you walk looking just a yoke's

[1] *i.e.* compassion is better.

[2] A small lump represented on the Buddha's head. Dh.S. lxxxiii. 23.

length before you, O Blessed One, wandering over the mountain slopes of the earth. A body, Blessed One, covered with lucky marks, skin soft and like gold in colour. The world has never enough of looking at thy lovely form, O thou of form incomparable. Thou hast fulfilled vows and austerities through ages past, thou art devoted to all unselfishness, self-control, generosity; thy mind has mercy and compassion for all creatures: I praise thee, the most compassionate. Thou delightest always in generosity and in virtue, thou delightest in tranquillity and fortitude, firm-set, thou hast meditation, wisdom, glory: I praise thee, possessor of wisdom unequalled. Thou art great in eloquence, subjugator of the wicked, thou roarest like a lion in the assembly, thou art the chief physician, the death of the three uncleannesses: I praise thee, chief inspirer of love. O Sage, pure in voice, body, and mind, in the three worlds like an undefiled water-lily; O thou that hast the voice of Brahma, thy voice is like the cuckoo: I praise thee, who hast passed beyond the three worlds. This world is all illusion, thou knowest it to be like a stage play, or a dream: no self, no being, no life, all things are like a mirage or the moon reflected in water; the world, knowing not the truth of emptiness and peace, rolls through the transmigrations: thou through thy pitifulness dost deliver them by hundreds of devices leading to their salvation. [320] Having seen the world perplexed always by many hundreds of passions, thou walkest like a physician incomparable, O auspicious one, freeing hundreds of creatures. Having seen the world destroyed by birth, old age, death, and sorrow, always diseased by countless lamentations for separation from what is dear, O Sage, thou walkest freeing it by thy pity. Like a cart-wheel all the world rolls round, in animals, in the hell of ghosts, in bliss, foolish, unguided, helpless; thou showest it the best way. This is the same holy path in the olden time told by those who were formerly Conquerors, righteous lords and doers of good in the world, this that thou showest, O mighty one unequalled, a road charming, smooth, pleasant, choice, excellent in holiness, causing supreme delight; this song thou singest surpassing Gandharvas, the best Kinnaras, and Āpsarasas, a voice purified by ways of salvation consisting in truth and rectitude incorruptible, with endless merits; hearing which myriads of beings cherish tranquillity through the three Vehicles. By thy worship they get bliss of various kinds, divine; thus amongst men one becomes rich, wealthy, powerful, a king doing good to the world, an emperor, lord of a continent, covering the world with the ten blessings;[1] he gets the seven jewels, most auspicious by confidence in thee, unparalleled. [321] Brahma also and Śakra he becomes, lord of the world, a happy lord of the gods, appointed also lord of Yāmas, and by thy worship he becomes Conqueror. Thus thy worship is unfailing, the sight and hearing of thee is unequalled, and thy footstep excellent and pure touches the world full of all kinds of pain. O Blessed One, knowing the road and skilled in it, thou keepest this world from the wrong path; thou dost establish the world, O Blessed One, in a holy path, safe, auspicious, clean. Imperishable for ever is the meritorious conduct of thee, rich in merit, a treasury of merit; in countless æons it fails not until it attain the chiefest wisdom. He attains a purified field, delightful, the pleasing glory of the highest heaven;[2] people become pure in body, voice, and mind, in that wonderful field. So thus the man receives choice virtues of all kinds as a result of praising the Conqueror; at the end of paradise he receives bliss amongst men, and he is a treasury of merit in all the world. The auspicious Conquerors ever proclaim thy praise and glory, far and wide in all regions, over hundreds of fields, thy renown in the assemblies, their afflictions gone, deliverers in the world, with their pleasant doctrine, compassionate beyond all, their senses calmed, devoted to tranquillity. O Blessed One, I praise thee, chiefest and best of men. [322] When I have received the five transcendent faculties, poised in the sky, O Conqueror, having heard thy voice, I shall be a hero like the Auspicious One, I shall dispense pure doctrine to the world, praising and blessing the Auspicious One who transcends all virtues, honoured by men, gods, and

[1] See Childers, s.v. *Kusalaṃ*.

[2] Childers, 336*a*.

nāgas. May the world also receive this wide merit that is acquired, and the Buddha's footstep." [1]

Or as it is told in the holy *Dharmasaṅgīti Sūtra*: "Moreover, the Blessed Buddhas are possessed of great merit and wisdom, they are full of great mercy and great compassion, they protect a mighty host of creatures, they remove thorns with their potent remedies, they have a quiet mind and tranquillity for all creatures. By Nirvāṇa they set free from transmigration, . . . like mother and father, with hearts like a friend's . . . unconquered by all the world, the glory of all the world, possessed of mighty powers, magnanimous, followed by multitudes, with excellent followers, courteous in giving sight or hearing without hindrance, regardless of their own happiness, loving to quench others' pain, loving the Law, bringing the Law, fetching the Law, healing by the Law, lords of the Law, masters of the Law, generous givers of the Law, ever devoted to unselfishness, ever vigilant, ever bent on discrimination, ever ready to open the way to instruction, like a royal road, . . . lovely in look are the Blessed Buddhas. Thus he calls them to mind; and thus having called them to mind he fixes the memory in order to develop their virtues. This is meant by calling the Buddhas to mind."

In the same place he describes remembering the Law. "Here this thought comes to the Bodhisatva: 'These Blessed Buddhas who are possessed of virtues endless and unlimited, are born from the Law, have the Law as their abode, created by the Law, have the Law as their principle, as their light, as their field of activity, their resource, are accomplished by the Law, . . . and all the blessings that are in this world and beyond it, [323] they also are born of the Law, produced by the Law. Therefore must I be desirous of enlightenment, valuing the Law, reverencing the Law, taking refuge in the Law, finding support in the Law, getting vigour from the Law, going according to the Law, entered into the Law.' This is what is meant by the Bodhisatva's remembering of the Law. Again, this thought comes to the Bodhisatva: 'Equal is the Law, equal for all

[1] Correct 322[1] first word to लद्धा, the Pali form: it is a misprint in the text.

creatures; the Law has no respect unto low, middle, or distinguished. As the Law is, so must I keep my thought. The Law has nothing to do with regard for the pleasant; impartial is the Law; as the Law is, so must I keep my thought. The Law does not depend upon time, for above time is the Law, self-evident, to be experienced by each for himself; as the Law is, so must I keep my thought. The Law is not in the lofty, without being also in the low, the Law is without bending up or bending down; as the Law is, so must I keep my thought. The Law is not in things pure without being also in things damaged, it is remote from superiority and inferiority; as the Law is, so must I keep my thought. The Law is not in saints without being also in worldlings, it has no respect to fields; as is the Law, so must I keep my thought. The Law is not in the day without being also in the night, or in the night but not in the day, the Law is established always; as the Law is, so must I keep my thought. The Law does not let slip the season of conversion; there is nowhere procrastination in the Law; as the Law is, so must I keep my thought. In the Law is neither emptiness nor fullness, for the Law is immeasurable and limitless, like the air it wastes not away and grows not; as the Law is, so must I keep my thought. The Law is not defended by any creature, it defends all creatures; as the Law is, so must I keep my thought. The Law seeks no refuge, the Law is the refuge of all the world; as the Law is, so must I keep my thought. There is no resisting the Law, for the Law is irresistible; [324] as the Law is, so must I keep my thought. The Law implies no inclination, for it is without inclination; as the Law is, so must I keep my thought. The Law fears not the danger of transmigration, nor is it pleased with Nirvāṇa, for the Law is without affection always; as the Law is, so must I keep my thought.' Thus the Bodhisatva remembers the Law, like the Law. This is the meaning of remembering the Law."

In the same place he says: "For the Order speaks the Law and does the Law, has the Law in the heart, it is the field of the Law, it supports the Law, takes refuge in the Law, worships the Law, does the duties of the Law, behaves according to the Law; is upright in nature and pure in nature, compassionate, merciful according to the Law, always behaves with discretion, always has support in the Law, acts clearly always, and so forth. Then as the Bodhisatva remembers the Order, this thought comes to him: 'The qualities that belong to the Order, those must also be brought about for myself and all creatures.'"

As the Bodhisatva's qualities are described in the holy *Vimalakīrti-nirdeśa*, so must we keep the Order in remembrance.

"All the aspects of all creatures, whatever be their voice or their words, the Bodhisatvas are so clever as to display them in one instant. They become old and diseased and show death in themselves, for the ripening of living creatures displaying illusory appearances. They show the secular conflagration, burning up the world; to mortals who think that things are permanent they show their impermanency. Invited by a hundred thousand beings in one kingdom, they eat in the houses of all and incline all to wisdom. If there be any skill in charms or in manual arts of all sorts, in all these they everywhere attain perfection and bring happiness to all beings. [325] If there be any sectaries [1] in the world, they become members of these; thus they bring to ripening all creatures by following after divers heretical ways. They become the moon or the sun, Śakra and Brahma lords of all creatures, they become water and light, earth and gods. In the intermediate ages of disease, they become medicine, those supreme ones, by which those beings are set free, and become happy and healthy. In the intermediate ages of famine, they become food and drink; dispelling hunger and thirst they preach the Law to all that have breath. In the intermediate ages of warfare they are intent upon compassion; they persuade hundreds of myriads of beings not to do harm. In the midst of great conflict they are impartial; they approve union and reconcilement, these mighty Bodhisatvas. Whatever hells there are in the infinite fields of the Buddhas, of set purpose they go

[1] Tib. ya mt'san, "miracle men."

thither for the good of all beings. In all the states of existence as animals that are known, everywhere they preach the Law, therefore are they called Guides.

"They practise enjoyment among the sensual, they show meditation amongst those who meditate; they destroy Māra and give no opening to him. As a lotus in the fire exists not,[1] even so they show that desires and meditation exist not. [326] Of set purpose they become a courtezan to draw men, and alluring them by the hook of lust, establish them in the Buddha's wisdom. They become villagers at any time, or merchants, or chaplains, courtiers great or small, for the good of the world. For the poor they become treasures inexhaustible, and giving them gifts, produce the thought of enlightenment. Amidst those who are stiff in pride they become mighty athletes; they seek the supreme wisdom that destroys all pride. When any are tormented with fear they stand ever before them, they give them security, and ripen them for wisdom. Becoming the five kinds of transcendent knowledge, virtuous sages, they school all beings in virtue in the effort of mercy and tenderness. They look on the reverend who need service in this world, they become clever servants or slaves and render obedience. They do everything clever in every kind of service to make one become a lover of the Law. [327] Whenever there is need of endless training and endless practice, they have endless knowledge and release endless creatures. Not in myriads of ages, nay hundreds of myriads, even when the Buddhas speak, would there be an end to the sweet tale of their virtues."

As in the holy *Ratnolkadhāraṇī* the qualities of Bodhisatvas are told, so must they be cultivated. "Emitting light, with quantities of garlands, garland-crests, garland-masses, all sorts of garlands scattered everywhere, the great-souled do the worship of the Conqueror. Emitting light, heaps of aromatic powder, lumps of powder, masses of powder, all sorts of powder scattered everywhere, the great-souled worship the Conqueror. Emitting light, garlands of lotus, masses of lotus, quantities of lotus, all sorts of lotus scattered everywhere, the great-souled

[1] Tib. read ते in 19.

worship the Conqueror. Emitting pearls, masses of pearls, heaps of pearls, all sorts of pearls scattered everywhere, the great-souled worship the Conqueror. Emitting light, banner-tops in array, the banners yellow, red and tawny, some blue, variegated flags. The Conqueror's fields are adorned with banners, these are arrayed with nets of jewels, pennons and flags hanging down like strings, nets of bells resounding the Conqueror. They hold up sunshades over the Tathāgata's head, as they do for the One Conqueror, and so with the palm of the hand they do infinite worship to all the remaining Conquerors.

This is the miraculous tranquillity of the sages; these the miracles of the popularity and knowledge of the Conquerors, devoted to supreme tranquillity, homage and service are accomplished by them. [328] Some instruct all creatures in a thousand expedients by means of the Tathāgata's worship, by means of infinite gifts and generosity, by means of the practice of all asceticism, some by means of patience indestructible and imperturbable, by means of the heroism of austerity and vows, by means of meditation and calm in the hermitage, by means of the knowledge of discriminating what is good, by means of thousands of expedients, by means of transcendent good-will, by means of well-wishing, the elements of popularity, by means of knowledge of accumulation of merit; some by means of truth, of dependent origination, and deliverance, by means of powers and senses, by means of release by the Disciples' Vehicle, by means of purification by the Vehicle of the causes,[1] by means of the miracles of the supreme Vehicle, some by means of impermanence and suffering, some by means of not-individuality and not-life, by means of detachment following on the idea of loathsomeness; [2] as many as are the ways of conduct in the world, in so many ways of Law they enter in [3]; as many as are the means of universal deliverance, they convert all creatures according to their dispositions in the world; but these who by means of universal deliverance

[1] =*pratītyasamutpāda*. [2] See Childers, s.v. *asubha*.

[3] Read ०यन्ति.

instruct all creatures according to their dispositions in the world, it is impossible to recognize; this is the miracle produced by meditation. These show the excellent meditation of the palace of pleasure,[1] suitable for ripening all the world; they show all pleasure, joy and delight on purpose, and thus they convert all. When in time of famine all the goods that bring happiness to the world are hard to get, then by accomplishing the wishes of all they give gifts, and work the good of the world by the best of choice food, drink and flavours, by a variety of jewels to fasten their clothes, by renouncing kingdoms, wealth and what is pleasant to themselves, [329] and convert all those who are devoted to liberality. Their limbs are distinguished by choice marks, with most beautiful ornaments, choice heroes, adorned with wreaths and anointed with perfumes. Showing beauty of form, they convert all creatures who are delighted in pleasantness and joy; choice of form, beautiful, wise, showing the perfection of beauty, they convert the people who delight in beauty; with sparrow-chirpings like honey, with the note of cuckoo, wild swan, and Himalayan pheasant, with voice of drum, kinnara, and brahma preach the law amongst all that delight in these things. The four and eighty thousand, through whom the Conquerors accomplish the good of the world, these everywhere with voices that disclose doctrine convert all creatures in the world according to their disposition. They give help in weal or in woe, they are helpers in good or in evil fortune, helping in all needs they convert all creatures with the voice of help. They support the inconveniences made by pain and calamity with the object of helping, their help overcoming pain for the good and happiness of all the world; and where there is no going forth as ascetics, no law known, no deliverance in the forest, there, helpers in royalty and prosperity, their minds peaceful in their going forth houseless, [330] to release all the world from the bondage and thirst of the household life, themselves free from abiding in sensual pleasures of all sorts, they preach deliverance by going forth from the household life; they following the ten

[1] Tib. read ते रति०

kinds of good conduct, walk in the law of the great men; following all the behaviour of the sages without exception, they work the good of the world; where living creatures are of immeasurable age, filled with felicity, and of few faults, there burdened with age, laden with disease, they show the power of death, themselves free; showing the world ablaze with passion, ablaze with sin, ablaze with the great fire of delusion, aflame with old age, disease, and death, they instruct all creatures, with the ten powers, the four kinds of confidence,[1] and the eighteen excellences in Law, pointing out the Buddha's greatness of soul, by the Buddha's virtues they work the good of the world. By miracles manifesting the supernatural power of the Tathāgata, by their power over form on all sides, they convert all beings by transformation that comes from their supernatural power. They walk the earth working the world's good by all kinds of ways and means; like a lotus unsoiled in the water [2] they go doing pleasant and gracious things; they are poets and kings of poets, they are actors and dancers, musicians and wrestlers, fakeers, cleaners, dancers, robbers, jugglers, showing these many shapes, [331] they become villagers, guides, and charioteers, they become traders, merchants, householders, kings, courtiers, chaplains, messengers, learned physicians, men versed in the scriptures; they become great trees in the forest, herbs, treasures of immortal jewels, the wishing-gem, trees that give all desires, guides to those that go astray. May those who know not all these arts and crafts speedily see these in the world. They teach in the world how to be husbandmen or tradesmen, and artisans of all sorts, who not harming or hurting any are the bringers of all bliss and praised for wisdom; all kinds of learning in science and potent herbs are produced by those sages, who become masters in the rules of the sages to which this world and the gods are devoted, who are strict of will, foremost in austerity, all this is produced by these wise men; [3] they become sectaries, Caraka or Parivrājaka, or observers of the ascetic Gotama's vow of silence,

[1] See Childers, s.v. *vesārajja*.

[2] Tib. read *padmam*.

[3] See J.R.A.S., 1901, p. 124.

or the devotees of the naked unclothed Guru: they become leaders of the sects. [332] Or they may belong to such as observe the Ajīvika system, whether those who have or those who have not the higher aim, those that have long coils of hair, those who took the vow as youths, amongst these also they become leaders. Among the ascetics who endure the five fires, turning to the sun, those who have the dog-vows and cattle-vows, those who act as beasts of the chase, followers of some of the observances of the thirty sects, amongst these too they become leaders. For such as delight in initiation into the knowledge of the deity, for those who travel from place to place exhibiting the sects, they live on roots, fruits, and water and also become masters in these endless systems. For those who remain squatting upon their heels, or who wander alone, whose bed is on thorns, ashes, or grass, who rest on a pestle-pole and so live, amongst these too they become leaders.

"If there be worldly sectaries who are outside the pale, amongst these observing the faith, by sharp, dangerous, and cruel penances they instruct the sectaries how to get rid of unhappiness. [323] Knowing that people are troubled with heresies, sectaries plunged in all heretical doctrine, they teach them by subtle verses with which all creatures are enlightened; to some by charms of Drāmiḍa,[1] they preach the truth by secret verses; some by words straight and clear, and to some also by words that are mysterious, to some by words in separated syllables and to some by thunderbolt verses with determination of sense, to some by words of wisdom that crush the adversary, to some by words setting free from unrighteous books, to some by words of human charms, by words in all manner of languages, to some by words in the language of gods, by words in the language of Nāga or Yaksha, by words in the language of Rākshasa or Gandharva, of demons, goblins, or great serpents, words of Kinnara, Apsara, or Garuḍa, they bring truth, enlightenment, and deliverance. They also, knowing the rules of interpretation according to truth, they who are of the

[1] That is, the Dravidian country.

Conqueror's fashion wholly, knowing the path of speech to knowledge beyond thought, preach the miracles of tranquillity

"They, because of the world's welfare, earnestly desiring tranquillity for all the world, emitting glory beyond thought, shedding rays of glory, convert all creatures ; to those creatures who see the glory there comes a beautiful and fruitful and transcendent source of wisdom. They show the Buddha, they show the Law, they show the Order, they show the road to men ; they show the images of the Conqueror in the shrines, so that they emit the ray of beauty in perfection. [334] They emit the ray called Splendour-making, which makes the curved splendour of the Maruts, and dispelling all mist and darkness, this blazes in splendour for those that are dear to the world. Incited by that ray, all beings keep alight the lamp of worship for the Conqueror. They also keeping the lamp of worship for the Conqueror, become conquerors who make lamps for the world, giving oil-lamps, ghee-lamps, lights of wood, grass, reeds, bamboos, lamps of perfumed and precious plants, when they have received the splendour-making ray amongst the Conquerors. They emit the ray called Ferrying-over. Incited with this brilliancy people [1] . . . ferrying in a ship on the paths of the river. Things material are despised, tranquillity is praised ; so that the Ferrying ray is brought to fulfilment.

"The ray named Thirst-dispelling : with this brightness people being incited cast off the thirst for sensual objects and desire the choice flavour of righteousness and deliverance, they become Buddhas, they rain the water of immortality, dispelling thirst and craving for all the world, they make rivers, pools, tanks full of lotus, springs welling forth, the causes of wisdom ; desire is blamed, meditation is praised ; thus the Dispelling of Thirst is accomplished. When they emit the ray Causing Delight, by this brightness people being incited, spreading delight, produce thought causing spontaneous delight, [335] the body of these beneficent beings resting upon a lotus adorned with lucky marks, proclaiming always the Buddha's virtues ; thus the ray Causing Delight is accomplished.

[1] The Tib. shows that several lines have dropped out.

"They send forth a ray named Pleasure-causing: people awakened by this brightness are always pleased with the Buddha, the Law, and the Order, they are always pleased with those three saints among the righteous company who consort with the Buddha, all those many beings who attain resignation to the idea of not being reborn,[1] and so they are incited and reminded, saints among the righteous company who remember the Buddha, having developed and displayed the virtues of enlightened thought. Thus the Pleasure-causing ray is finished.

"They emit the ray Accumulating Merit. People incited by this brightness give all manner of gifts, craving supreme enlightenment, to fulfil the wish of suitors; their sacrifice is unhindered as they perform it; having given gifts according to every wish, the ray of Accumulating Merit is accomplished. They emit the ray which is Full of Wisdom: people are stirred by this brightness. This discloses in a moment the fact that Righteousness is one, though it is approached in many ways. [336] This ray gives to creatures who are seduced by the variety of things a share of knowledge in the discrimination of objects, making an illumination of the meaning of religious texts; thus this light of wisdom is finished. They emit the ray of Brilliant Wisdom. People incited by this brightness have recourse to the void, they see that things are without substance, unborn and undying, without being or property, like mirage and illusion, like the moon in the water, like sleep, or reflections in a mirror, void, without owner, indifferent: the ray of Brilliant Wisdom is finished. They emit the Ray of Holy Miracles; by this ray incited, people having received the indestructible treasure of the charm, they receive the treasures of all the Tathāgatas, they do reverence to all the supporters of the Law, they make a pious support of the sages, they protect the Law of the world: the Ray of Miracles is finished. They emit the Ray of Renunciation. Those greedy ones who are incited by this learn that enjoyments are unlasting and impermanent, and become devoted to renunciation. Persons greedy, hard to tame, unsubdued, knowing that wealth is the stuff

[1] Anutpattikakshānti, Dh. S. cvii.

of sleep or clouds, are pleased in mind with the growth of renunciation: the Ray of Renunciation is finished. They emit the Ray Incombustible. By this vicious persons incited become established in purity of manners, and they conceive the thought, 'May I become Buddha.' [337] In the good and virtuous path of action, they undertake virtues by solemn vow, which awakens the minds of many persons by their vow: thus the Ray Incombustible is accomplished. They emit the Ray of Patience made Manifest. By this unrestrained persons are affected. Leaving all anger and undue self-conceit they become always devoted to patience. Patience in misery, unshaken mind in those who are unfortunate for the sake of enlightenment; the virtues of patience are always praised. Thus the Ray of Patience made Manifest is finished. They emit the Scorching Ray by which apathetic persons are incited. They do the right and proper worship to the Three Treasures, not weary in well-doing; thus doing right and proper worship to the Three Treasures, not weary in well-doing, they pass by the four ways of Māra and soon touch the supreme enlightenment. Because one has made many beings take on heroism; having done worship to the three Treasures, he has upheld doctrine at the time of destruction: thus the Scorching Ray is attained. They emit the Tranquillizing Ray, by which restless persons are affected. Amongst them is neither passion nor wrath nor delusion, they become enlightened, their thoughts steadfast, thus shaking themselves free from association with sin, bad friends, and wickedness in their conduct they praise meditation, tranquil in the forest: thus the Tranquillizing Ray is accomplished. They emit the Ray of Wisdom made Manifest, by which unwise persons are affected; in this way, the Truth, dependent origination, deliverance, they attain the moral qualities and perception.[1] [338] Having attained the faculty of perception[2] . . . having attained the Sun-illumination trance, they become Conquerors, kindling the brightness of

[1] Reading इन्द्रिय as in next verse. See Childers, s.v. *indriyam.*

[2] A line is omitted.

wisdom, by renouncing kingdom, wealth, and what is dear to themselves, respecting the Law which is sought as the cause of enlightenment, they manifest that Law. Thus the Ray of Wisdom made Manifest is finished. They emit the Ray of Buddhas, by which brightness people are incited. Many thousands of Buddhas, thousands beyond thought, they behold, seated on forests of lotuses, they declare the Buddha-release of the great-souled Buddha, the Buddha's innumerable miraculous transformations, disclosing the increase of the Buddha's power : thus the Buddha-Ray is accomplished. They emit the Safety-giving Ray, by which touched, beings, tormented by fear,[1] hurt, stricken, held in bonds by evil spirits, are set free from all misfortunes. Those to whom safety is offered are kept from killing living creatures ; saved are the terrified because they have found a refuge : thus the Safety-giving Ray is accomplished. They emit the Ray that gives All Blessings, by which the sick and suffering are affected. Wholly delivered from disease and pain, they receive the blessings of the trance of meditation ; they drive away sickness, giving roots and fruits, healing herbs, precious flavours, sweet ointments, fruits, sap, honey, ghee, oil, for eating and drinking.

[339] "They emit the Ray of the Vision of Buddhas ; beings touched by this ray at the end of the waning of life remember Buddha, they see Buddha, being reborn they go into a Buddha's field. They die, and remembering the Buddhas, see apparitions of Buddhas, which cause joy ; as at death they cry 'refuge in Buddha,' they attain the Ray of the Vision of Buddhas. They emit the ray called the Exposition of the Law, by which brightness people are affected. They recite the Law, hear it, write it, they become always devoted to the Law. When the Law is scarce, they declare the Law ; the hope of those who search for the Law is fulfilled ; do they but say, Produce aspiration and apply yourselves to the Law, they obtain the Ray called the Exposition of the Law. They emit the Sounding Ray to stir up the sons of Buddha ; and whatever be the volume of sound in the three worlds, all hear the voice of the Tathāgata :

[1] Reading तेन भयार्दित.

thy praise the great sages with a loud noise, by the offering of lutes and mighty bells, they make a din to sound the noise of the Conqueror throughout all the world: the Sounding Ray is accomplished. They emit the Ray that gives Immortality, by which illumination the people are moved; by renouncing the practice of distraction,[1] they attain possession of all virtues; they declare that things composite are full of much pain and calamity and always unstable, but the joy of peace and painlessness is always stable; by this declaration the Ray that gives Immortality is accomplished. They emit the Most Excellent Ray, by which brightness people are moved. They hear the excellent virtue, the excellent meditation, the excellent wisdom of the Conquerors: [340] chief in virtue, chief in meditation, chief in wisdom is the great royal sage, who is praised and lauded as the cause of enlightenment; thus the Most Excellent brightness is accomplished.

"They emit the Ray of Manifestation of the Treasures, by which brightness people are moved. Having received the deposit of the imperishable treasure they worship the great sages with choice treasures, lavishing treasures upon the Conqueror and the Conqueror's shrine they attract all people by the treasures, bestowing treasures on the Conquerors: the Ray of Manifestation of the Treasures is accomplished. They emit the Ray of Splendid Perfumes, by which brightness people are moved. From the odour of superhuman and delightful perfumes there arise Buddha-virtues innumerable; because they have done worship to the lords of men with perfumes and ointments human and divine, the Conqueror's shrines are all perfumes: the Ray of Splendid Perfumes is accomplished. They emit the Ray of Manifestation of Many Colours, the many-coloured banners and flags of Indra, with resounding of music and wafts of perfume, brilliant and divine flowers scattered abroad, they approach the worship of the Conquerors with music, flowers and ointments, incense and powders, spreading of parasols, flags and banners: thus the Ray of Many Colours is accomplished. They emit the Ray of Delighting. The

[1] Tib. implies something like प्रमादचर्यो, not स्थिरं.

earth stands as smooth as the palm of the hand as they cleanse the hermitage-shrines of the sages,[1] and thus the Ray of Delighting is accomplished.

"They emit the Cloud-like Ray; there are the clouds showering perfumes; they sprinkle the path about the shrine with cinnamon and scented water: the Cloud-like Ray is accomplished.

"They emit the Decoration-manifesting Ray; the naked become clothed [2] and ornamented. They give various clothes, girdles, necklaces: the Decoration Ray is accomplished. [341] They emit the Ray of Choice Flavours; the hungry receive food of choice flavours, they give all manner of food and drink of choice flavours: the Ray of Choice Flavours is accomplished. The Ray that shows Wealth they emit; the poor receive gifts of treasures: by giving plenty of the three imperishable treasures the Ray of Wealth is accomplished. They emit the Eye-cleansing Ray; then the blind see all manner of shapes: by giving of lamps to the Conqueror and the Conqueror's shrine the Eye-cleansing Ray is accomplished. They emit the Ear-cleansing Ray, and those without hearing hear many sounds: by giving music to the Conqueror and the Conqueror's shrine the Ear-cleansing Ray is accomplished. They emit the Smell-cleansing Ray, and they that smelt not before smell sweet perfumes: by giving perfumes to the Conqueror and the Conqueror's shrine, the Smell-cleansing Ray is accomplished. They emit the Tongue-cleansing Ray, and they praise the Buddhas with dear and lovely words; evil speech is prevented, gentle words are said, and this Ray is accomplished. They emit the Body-cleansing Ray, and those without senses receive good senses: by bowing the body to the Conqueror and the Conqueror's shrine the Body-cleansing Ray is accomplished. They emit the Thought-cleansing Ray, and all the insensate receive the power of thought: by bringing the thoughts within the power of meditation the Thought-cleansing Ray is accomplished. They emit the Form-cleansing Ray; and one sees the bodies of the lords of men transcending

[1] By scented water: marginal note.

[2] So Tib.

thought; this is obtained by making shrines and various coloured pictures of the Buddha's bodies. They emit the Sound-cleansing Ray; and one understands that sound is not sound and void: this ray is obtained by teaching that sound is produced from causes and like an echo. They emit the Scent-cleansing Ray, and all evil smells become sweet smells; this ray is obtained by bathing the shrines of the Conqueror and the Bo-tree with waters [1] perfumed with the choicest perfumes. [342] They emit the Taste-cleansing Ray; poisonous tastes lose their poison and become excellent; that ray comes by giving all fine flavours to Buddha and disciples and to the spirits of one's ancestors.

"They emit the Touch-purifying Ray; hard becomes soft and pleasant to the touch; showers of spears and tridents, lances and swords become soft garlands of lotus flowers, they walk on a road overspread with soft tapestries pleasant to the touch; that light is the giving to the Conquerors of garments soft with flowers and perfumes and good store of garlands. They emit the Concept-cleansing Ray from every pore; they think of the objects when they hear it emanating from those benefactors of the world, pleasing the intentions of the Conquerors; things born from a cause are not born, the real body of things is a body not born; the true nature of things is everlasting, like as the sky: the Concept-cleansing Ray is accomplished.[2]

"They produce the Ray called Joy-first; from the opening of each pore of the sages these rays issue forth as many as the sands of the Ganges, and each achieves a special purpose; just as they issue forth from the orifice of each pore, as many as the sands of the Ganges, so from all the pores of the sages [3] without exception on all sides (such is the miraculous working of meditation) he emits each ray towards those who have previously been companions in the quality which causes each ray to be emitted; such is the miraculous display due to the

[1] Reading जलै°.

[2] Compare for the doctrines alluded to Vajracchedikā, p. 43.

[3] Read रोमादेष.

knowledge of the sages. Those who have been previously companions in their merit, who have rejoiced in this merit and prayed for it, who having seen it have accumulated good deeds, those men perceive this ray. Those who have accumulated good deeds and done meritorious actions, who have again and again worshipped the Buddhas, desiring a Buddha's qualities and greedy for them, these men the ray succeeds in stirring up.

[343] "As one born blind sees not the sun, yet does the sun not cease, yet he rises upon the world, but he that hath eyes sees its rising and prepares for all his business; even so is the Ray of the Great Ones; there it is, but the vulgar see it not, even when they have left the world,[1] because they are plunged in falsehood, without aspiration. Even for the high-minded these rays are hard to obtain. Ornaments, precious stones, palaces, jewels, elixirs, ointments, perfumes, these belong to the great and high-minded, they are very hard to obtain for those in poverty: even so is the Ray of the Great Ones, there it is, and the vulgar see it not, being plunged in falsehood, without aspiration. Hard to obtain are these things, even for the high-minded. Whosoever having heard the analysis of these Rays has faith, aspiration, and contentment, for him there must be no more doubt, no more anxiety, nor indeed will he fear any more, saying, 'I shall never be a great banner of virtues'; they practising the Meditation called the Creation of an Army, show to all the ten quarters incomparable sons of Buddha as their surrounding. Those masses of Rays create a beautiful lotus as large as the universe of three thousand worlds; they appear seated upon this blossoming lotus; such is the magical display of this Meditation. They raise up other lotuses as many as the atoms of dust in ten fields of Buddha, together with a surrounding company; for they are surrounded with the sons of the Buddhas, some in a state of meditation and some not. Beings who have been ripened by these sages, and perfected by them in a Buddha's virtues, surround the

[1] Tib. adds the equivalent of *pravrajitāpi*. It goes on: "But the high-minded see them."

great lotus, and stand in the celestial regions with outstretched hands.

[344] "They enter into meditation with a child's body as the object of their contemplation, and they arise when it has become a vigorous youthful body. Concentrating their thought upon a vigorous youthful body, they arise when the body has grown old. Concentrated upon a body grown old as their object, they arise from the bodies of faithful female disciples; concentrated in thought upon these, they arise from the bodies of Sisters; concentrated upon these, they arise from the bodies of famous Brethren; concentrated upon these, they arise from the bodies of Brahman pupils and not pupils; concentrated upon these, they arise from the bodies of Pratyeka Buddhas; concentrated upon these, they arise from the bodies of pre-eminent Buddhas; concentrated upon these, they arise from the bodies of divinities; concentrated upon these, they arise from the bodies of great nāga sages; concentrated upon these, they arise from the bodies of all sorts of beings; concentrated upon these, they arise from one single pore; concentrated upon one pore, they arise from every pore; concentrated upon every pore, they arise from one hair-hole; concentrated upon one hair-hole, they arise from all hair-holes; concentrated upon all hair-holes, they arise from one atom of dust; concentrated upon one atom of dust, they arise from all dust-atoms without exception; concentrated upon all atoms of dust, they arise from the surface of the sea-water; [345] concentrated upon the surface of the sea-water, they arise from the fruits of the jewel-tree; concentrated upon the fruits of the jewel-tree, they arise from the Rays of the Conqueror; concentrated upon the Conquerors' Rays, they arise from the rivers and sea-water; concentrated upon the water, they arise from the glorious path as Mahātma; concentrated upon the paths of fire, they arise from the path of the mind intent on remembrance; concentrated upon the path of the mind, they arise from the surface of the earth as Mahātmas; concentrated upon the surface of the earth, they arise from every divine mansion; concentrated upon all divine mansions, they

arise from the sky [1] intent on remembrance. The spiritual exaltation [2] is infinite for those who have accumulated virtues infinite; even if explained by the Conquerors for infinite ages it cannot be exhausted. The ripening of the world's action is infinite. The miraculous display of nāgas, the miraculous display of Buddhas, the miraculous display of meditation in one who uses it, is infinite, though explained by all the Jinas. Placed in the power of the Eighth Deliverance, from being of one body they become of many bodies, and being many they become one again, and meditate amidst the blazing sky; and though without great compassion, not desirous of wisdom, indifferent to the world, yet they show infinite transformations of the body; then what cannot he show who desires the welfare of the world? Sun and moon moving in the sky show their reflection in spring, lake, pool, well, or tank, in vessel, jewel, ocean, or river, of all parts. [346] In the same way, these heroes show their bodies infinite in all the ten regions, knowing all ways of meditation and deliverance, where the Tathāgata is visible in his own essence. The deity of the ocean named Rutāvatī charms by her voice all beings sprung from the sea, that understand music. And this Rutāvat, full of passion and sin, in all sound knowing the rules of counter-notes, having got in her power the mighty law of incantations, whom did she not delight of men and gods both? as making illusion with accomplished skill she showed various endless forms, at any one moment in night or day showing whole months, or a hundred years, bright with light. Then making illusion, full of passion and sin, as she delighted the world, transforming by illusion, well taught in meditation and transcendent knowledge and deliverance, whom did she not delight with her knowledge of the rules of conduct? As she made by miracle many forms at will, having put a thunderbolt on his foot as a phylactery, she showed a stature reaching from sea to sky, and her head equal with the top of Sumeru. And as full of passion and sin and delusion, he showed mighty powers equal with Rāhu,

[1] Reading गगनात्तु°.

[2] The Eight Spiritual Exercises: Childers, s.v. *Vimokkho*; see below.

crushing Māra, enlightening the world, to whom did not he show his endless power? In the infinite transformations of Śakra in the battle of Gods, Asuras and Indra; as many as the billions of Asuras, so many bodies of himself did Śakra make. [347] Each of all the chiefs of the Asuras thinks that Śakra himself is before him; all fall into confusion or terror, thinking, Here is one is caught by him who wields the thunderbolt. Beholding Sakra, who shows a thousand frightful eyes, emitting flames, holding the thunderbolt, his body clothed in armour, the power invincible, the chiefs of the Asurās flee away. Thus Śakra shows miraculous transformations in his desire for the victory of the gods, although the strength of his merit is weak; how should there not be a miraculous display in the case of a being of merit inexhaustible, who works for the protection of the whole world? Clouds born of the wind give rain; again, clouds are dispelled by the wind; by the wind the corn grows in the world, wind brings blessing to all creatures in the world. And this wind is unpractised in the highest perfections, unpractised in the Buddha's virtues. Why should not they who show infinite ripening for the world, who have obtained the best, show miraculous transformations?"

CHAPTER XIX

INCREASE OF HOLINESS

[348] ANOTHER cause of the increase of merit is to be practised: that is the weal of all at all times.[1]

As it is said in the holy *Ratnamegha*: "He giving at a Tathāgata's shrine or Tathāgata's image a flower or incense or perfume, applies this so as to annul the wickedness of unsavouriness or dirt of all beings, and to get the Tathāgata's quality. By accomplishing the act of cleansing and anointing he dispels ungracious ways of deportment, and causes the acquiring of gracious ways of deportment for all beings. By uplifting a flowery shelter, he accomplishes for all beings the dispelling of all passion and sorrow. As he enters the monastery he conceives this thought: May I make all beings enter the city of Nirvāṇa. As he goes forth, he conceives this thought: May I make all beings go forth from the road of transmigration. When he opens the door of the house[2] he conceives this thought: May I open to all beings the door of the good way to Nirvāṇa by transcendental knowledge. When he closes it, he conceives this thought: May I close all the doors of sin for all beings. When he sits down he conceives this thought: May I make all beings sit in the seat of wisdom. As he lies on the right side he conceives this thought: May I bring all beings to Nirvāṇa. As he arises thence he conceives this thought: May I make all beings to arise from going about to sin. As he goes to attend to his bodily needs he conceives this thought: May all beings go as the Great Being goes. As he sits there he conceives this thought: May all beings find as easy a purging of all lust and

[1] Kārikā 26[1].

[2] Read लयन०. Tib. gnas khaṅ.

wickedness and delusion. As he makes all clean he conceives this thought: May I purify all beings from the dirt of sin. As he cleanses his hands he conceives this thought: May I take from all beings [349] the desire for all sins. As he cleanses his feet he conceives this thought: May I take away from all beings the dirt of sin in its many kinds. As he cleanses his face he conceives this thought: May I make clean for all beings all the ways of access to righteousness. As he rubs his teeth he conceives this thought: May I take away from all beings the various kinds of sin's defilements. He uses every position of the body for the good and blessing of all beings. As he greets the Tathāgata's shrine he conceives this thought: Be all beings greeted in heaven and in earth."

Or as it is in the holy *Prajñāpāramitā*. "Again, Śāriputra, when the Bodhisatva, the Great Being, is in the midst of a forest of wild beasts, he must not fear, he must not be afraid, he must not fall into terror. And why not? Because he has renounced all for the sake of all beings. Therefore he must thus think: If ravening beasts should eat me, let that be my gift even to them; and my perfection of charity will thus be fulfilled, and the supreme and perfect enlightenment will be attained;[1] and thus I shall bring it about, that when I have been enlightened with the supreme enlightenment, in that Buddha's field there shall be and shall be known no beings whatsoever to have entered into the bodies of animals. When Śāriputra, the Bodhisatva, the Great Being, is in the midst of a forest of robbers, he must not fear, he must not be afraid, he must not fall into terror. And why not? Because all these Bodhisatvas, Great Beings, are ready to renounce all that is theirs, and a Bodhisatva must abandon even his body, must renounce even the means and necessaries of life. Thus he must think: If these take from me the means and necessaries of life, let that be my gift even to them. If any persons should uproot me out of life, then I must not feel hatred or anger; I must not offend even against them with body, voice or mind; thus by me at that moment will be fulfilled the perfection of charity, the perfection of virtue

[1] Inserted from lines 18–19 below.

the perfection of compassion; and the supreme and perfect enlightenment will be attained. So will I do and so will I behave, that when I have attained the supreme and perfect enlightenment in that Buddha's district those and other faults shall not at all or in any place be found or seen. And, Śāriputra, when the Bodhisatva the Great Being is in a waterless forest, [350] he must not fear, he must not be afraid, he must not fall into terror. And why not? Because the Bodhisatvas are of will unterrified. And thus must he think: I must teach all beings how to destroy all thirst. A Bodhisatva, a Great Being, must not fall into fear. If I shall perish by thirst, yet nevertheless before all the world I shall conceive the thought of great compassion; alas, these beings have small merit that in their world such waterless forests are known; but I will so do, and so will I behave, that when I have attained the supreme and perfect wisdom, in that Buddha's field waterless forests shall no more ever be known anywhere. So will I endow all beings with merit, that they shall have most excellent water.[1] So will I lay hold of firm courage on behalf of all beings, that the perfection of courage shall then and there be fulfilled. Again, Śāriputra, when the Bodhisatva the Great Being is in the midst of a foodless forest, he must not fear, he must not be afraid, he must not fall into terror. Thus must he resolve: So will I lay hold of firm courage, so will I cleanse my own Buddha's field, that when I have attained the supreme and perfect wisdom, there shall no more be or be known in this Buddha's field any such foodless forests anywhere. Those beings shall be happy and provided with all requisites, filled with all happiness; and so will I do that whatsoever shall be the wish of those beings, whatsoever they shall desire in their mind, that shall come to pass; just as all is brought to pass by the mind of the Thirty-three gods, so by their mind it will arise. So will I lay hold of firm courage for the sake of all beings, that the perfection of energy shall obtain full development at such a time. And there shall be no lack of the necessaries of life for all beings everywhere and at every time."

[1] The phrase *ashṭāṅgopeta* occurs in Divyāvadāna, 127[19].

So this, "all beings' weal in every circumstance," [1] is the cause of the growth of merit; and it is to be seen in detail in the holy *Gocara-pariśuddhi Sūtra.*

Moreover, "the pious and unworldly gift" [1] is a means for the growth of merit.

[351] As it is said in the holy *Adhyāśaya-saṃcodana Sūtra:* "When Maitreya gives the gift of righteousness, desiring no profit or honour, there are twenty advantages for his disinterested gift. What are these twenty? To wit: He is thoughtful, mindful, wise, intelligent, steadfast, prudent; he fully understands the transcendental wisdom; he has little passion, little hatred, little delusion; Māra has no opening against him; he is held in regard by the mighty Buddhas, and the supernatural beings protect him; the gods place power in his body; his enemies have no opening against him; his friends are faithful to him; his word is to be trusted; he gains the four kinds of confidence; [2] he is rich in spiritual joy, praised by the learned; that gift of his is one to be remembered. These, Maitreya, are the twenty advantages."

And in the holy *Prajñāpāramitā* he says: "If, Ānanda, you should preach the Law in the Disciples' stage to men of the Disciples' Vehicle, and if at that preaching all the beings in a Trisāhasramahāsāhasra [3] world should attain to sainthood in your sight, yet the disciple's duty would not be done by you, my disciple. But if, Ānanda, you should preach and reveal even one verse connected with the supreme perfection of wisdom to a Bodhisatva, a Great Being, thus I should be content with you, my disciple; and if all the beings in that aforesaid world should by that former preaching attain to sainthood, then all that meritorious action of those saints, in gifts, in morality, in meditation, would be a great body of merit. [4] What think you, Ānanda, is this a great store of merit? He said: Yes, great, Blessed One, great, Blessed One. The Blessed One said: But, Ānanda, that man of the Disciples' Vehicle who preaches somewhat connected with the perfection

[1] Kārikā 26, 1.

[2] See Childers, s.v. *vesārajja.*

[3] Name of a Buddhist world.

[4] Vajracchedika, p. 39.

of wisdom to the Bodhisatvas, the Great Beings, gains greater store of merit than he; and greater still than this, Ānanda, gains a Bodhisatva, a Great Being, who preaches to another Bodhisatva somewhat connected with the perfection of wisdom, even one day. [352] Not to say one day, Ānanda, even one forenoon. Not to say one forenoon, Ānanda, even one half-hour, even one instant of time, etc. . . . this gift of the Law, Ānanda, to a Bodhisatva, a great Being, becomes a root of good for all those of the Disciples' Vehicle and of the Pratyeka Buddha's Vehicle. Thus the Bodhisatva, a Great Being, obtains a root of good. Possessed of such a root of good, it is impossible and out of the question that the Bodhisatva, the Great Being, should turn away from the supreme and perfect enlightenment. That is not possible."

How is the gift of the Law to be given? As it is set forth in the holy *Saddharma-puṇḍarīka*.[1]

"The sage, having meditated for a time, within his house with the door closed, after surveying all the Law in profound thought, should arise and preach with courageous heart. He is always in a proper position, conspicuous and well seated, when he preaches the Law, having prepared a lofty seat suited for him in a clean and pleasant place. He is clothed in a clean robe, well dyed with pleasant colours, covered with a black dust-cloak and robed in a full cassock. [353] He sits on a seat provided with a footstool, strewn with various drapery; his feet well washen he mounts thereupon, his head and face anointed. Seated there on the pulpit of the Law, seeing all beings assembled and attentive before him, let him utter various discourse to the Brethren and Sisters. He should put laziness far from him, and he knows not the name of weariness; the sage should put away all displeasure, and implant the power of Compassion in the assembly. The sage should speak of the excellent Law both night and day, with the aid of countless myriads of examples; he should delight and also please the company and never ask anything at all there. Food and nourishment, meat and drink, clothes, beds and seats,

[1] Chap. xiii., stanzas 24, 26–29, 32–35.

vestments, physic for disease should not trouble his thoughts, and he should not say anything about them besides in the assembly. [354] Only he should always be thinking in his enlightened mind: May I become Buddha, and these beings also! This is for me the means to attain all happiness, that I declare the Law for the good of the world."

In the same book he says: "To no one even through love of the Law does he show any especial favour."

In the holy *Candra-pradīpa Sūtra* he says again: "If they should supplicate thee to obtain the gift of the Law, first say unto them, I am not taught in the greater scripture. Thus speak thou: You are wise in knowledge; how can I speak before those of great soul? Speak not hastily to them, but examining the recipient, if you discern a fit recipient then preach even uninvited. If you should see wicked persons many standing in the assembly, do not preach austerity, but praise the virtues of giving gifts. If there should be persons of moderate desires, pure, established in virtue, you should win their friendship [1] and [355] preach austerity. If there be a few that desire sin and many virtuous there, take your side and praise the quality of virtue."

It is said also in the holy *Sāgaramati Sūtra*, to wit: [2] "Peace, tranquillity, conquered foe, plant, mirror, Māra's defeat, terror, meditation river, candid purity, washing away of dirt, the harmless, ejecting the harmful, swallowing, face averted, face turned to, all attacks and all bonds nullified, all false teachers held fast, Māra's snares unbound, the seals of Buddha established, all Māras destroyed; all deeds of Māra disappear by purification of the immovable stage. These, Sāgaramati, are the charms duly performed by a preacher of the Law, by a preacher in the pulpit, by a preacher seated who diffuses through the whole assembly compassion which has attained the state of enlightenment. One should liken oneself to the physician and the Law to medicine, and the hearers of

[1] So Tib.

[2] These words are incoherent and sometimes nonsense, giving sound jingles as usual. They are simply transliterated in Tib.

the Law to patients, and the Tathāgata to the Good Being, convinced that the eye of the Law will last long, then bringing these magic charms to bear, one should preach the Law. Around him for a hundred leagues no Māra, no deity of Māra's retinue, will come nigh to cause blindness, and whatsoever do approach cannot hinder him."

In the same place he says: "A preacher of the Law should be clean, of pure behaviour, well bathed, cleanly housed."

The giving of the Law is after this fashion:

[356] "The mind of true enlightenment,
this increase gives to holiness." [1]

As it is said in the holy *Ratna-karaṇḍaka Sūtra:* "For example, Mañjuśrī, as trees grow with various odours when they are nourished by the four elements; even so, Mañjuśrī, is the Bodhisatva's root of good, accumulated by his various tasks; it grows when nourished by the thought of enlightenment, directed towards omniscience."

This kind of Bodhisatva-instruction has been always taught to beginners, to keep them in mind; and in detail it is a matter for the very Buddha; then of this instruction as described,

Perfection lies in self-denial;
by never leaving watchfulness
it comes by understanding full,
by mindfulness and deepest thought.[2]

Here, when wicked and evil things have not arisen, he forms a resolution that they shall not arise, he strives, he puts forth strength, he controls and fixes his mind; by this comes protection.

When they have arisen, he forms a resolution that they shall be destroyed; by this comes purification. And when good things have not arisen he forms a resolution that they shall arise, . . . and when they have arisen he forms a resolution that they shall abide and increase, and so forth. By this comes growth. And all these things are to be always surrounded by

[1] Kārikā 26b.

[2] Kārikā 27.

vigilance, because the quality of being the root of all merit belongs to vigilance.

As it is said in the holy *Candra-pradīpa Sūtra*: "All things that are praised as good, virtue and sacred knowledge, self-sacrifice and also patience, in all these the root is vigilance, that gains the treasure pointed out by the Blessed One."

And what is this vigilance? To be attentive to prevent destruction of what is wished or the approach of what is not wished: that is to say, as the attention of a servant who has taken a jar full of oil over a slippery place for a king ill-tempered and difficult to appease.[1]

[357] For it is said in the holy *Tathāgata-guhya Sūtra*: "Here what is this vigilance? A restraint of the senses. Seeing forms with the eye, one is not emotionally affected[2] by the primary or secondary marks. Thus while distinguishing objects with his mind he is not thus affected by their marks, he sees exactly as they are enjoyment and distress, and escape from transmigration. That is what is meant by vigilance. Again, vigilance is the mastery of one's own thought, consideration for other's thought, development of love of the Law by not ministering to the love of sin, all that is called vigilance. He that has faith and vigilance, Guhyakādhipati, must use courage accordingly, by which he perfects those things that cause vigilance and faith. He that has faith and vigilance and courage, Guhyakādhipati, must endeavour to attain full consciousness of what he is and does, so that he does not lose any of the things that belong to wisdom. He that has faith, vigilance, courage, Guhyakādhipati, with full knowledge of what he is and what he does, must earnestly make endeavour after a right state of mind;[3] for, Guhyakādhipati, the Bodhisatva that has the right state of mind recognizes what is as that which is, and what is not as that which is not . . .; the eye exists from the standpoint of experience."[4]

[1] See Jātaka, i. 393, Kathāsaritsāgara, vi. 27 (trans. p. 239), Lalita Vistara, 297–9, and Bodhicaryāvatāra, vii. 70.

[2] In Pali, *nimittam gaṇhāti* is used of falling in love: Jat. ii. 344, 6 etc.

[3] *Dharma-saṃgraha*, 108.

[4] *i.e.* it is empirical, conventional.

In the same place, he says: " Always vigilance is the root of immortality, and the thought of enlightenment the root of what belongs to all creatures' good, and the mind wholly detached and separated is the root of all happiness."

He said also: " One must exercise oneself in making no difference between others and self, if the thought of becoming a Buddha is to become strong. Self and not-self exist only relatively, just as the hither and further banks of a river, and therefore this is false. [358] That bank is not of itself the other bank; then in relation to what could this bank [1] exist? Self-hood is not of itself realised, then in relation to what should there be another?

" If you say, No hurt comes to me by another's pain, and do not protect him; why do you protect yourself so as not to be hurt by pain in a future body?

" To say: 'The same I will be then also,' is a false calculation, because he that is dead is one, he that is born is another.

" If another is born there, what is the use of merit? What is the use of a young body's piling up riches for an old one? When that which is in the womb is dead another is born, the child; when childhood is dead, boyhood; for the destruction of this comes the youth, by destruction of this the old man; how is it one body that is dead? Thus each moment the body is different, like the hair and nails and so forth. Then by the leaving of childhood the child becomes the boy. The body is to be called self-existing only if it has stability. If the body is something that has a shape, there is no body either in the embryo or in the cremated ashes; if you maintain that it does exist in a subtle form without gross existence, then it is not to be seen by itself, and it cannot be called a body. I am not concerned with such a thing at all; but the visible body is liable to destruction and it is only relatively true that there is a bond between the various stages. [359] If its [2]

[1] Read °पारता.

[2] *Tad* seems to be "a permanent substance." Some sayings in the scripture seem to imply such a substance; but others deny it, and so does reasoning; for the *pradhāna*, the permanent substance as the Sāmkhya school

existence is established by the scripture, it is nevertheless denied both by reasoning and by scripture because the primary nature does not exist independently of the qualities; nor are there three essential elements, and the qualities, if they exist,[1] are also each of three parts, and the rest of the world is nine-fold.[2] Without consciousness are such things as clothes; how can they consist of pleasure and so on? Cloth does not come from such things as happiness, but happiness, etc., comes from such things as clothes: as they are not the cause of clothes, they exist not, and how can they be happiness? Therefore by scripture and reasoning all that is composite is impermanent. Therefore the connection of cause and effect is not destroyed by evidence;[3] it is seen in the particular series of each being; how could it exist with permanent things? The atom is not a unity without parts,[4] because in such a unity there are no special divisions. Lamp-oil is used up and it is not seen being used up; so things are not seen being used up every moment. To liken the series of moments of consciousness and its aggregation to a group or an army is a mistake; nevertheless there is a notion of 'I' in reference to this series and aggregation because of our habit of considering them as 'I.' Why, then, could not such a notion be produced with regard to other beings?[5] [360] Therefore the world must be thus understood as an aggregation of spheres. The suffering of oneself and one's neighbour is to be prevented even if it be not really felt. Although not justified, if that suffering takes place in oneself and not in another, what is not justified must be eschewed

understands it, has no existence. P. is the equilibrium of the three guṇas; it has no existence independent of these three; it ought to be "three," and you deny it. Further, each of the three ought to be threefold, as it is mixed up with the two other guṇas. And the "rest of the world," that is the expanded or manifested universe, which according to the Sāmkhya is made of the three guṇas, would be ninefold.

[1] Tib. suggests सत्तो.

[2] Tib. ḥgro-ba chog-ma rnams dgur ḥgyur, *i.e.* नवविधं.

[3] Read बाध्यते with Tib. mi gnod.

[4] परमाणुन्तु is a misprint for °माणु°, which the MS. has.

[5] That is, we may school ourselves to consider our neighbours as ourselves.

whether in oneself or in other, with all one's strength. If much pain comes by pity, why should we make effort to produce this suffering? We answer: When we contemplate the pain of the world, how comes there much pain from pity? Thus when the mind has become accustomed to regard pain and pleasure as alike in another,[1] at the very going down into hell they are as wild geese going into a lotus plantation. When they are plunged in an ocean of joy at the deliverance of creatures, their satisfaction is complete; even deliverance is nothing to them if it be without flavour.[2] Even after this acting for others' good there is no exhilaration and no dismay. There is not even desire for the ripening of merit because of the thirst for others' good alone. The happiness of all creatures in the world is really his own, there is no doubt of that. There is no room even for jealousy for others' blessings, since he considers them as his own.[3]

[361] "The pointing out of sin is the same in others or in self; and so a delight in merit is a vehicle to take one to enlightenment. Thus comes about the application of all merit without exception; therefore merit is produced, infinite as animate nature. This is the last road, the beginning of the infinite joy of peace, bringing joy to the great multitude of the company of Bodhisatvas. And being always protected by the servants of Buddha with Vajrapāṇi as their supreme chief, causing fear to Māra's cohorts, the royal sons of the Buddhas, in the chariot of enlightenment, ride by that road, their praises sung by gods and others. Therefore identifying oneself with other creatures through constant practice for the sake of quenching others' pain one should renounce self and all such things. When one is in the grasp of desire, his pain is not quenched, because by preventing the application of merit he causes pain; and when the world is burnt in the fire of pain, what delight can there be in one's own[4] happiness? When

[1] Tib. zhi dgah=शम०, "having thus cultivated their soul by taking pleasure in appeasing the woes of others."

[2] *i.e.* Nirvāṇa is nothing without this beneficence.

[3] Tib. bdag-la phra-dog go skabs med, suggesting नात्मनीर्ष्यावकाशो ऽस्ति ॥.

[4] The MS. has स्वदुःखे.

one is burning all over, what happiness is there if one nail is not burned? Desire for selfhood is the chief root of all pains. Therefore I destroy just this for all creatures, by abandoning my own good.

[362] "Therefore desire,[1] known for the arch-procuress, must be conquered with every effort, by remembering the truth about self, by the thought how the chain of causation is produced. If [2] for fear I do not abandon this self there is danger in not giving it,[3] because each moment my body and thought are passing away. If wisdom can be received by the body, imperishable by perishable, pure by impure, then it is received by m .. Thus having abandoned self let him follow the good of all creatures, like an image of Bhaisajyaguru,[4] not thinking of worldly things. Let him apply his own knowledge to the service of all creatures; having duly guarded his wealth,[5] let him use it for all creatures. One must produce the suff-.ing which expels much suffering in oneself or another, and also that which produces much happiness.[6] But passions, since they hinder the enjoyment of creatures, are to be swept away with all earnestness as the corpses of snakes are swept from a holy place which is to be enjoyed by the good. 1hat holy place cleansed bears rich and abundant crops of blessing, it will rejoice the world tormented by a dearth of happiness.[7] Are not gain and honour and self renounced by me? What is the good to-day of anger or falsehood? That is what I ask. If there is hatred against those who destroy my things, how shall there be compassion? For even the cruel man is not angry if another's good is destroyed. [363] It is true that the sugar-cane and musk are contemptible, which when improperly treated by their cwner are uneatable. They do not think of requital thro' desire of the good of the owner, they do not incline him to give, they do not approach him for, enjoyment.

[1] Tib. śes khe ḇdod.
[2] yad=yadi.
[3] So Tib.
[4] The god of medicine.
[5] So Tib. nor.
[6] The substance of a verse which has dropped out after 11.
[7] So Tib.

Following and approaching [1] then, the miraculous sons of the Conqueror, great remedies of all organs and diseased humours, address and instruct the angry evildoers, and without abandoning their essential sweetness, they make happy even the unhappy. There are five elements called earth, water, fire, wind, voice; so long as beings exist, they do good to all, and even by the wickedness of these there is no [2] cessation from the doing good; thus I do no hurt to all these elements, even six.[3] So long as the world shall remain poised in the air, so long shall I continue doing good to the world, progressing onwards towards enlightenment. Myself my teacher, always instructing myself, like a good pupil, without myself asking myself with all my force. [364] Who would be unhappy by my unhappiness, fearful from my fear, or know my faults and evil propensities, as the self can do when it is the preceptor of self? How could a pupil be equally indefatigable and unwandering as oneself, or a subject for pity, and always ready? Bemused by trouble in this world, blind with perplexity, on a path full of pitfalls, stumbling at every step, both another and myself are deplorable always.[4]

"Men have the same failings as oneself; therefore to search for errors is not proper; nay, it is rather fit to admire virtues when we meet them. It is impossible for me alone to remove this great ocean of my faults; for that I have need of others. Then what leisure have I for others' faults? [5]

"I accept respectfully the voice of those clever at instructing others, who assist with unsolicited instruction; I am the pupil of all. I have to fight alone against many passions, my enemies; then while I am engaged in battle with one, others strike me easily. Then he who tells me a danger, in the rear or in some other quarter, whether he hate me or love me, he is a friend that gives me life.[6]

[1] Tib. rjes ḥbraṇs ñer soṅ; read °सृत्य in both words.

[2] Tib. mi ldog: the negation is necessary.

[3] The sixth is *vijñānadhātu*.

[4] Read °शाष्याद् for °शयष्याद् in line 15, p. 363.

[5] Read मे क्षणः

[6] Read स मे.

[365] "With the dark blue colour of a swarm of bees, wearing an ascetic's dress, carrying a chaplet of various sweet and blooming flowers, traversing a multitude of Buddha's fields in all directions at the same time, mighty, invincible,[1] taking away every obstacle, emitting the water of quenching for the fires of ghostly existence and hell, pursuing the good of beings who may be converted, standing in the abysses of transmigration, wearing the ornament of strength for causing the opening of the world's eyes, wise, strong in body, causing people to feel confidence. With all my being, glory again and again to that concentrated salvation which has for name Mañjuśrī, a great lake of joy for those tormented with different pains, a mighty cloud for satisfying the hells of thirst in the three worlds, a wishing-tree filling the ten regions with blooming flowers that the world desires, venerated by the lotus-eyes of the world, rejoiced by reaching their desires, praised by hundreds of Bodhisatvas their hair shivering with admiration. I revere Mañjuśrī with ever-increasing salutations. Honour to thee, Mañjuśrī, sorrow's physician, giver of the feast of happiness, by whom in every way we live.

[366] "Thus, having written of the life of the long line of Conquerors, most wonderful everywhere, good has been acquired by me; let there be happiness without end for embodied creatures thereby until the sovereignty of the Sugata extends over the infinite boundaries of heaven."

End of the Growth of Merit.

Here endeth the Śiksāsamuccaya set forth in a number of chapters for the discipline of Bodhisatvas.

[1] That is, बलिना, अप्रति०.

PRINTED BY WILLIAM CLOWES AND SONS, LIMITED, LONDON AND BECCLES, ENGLAND.

INDEX I

Titles of Works quoted.

INDEX II